OWN'S MARCH IN THE STREETS OF CHARLESTON, February 21, 1865.—[See Page 172.]

Voices of the 55th

The reverse of this tintype reads:

Segt. Jackson
55th Regiment

Voices of the 55th:
Letters from the 55th Massachusetts Volunteers, 1861–1865

Edited and annotated by
Noah Andre Trudeau

Morningside
1996

ISBN: 0–89029–327–9

Morningside House, Inc.

260 Oak Street
Dayton, Ohio 45410

1-800-648-9710
Fax: 513-461-4260

Contents

List of Maps/Diagrams

Editor's Note and Acknowledgements

If the quality of a Civil War regiment is measured by the selflessness of its admirers, than the 55th Massachusetts is blessed on every hand. Virtually every stage in the creation of this book was aided in no little measure by the generosity of those individuals who, like your editor, have become fascinated with the story of Massachusetts' "other" black infantry regiment.

The project got underway when Robert Younger of Morningside Books responded to my search for published material relating to black Civil War regiments with the comment that he had some letters from a private in the 55th and would I like to see them with an eye toward editing them for publication? The John Posey letters that soon arrived were valuable as the seldom heard voice of an enlisted African American private, but their personalized content and awkward construction meant that they alone could not bear the weight of an edited volume.

I had long been familiar with and an admirer of Edwin S. Redkey's volume of letters by black Civil War soldiers that had been published in the "colored" press of the day. That volume held a few more letters from the 55th, and a call to its editor brought the happy news that he had collected many more letters than he had published. Mr. Redkey cheerfully made this "stash" available to me, and from it a few more voices from the 55th were gathered.

During a research trip (on another, though related project) I learned that Harvard's Houghton Library held a complete run of the war-time issues of the *Weekly Anglo-African*. The microfilm was purchased, and another batch of 55th letters were in hand. By this time something approaching a real book was beginning to emerge from the growing pile of photocopies and transcripts.

I then chanced across Stephen D. Smith's wonderful pamphlet on the Folly Island encampment and cemetery of the 55th Massachusetts. A call to Mr. Smith brought another generous sharing of original materials and an introduction to Ms. Kathy Dhalle.

Who could have imagined that in a small upstate New York town there lived the person who is, in all probability, the foremost living expert on the men and history of the 55th Massachusetts? What had begun as a master's thesis had become something akin to an obsession that, over the years, had led to an accumulation of hundreds of bits of information, official documents, and primary manuscripts relating to that black regiment. Not only does Ms. Dhalle know just about all there is to know about the 55th, she has also tracked down and contacted an amazing number of proud descendents of this remarkable military unit. Her willingness to share everything with this Johnny-come-lately must elevate her to near sainthood. Thanks to her collection, I was able to add several letters culled from the pension files of 55th veterans, and some choice items from other sources as well.

Throughout it all, my researcher, Bryce Suderow, sifted through the holdings of the National Archives and located for me a small treasure of official documents and reports related to the 55th.

I have tried to follow common sense rules with most of the editing I have done for this book. Those letters culled from newspapers are printed as they appeared, though a few obvious misspellings have been corrected. The letters of John Posey required a fair degree of construction to make them easily readable, and in a few places I had to take some liberties with the text. In order to preserve the historic value of these letters I have included two versions of each; my edited version (as it might have appeared in a newspaper of that time once the local editor had "cleaned" it up) and a literal transcription of the original text. The direct transcriptions appear in an appendix. All other letters have been tidied up for publication, with spelling corrected, obvious name errors corrected, and some occasional formatting for purposes of clarity.

An early draft of this book was reviewed by Kathy Dhalle and Bryce Suderow, and ministered at Morningside Books by Kella Barnhill. I am grateful for all keen eyes, and cognizant that the final decisions were mine and are my responsibility.

My deepest and humblest thanks to all the friends of the 55th who contributed to this volume, and my sincerest hope that in some small way what I have produced justifies their generosity.

Introduction

As the subject of the film *Glory*, a PBS *American Experience* documentary, an episode on the A&E/History Channel series *Civil War Journal*, as well as several books and numerous articles, the 54th Massachusetts (Colored) Volunteers enjoys a contemporary name recognition equalled by few other Civil War infantry regiments. The story of its idealistic and heroic first commander, Colonel Robert Gould Shaw, and its futile, sacrificial assault against Confederate Fort Wagner on July 18, 1863, is truly the stuff of legend. Yet it is also true that the popular image of the 54th Massachusetts has overshadowed the service of the more than 116 other black infantry regiments that took part in the war. The 54th Massachusetts was not the first "colored" regiment to be created, nor was its attack on Fort Wagner the first major engagement for black troops. And the 54th was not the only regiment of African Americans to serve under the state flag of Massachusetts; there was a cavalry regiment and a second infantry regiment—the 55th Massachusetts (Colored) Volunteers.

The first men recruited for the 54th Massachusetts arrived in late February 1863 at Camp Meigs in Readville. Its ranks were filled by May 11; then, according to an officer of that regiment, "more recruits had arrived than were required, and the Fifty-fifth Massachusetts was begun with the surplus on the succeeding day."[1] On that day, May 12, Leonard C. Alden of Cambridge was commissioned and mustered in as second lieutenant of the regiment. Already present in camp were three officers originally slated for the 54th who now assumed command duties with the 55th: Norwood P. Hallowell, colonel; Alfred S. Hartwell, lieutenant colonel; and Charles B. Fox, major. Hallowell and Hartwell were Harvard men, and both had seen active service—Hallowell with the 20th Massachusetts and Hartwell with the Missouri militia, and later with the 44th Massachusetts. Hallowell had been severely wounded in the arm at Antietam, an injury that would contribute to his resignation from the regiment on November 2, 1863.[2]

1. Luis F. Emilio, *A Brave Black Regiment: History of the Fifty-Fourth Regiment of Massachusetts Volunteer Infantry* (New York, 1992; reprint of 1894 edition), p. 26.
2. Charles B. Fox, *Record of the Service of the Fifty-fifth Regiment of Massachusetts Volunteer Infantry* (Boston, 1868), pp. 1, 98.

9

Without the single-minded determination of Governor John A. Andrew, there would have been no 54th Massachusetts, and were it not for the particular genius of recruitment organizer George L. Stearns, there would have been no 55th. Andrew was a zealous abolitionist, and an early advocate of arming black men. Within a month of the formal issuance of the Emancipation Proclamation, Andrew obtained authorization from the War Department to raise infantry units made up of "persons of African descent."[3] Yet all of Andrew's considerable determination could not overcome a simple matter of arithmetic: according to the census of 1860, there were just under 2,000 free black males of military age living in the Bay State—not a large enough manpower pool from which to create a 1,000-man regiment. To overcome this hurdle, Andrew employed a privately organized recruiting committee headed by the well-known Massachusetts abolitionist Stearns.

George L. Stearns, a white man, turned to the black community for help. A number of leading African Americans joined the effort, including Martin R. Delany, John Jones, and John M. Langston. Like most recruiting agents, they worked on a commission basis. They addressed rallies and guided recruitment efforts that took place north and south of the Mason-Dixon line. The black press of the day was also utilized. This notice from the "Recruiting Committee" appeared in the June 13, 1863, issue of New York's *Weekly Anglo-African* under the headline "Fifty-Fifth Mass. Regiment":

> The policy of using the colored man in the War for the Union has been definitively adopted by the Government. For the future he has to share the trials and glories of white men in this sacred contest for civilization and freedom, and the maintenance of Republican Government.
>
> His hearty co-operation and usefulness are attested in every form and on all occasions. The Generals of every military department now freely acknowledge his value. High official recognition of his aid has also been given in the dispatch of the Honorable Secretary of State to

3. Dudley T. Cornish, *The Sable Arm* (New York, 1956), p. 105. Emilio, *A Brave Black Regiment*, p. 2.

our Minister to England, in his announcement that "Everywhere the American General receives his most useful and reliable information from the negro, who hails his coming as the harbinger of freedom."

Massachusetts early recognized this truth. Her sagacious chief magistrate first urged upon the War department the advantage of enrolling colored men into the service of their country. His appeals in this were answered. Authority was granted to raise one regiment of blacks in Massachusetts; and more rapidly than any other in the State, the Fifty-fourth has been recruited to its maximum, and is now on the eve of departure for the seat of war. All witnesses testify that in deportment and proficiency it is second to none to the contingent of Massachusetts. Its officers are men of character and position, and the promise of usefulness is most gratifying.

A second regiment of colored men—the Fifty-fifth—has now been authorized. Already is the nucleus in camp. It will be speedily recruited and dispatched for active service. Every man thus enlisted is credited to the quota of the State.

That same issue of the *Anglo-African* contained this enthusiastic report from recruiter Uriah H. Brown in Cadiz, Ohio:

The colored people of the great West are determined to vie with their brethren of the East in the promptness and alacrity, with which they seize the opportunities of the age, and spring to the help of [the] government under which they live. Volunteering goes bravely on in different sections of this state. Recruiting officer Brightwell has recently been in this and the adjoining county of Belmont, engaged in the work. On last Thursday evening he arrived in this place, on his return from the latter country with eighteen or twenty recruits. A spirited meeting was held here on that evening, at which addresses were delivered by Hon. John A. Bingham, Mr. Rivers and Mr. White. Much enthusiasm existed, and what has been done is only a promise of what is yet to be accomplished before the work ceases.

On Friday morning, Officer Brightwell, with his men to the number of twenty one, left amid many tears and good wishes for the place of rendezvous—the number to be increased by squads at different points on the road.

These volunteers are for the 55th Massachusetts Regiment.

Camp Meigs, located some 10 miles from Boston, had been established by Governor Andrew as a rendezvous point in his Special Order 790, issued in September, 1862. Several white regiments had already been formed and transferred to the front from Readville before the black recruits arrived, including one of the state's finest fighting outfits, the 20th Massachusetts. Luis F. Emilio, an officer in the 54th Massachusetts, remembered the Camp Meigs site as "flat, and well adapted for drilling, but in wet weather [it] was muddy, and in the winter season bleak and cheerless. The barracks were great barn-like structures of wood with sleeping-bunks on either side."[4]

The official history of the 55th Massachusetts includes this recollection from its Readville encampment:

> On the evening after the arrival of the first squad of recruits, at the conclusion of the tatoo roll-call, and before the ranks were broken and the men dismissed for the night, a striking and unusual scene occurred. One of their number stepped from the ranks and made a simple and appropriate prayer, and the whole squad joined in singing one of their peculiar hymns. The practice thus commenced was continued, and adopted by each company in succession, and was seldom omitted during the stay of the regiment at Readville; but continued with increasing interest, partly on account of the really fine singing, until it became a great attraction to the friends of the officers and men.[5]

Serious drilling by squads and companies began immediately,

4. Emilio, *A Brave Black Regiment*, p. 21.
5. Fox, *Record of the Service*, p. 2.

and by June Major Fox was directing full-scale battalion drill. For the next month, notes the regiment's history, "battalion-drill became the regular duty of every pleasant afternoon, and was omitted only on such days as practice marches of from four to six miles were made over the roads of the surrounding country."[6]

The black men who filled the ranks of the 55th Massachusetts came largely from Ohio, Pennsylvania, and Virginia—only twenty-two out of 880 were natives of the Bay State. Also present was Nicholas Saib, born in Africa, who had once served the Russian minister to Constantinople as his slave.

The recruits for the 55th were overwhelmingly farmers, with an average age of twenty-three years, three months, and an average height of five feet seven inches. Slightly more than half joined the regiment knowing how to read, and about a quarter were married at the time of their enlistment. Not everyone was motivated by an unselfish patriotism. The regimental history admits that a few desertions did take place while the men were camped at Readville, though, "the deserters were men of such character that their officers had no desire to retake them." The regiment's roster identifies only three men as having deserted while at Readville; one later returned to duty, while another, John M. Smith of Company A, was arrested and eventually hung for rape on February 18, 1864.[7]

But these were a few bad apples in a barrel of remarkably good ones. Among the young men joining the regiment in this period was a twenty-two-year-old farmer from Vincennes, Indiana, named John Posey. According to the descriptive book of Company D, Posey was five feet eleven inches tall, with brown eyes and black hair. His enlistment was for three years. Another recruit was Charles Hicks, a twenty-year-old farmer from Cambridge, Ohio; while still in camp he contracted a disease that left him virtually blind. As Captain Charles C. Soule, his company commander, noted: "Hicks is peculiarly an object of charitable consideration, as he came from the west to enlist in the 55th Regiment,—and just as his pleasant and manly disposition and soldier-

6. Fox, Record of the Service, p. 3.
7. Fox, Record of the Service, pp. 110-112. Steven D. Smith, Whom We Would Never More See: History and Archaeology Recover the Lives and Deaths of African American Civil War Soldiers on Folly Island, South Carolina (South Carolina, 1993), p. 8.

ly conduct were made manifest, [he] was stricken by an incurable malady, under which he has since suffered for the larger portion of his time among strangers."[8]

Companies A, B, C, D and E of the 55th Massachusetts were mustered into service on May 31, Companies F and G on June 16, followed on June 22 by Companies H, I and K.[9] On July 18, 1863, the men and officers of the 55th Massachusetts were presented with their regimental flags by a delegation headed by Governor Andrew. Befitting the large Buckeye contingent in the regiment, two flags were gifts of the "colored ladies" of Ohio. As part of his remarks, Governor Andrew said: "I know not when, in all human history, to any given one thousand men in arms has been committed a work so proud, so precious, so full of hope and glory, as the work commited to you."[10]

On July 21, the men of the 55th Massachusetts marched into Boston where they boarded the steamers that would convey them south. They were going to war.

The U.S. transport *Cahawba* carried the regiment to Morehead City, North Carolina, where the men disembarked on July 25 and climbed aboard railroad cars taking them to Newberne. There the regiment became a part of the "African Brigade" commanded by Brigadier General Edward A. Wild.[11] A Harvard man himself, Wild was an experienced surgeon who had passed up medical duty in favor of active combat service with the 1st Massachusetts. He was severely wounded at the battle of Seven Pines in early 1862. Soon after his recovery he mustered out of the 1st and re-mustered as colonel of the 35th Massachusetts, a regiment he led at the battle of South Mountain where he was again seriously wounded, this time losing an arm. After recovering from this wound, Wild was commissioned brigadier general of volunteers, with a special brief to organize a unit of black soldiers. An ardent abolitionist, Wild exercised his command authority with a zeal

8. National Archives: Service Record, John Posey. Military Officer's Records, Volume 2, Massachusetts National Guard Supply Depot, Natick, Massachusetts.
9. National Archives: Compiled Service Records, 55th Massachusetts, Field & Staff Record of Events through August 31, 1863.
10. Fox, *Record of the Service*, p. 3. Charles H. Wesley, *Ohio Negroes in the Civil War* (Ohio, 1962), p. 31.
11. Compiled Service Records, 55th Massachusetts. *The War of the Rebellion: A Compilation of the Official Records of the Union and Confederate Armies* (Washington: Government Printing Office, 1880-1901), series I, volume 28, part 2, p. 75. [Hereafter cited as *OR*]

that often put him at odds with his superiors. In one notorious incident, he ordered the whipping of a captured slave owner—the order to be carried out by former slaves who had themselves been whipped by the man.[12]

For the next four days, the 55th took part in brigade drills with the other units under Wild's command—the 1st North Carolina Colored, a detachment of the 2nd N.C.C., and a company of the 3rd. Then, on July 30, 1863, "in the midst of a pouring rain," Wild's African Brigade boarded ships bound for Charleston, South Carolina. Companies D, G, I and K of the 55th boarded the schooner *Recruit*, while the remaining six companies went by way of the steamer *Maple Leaf*. The steamship arrived at Stono Inlet, off Folly Island, South Carolina, on August 3, followed six days later by the *Recruit*, which had battled head winds all the way. Wild's brigade now became a part of Brigadier General Israel Vogdes' division, which otherwise consisted mostly of New York troops in brigades led by Colonel Samuel M. Alford and Brigadier General Robert S. Foster.[13]

Wild's African Brigade was a small cog in an operation that had been underway for more than a year aimed at capturing the citadel of secession, Charleston. A series of land and naval actions had punished but failed to break the Confederate defenses protecting the city. With slim prospects for a battlefield victory, the officer heading the operation, Brigadier General Quincy A. Gillmore, planned to shell Charleston into submission. To accomplish this he had to seize Morris Island, which commanded the southern approaches to Charleston Harbor. From his headquarters on Folly Island, Gillmore launched his assault on adjacent Morris Island on July 8. The southern end of the island fell quickly on July 10 after sharp fighting, but Gillmore found his attempt to possess the all-important northern end blocked by a low lying, sand-walled Confederate redoubt known as Fort Wagner. An attack made on July 11 was repulsed with heavy casualties. A second, heavier assault was launched a week later. The storming column this time was led by a black regiment, the 54th Massachusetts. This attack too was a failure, with the 54th taking heavy

12. Ezra J. Warner, *Generals in Blue* (Louisiana, 1964), pp. 557-558. United States Military History Institute, Carlisle Barracks: Edward A. Wild Papers.
13. *OR*, vol. 28, pt. 2, p. 75. *Record of the Service*, pp. 10-11.

losses, including its young commander, Colonel Shaw. Gillmore next turned to classic siege tactics, requiring prodigious labor to dig the necessary trench systems and fortifications.

Fatigue duty was the order of the day, day after day, for the newly arrived troops of Wild's African Brigade. According to the 55th's history: "These details were employed in cutting timber, making gabions, building wharves, loading and unloading stores, artillery, and ammunition, hauling heavy guns to the front, and working in the trenches on Morris Island." A notation in the monthly regimental return for August 1863 says, "The Regiment since its arrival has been engaged [in] continuous fatigue duty on Morris Island, parties averaging over 400 per day." A check of the bimonthly company records of events shows that in addition to their work on Morris Island, details of the 55th labored on Folly Island, Long Island and Botany Bay Island.[14]

It was the racially prejudicial view of the white command establishment that blacks were "naturally" suited to labor in the humid swamps of the Charleston barrier islands, a policy that was tragically misguided. In the first seven weeks of fatigue duty, the 55th lost a dozen men to disease; by December, that total had risen to twenty-three. Most of the dead were laid to rest in the brigade cemetery which would be rediscovered in the summer of 1987 when a building contractor uncovered some of the graves. A subsequent examination of the site was undertaken by staff of the South Carolina Institute of Archaeology and Anthropology at the University of South Carolina.[15]

The price paid by the men of the 55th because of their assignment to semi-permanent fatigue duty might be gleaned from an entry from the diary of the regiment's surgeon, Dr. Burt G. Wilder:

> There are several minor surgical cases under my care just now; a toe nearly crushed off, a finger crushed yesterday, a foot that had to be lanced this morning, and a hand accidentally shot a few days ago; the man whose arm was dislocated some time ago has been on duty for several days.

14. Fox, *Record of the Service*, p. 11. Compiled Service Records, 55th Massachusetts.
15. Smith, *Whom We Would Never More See*, p. 10.

Dr. Wilder also related an incident involving the African Brigade's division commander:

> Brig. Gen. Vogdes, in command of the island, called while I was studying our sick list this morning and said it was too large; and hoped I did not allow men to impose upon me and when not really ill; it makes me somewhat indignant for he has been taking our men, 400 or 500 at a time, and many of them have been out four or five nights in succession at hardwork; I am determined that none shall go who are unfit.[16]

Assignment to fatigue details did not mean that the men were relieved from their military obligations. Quoting again from the history of the 55th Massachusetts: "From Sept. 17 to Oct. 28, in addition to guard, picket, and fatigue duty, the whole regiment was required to be under arms at four A.M., and remain until daybreak enabled the outposts to see across the marshes."[17] Ten days before this particular assignment began, the Federals finally completed their control of Morris Island when the Confederate defenders of Fort Wagner—battered by months of artillery shelling and only too aware that the Union trenches had been pushed to within storming distance of the bastion—evacuated the post. Soon Gillmore had his heavy guns ranging freely over Charleston, but neither the threat nor the reality of Yankee cannonades weakened the city's fierce determination to resist. Lacking enough troops to mount a full-scale assault on Charleston, Gillmore's offensive dwindled to a program of long range shelling, accompanied by cat-and-mouse raids along the waterways south of the city. This wearying regimen proved to be too much for Colonel Hallowell, who was suffering greatly from his Antietam wound. By Special Order 487 he was honorably discharged from the service of the United States.[18] Alfred S. Hartwell now assumed command of the 55th.

With a stalemate at Charleston, attention now turned to other theaters of operation along the coast. On February 13, 1864, three

16. Both this quote and the preceding one from Smith, *Whom We Would Never More See*, p. 30.
17. Fox, *Record of the Service*, p. 12.
18. Compiled Service Records, 55th Massachusetts.

companies of the 55th Massachusetts went on board a steamer bound for Jacksonville, Florida. They were followed the next day by the remaining companies.[19]

It is difficult to be charitable regarding the Federal Florida Campaign of 1864. Concocted out of a political agenda shaped by stubborn misconceptions and false assumptions, operating with military goals that were vague and tentative, the entire affair was doomed to failure. Militarily, it reached its high (or low) point on February 20, 1864, when a Union expeditionary force was savaged at the battle of Olustee. Three black regiments were especially prominent in this action—the 8th USCT (United States Colored Troops), the 35th USCT (formerly the 1st North Carolina Colored), and the 54th Massachusetts. Combined, these regiments lost more than 1,800 men.[20]

The 55th Massachusetts arrived in Jacksonville on the evening of February 15 and was soon employed performing picket, provost and fatigue duty. With this kind of service it was inevitable that the regiment would be broken up to cover a wide area. Two companies, B and I, were posted at Yellow Bluff, about halfway between Jacksonville and the mouth of the St. John's River. Back at Jacksonville, Company F became the garrison for Redoubt Fribley, part of the city's outer defenses. In early March, the remaining companies of the regiment joined an expedition that went up the St. John's River as far as the town of Palatka, which they would help garrison for a month. It was around this time that Wild's African Brigade was disbanded, and its two regiments were assigned to different commands.[21]

The period the 55th spent in Florida was not without its incidents, both tragic and heroic. Of the former, there was the death of Lieutenant Dennis H. Jones of Company I, killed by the accidental discharge of a gun while on a scouting party. Of the latter, the regimental history has only this cryptic note: "Capt. [Robert James] Hamilton made a daring excursion from Pilatka,

19. Fox, *Record of the Service,* p. 21.
20. For the most incisive examination of this campaign see: David James Coles, "'A Fight, a Licking, and a Footrace,' The 1864 Florida Campaign and the Battle of Olustee." (M.A. thesis, Florida State Univ., 1985).
21. Fox, *Record of the Service,* p. 24. Compiled Service Records, 55th Massachusetts. Smith, *Whom We Would Never More See,* p. 10. *OR,* Volume 35, Part 1, p. 492.

with a rebel deserter, some forty miles into the interior, visiting the neighborhood of the rebel camps, and being absent several days."[22]

Also occurring at this time was the execution of three members of the regiment, taking place shortly after the first landing. The condemned men, found guilty of raping a white woman, were John M. Smith of Co. A and John M. Cork and Spencer Lloyd, both of Co. B. Cork and Lloyd were hanged February 18 at Camp Finegan. Smith, who had deserted the regiment while it was at Camp Meigs, had been arrested and returned to the 55th in October. His hanging took place in Jacksonville. "This latter execution," noted one of the regiment's officers, "necessarily by the dim moonlight, as the troops marched at dawn, was a solemn and impressive scene."[23]

The 55th's Florida sojourn came to an end in mid-April when its scattered parts were put aboard the steamers *Sentinel* and *Neptune* and returned to Folly Island on April 18 and 20, 1864. This time the men and officers found themselves with much more elbow room, as the bulk of General Gillmore's command was in the process of moving north to Virginia, where it would fill out the Tenth Corps of Major Benjamin F. Butler's Army of the James, and take part in what would become known as the Bermuda Hundred Campaign. Gillmore began moving his first units to Virginia on April 13, and would spend the rest of the month transferring the others assigned to that front. He and his staff then followed, leaving the command of the troops posted to Morris, and Folly and the other islands to Brigadier General Alexander Schimmelfennig, a veteran officer who had served with the ill-fated Eleventh Corps at Gettysburg. The 55th Massachusetts was now teamed with the 103rd New York in a brigade commanded by Colonel William Heine.[24]

"The duty assigned to the regiment until May 8th was severe," notes the regiment's history. "On the night after the arrival of the first detachment, two-thirds were at once ordered to relieve the pickets, and for several weeks the details continued excessive," a statement echoed in the Record of Events for that period. On

22. Fox, *Record of the Service*, pp. 24-25.
23. Fox, *Record of the Service*, pp. 22, 116-119.
24. Fox, *Record of the Service*, pp. 25-27. *OR*, volume 35, part 2, p. 78. Herbert M. Schiller, *The Bermuda Hundred Campaign* (Dayton, Ohio, 1988), p. 39.

May 8th the various details of the 55th were relieved by the 54th Massachusetts, and the regiment moved to Stono Inlet, where it set up camp. According to the regiment's official record, "The water was good and this location the most comfortable, as it was that longest occupied by the regiment on Folly Island."[25]

As if seeking to compensate for the reduced size of his force through increased activity, General Schimmelfenning ordered a series of raids and probing actions that, for the first time, took the 55th Massachusetts into harm's way. Excerpts from the Regimental Return and Company D Record of Events tell the story:

> A Reconnaissance in force was made on the night of the 20th on James Island composed of Companies D, E, G & H under command of Col. Hartwell united with the 103 New York Volunteers under command of Major Morrison of the 103 New York Volunteers.
>
> The party advanced from Long & Tiger Islands about daybreak, upon crossing a deep marsh skirmishers were thrown out and advanced drawing the fire from the enemy in the woods and rifle pits. Company D by a flank movement drove them from the woods and came in upon the open flank of the rifle pits and driving them to their second line of entrenchments.
>
> The entire force crossed the lower end of James Island, returning on the afternoon of the 22d by the way of Coles Island. But one casualty occurred, viz; Phineas T. Corst, Company "E" wounded in the leg. On the 23d a party of 300 men were sent up the Stono River on steamboats "Golden Gate" & "Standish" for the purpose of making a demonstration towards James Island from Battery Island.
>
> The party returned at midnight.
>
> * * *
>
> Skirmish on James Island S.C. May 22 1864 in which this company done their full share. The men fought like veterans.

All was not quiet in the ranks of the 55th at this time, however.

25. Fox, *Record of the Service*, pp. 26-27.

The unwillingness of the Federal government to pay black soldiers the same amount it paid whites had been an issue with all African American troops for months. Governor Andrew had attempted to mitigate the sting for the Massachusetts regiments by offering to have the state pick up the difference, but the soldiers of the 54th and 55th refused to accept this compromise. The damage the Federal policy did to black troop morale was substantial. In his fitness report for the month of April, 55th surgeon W.S. Brown notes: "The non-payment of the men produces in some a marked feeling of insubordination, and exerts on all a depressing influence." There had been several instances of mutinous behavior at various points in the 55th's service in South Carolina and Florida, but nothing that resulted in any severe punishment. This was true until June 18, 1864, when Private Wallace Baker, having been tried and found guilty of mutiny, was executed "by a detail from his own regiment."[26]

The next combat action involving the 55th was of a larger scale than the May 22 action. It was emblematic of overall Federal operations against Charleston in the period following the evacuation of Fort Wagner: well conceived but poorly executed. Believing that the Confederate defenses had been greatly weakened by the reassignment of troops to other fronts, a triple advance was designed to pressure them. One portion, under Brigadier General John P. Hatch, moved up the North Edisto River, landed on Seabrook Island, and crossed to John's Island with the intention of disrupting the Charleston and Savannah Railroad. At the same time, Brigadier General William Birney led a smaller force in a landing further up the river with instructions to destroy the C&S Railroad bridge over the South Edisto. In the meantime, a third force, commanded by General Schimmelfenning, was to test the enemy's defenses on James Island.[27]

Hatch's deployment and march were fatally slowed by the heat and by the time he reached his target, Confederate defenders were waiting for him. Birney, failing as well to move promptly and decisively, was also stalemated and withdrawn. The fate of the third element in this operation was recorded in the July 14 issue of the *New York Herald*:

26. Military Officer's Records, Volume 2, Massachusetts National Guard Supply Depot, Natick, Massachusetts. Fox, *Record of the Service*, p. 29.
27. Fox, *Record of the Service*, p. 29. *OR*, volume 35, part 1, p. 14.

On Saturday morning, the 2d [of July], as a co-operative movement, General Schimmelfenning, commanding the district of Morris and Folly Islands, crossed over to James Island from Folly, with a part of his force, and drove in the rebel pickets after a skirmish. The troops were then formed into column and advanced toward an old battery, not until recently occupied. The Thirty-third United States colored infantry, and the One Hundred Third New York, were placed in the advance. When they arrived very near the fort the rebels opened with two brass field pieces, with canister, creating considerable havoc and causing some confusion. The Fifty-fifth Massachusetts had been formed in line for the purpose of charging on the fort, and as soon as the fire had been drawn they advanced at double quick. Theirs was a delicate duty to perform; for they had to charge through retreating white and black troops, in the face of a murderous fire. But they never flinched. The rebel fire was quite high, and nearly all who were wounded were hit in the head. With a shout and the intrepidity of veterans they rushed over the parapet, driving the rebel forces before them into the woods, and capturing two guns. As this was the first time this regiment was ever under a hot fire their conduct was especially praiseworthy. They have nobly sustained the reputation won for the Massachusetts colored troops by the Fifty-fourth at Wagner and at Olustee.

The losses, according to the history of the 55th, were: "Killed, —enlisted men, seven. Mortally wounded,—enlisted men, two. Wounded,—commissioned officers, two; . . . enlisted men, seventeen, one of whom afterward died at Beaufort."[28]

After the 55th returned from this expedition it fell into the difficult routine of garrisoning a post that was in direct contact with the enemy. Long spells of manning redoubts and picket lines under a steady desultory fire would be interrupted only by expeditions into enemy country in search of forage or information. And conditions on the islands were far from idyllic. According

28. Fox, *Record of the Service*, p. 31.

to one officer's diary entry made during this period, the men were "Awfully tormented with mosquitos, fleas, sand and sun." Adding a bitter edge to the whole was the pay issue, which continued to rankle both officers and men. Matters came to a sudden boil in mid-July when, according to the regiment's history, "two partial combinations among the enlisted men to refuse duty took place." "In point of fact," Colonel Hallowell related after the war, "the Fifty-fifth did stack arms one morning, not in an angry, tumult-uous way, but in sullen, desperate mood that expressed a wish to be marched out to be shot down rather than longer hear the cries from home and longer endure the galling sense of humiliation and wrong. But better counsels prevailed, and a grand catastrophe was averted by the patriotism and innate good sense of the men, added to the sympathy and firmness of the officers."[29]

The entire controversy began to move toward a resolution in late August when orders were received that equalized the pay of black and white troops. But there was fine print to the new in-structions—the full scale was limited to those African Americans who had been free "on or before April 21, 1861." If followed liter-ally, this provision would have allowed only those who had been free before the war to receive full pay for service rendered in 1862 and 1863. Protests were made, but one of the more effective responses was developed by Colonel Edward N. Hallowell of the 54th Massachusetts. Known as the "Quaker Oath," it required officers ask their men to affirm that each of them did "solemnly swear that you owed no man unrequited labor on or before the 19th day of April, 1861." As clever as Hallowell's oath was, it could not mitigate the slap in the face the payout order repre-sented to black troops. When the 55th was drawn up to take the oath, several of the ranks refused, but most went along. The necessary papers were soon wending their way through the mili-tary bureaucracy, and on October 4 the paymaster began the long awaited cash disbursement. The event was observed in the regimental history as being "like the loosening of a cord, long drawn to extreme tension."[30]

29. Massachusetts Historical Society, Massachusetts 55th Volunteer Association of Officers Record: Extracts from the diary of Lieutenant George T. Garrison, entry for June 4-5, 1864. Fox, *Record of the Service*, p. 33. N.P. Hallowell, *Selected Letters and Papers of N.P. Hallowell* (New Hampshire, 1963), p. 9.
30. Fox, *Record of the Service*, pp. 35-37. Joseph T. Glatthaar, *Forged in Battle* (New York, 1990), p. 174.

The duties of the 55th before Charleston continued through the summer and into the fall. "The weather was now growing cool, heavy gales and cold storms from the north were frequent, and it was with difficulty that fuel could be obtained," notes the history of the regiment. On November 23, orders were received for the regiment to be ready to move at a moment's notice. Something other than the promise of winter was in the wind.[31]

The plan for the operation that would bring the 55th Massachusetts into its toughest battle was apparently simultaneously conceived in South Carolina and Washington, though its catalyst was the approach of Sherman's army on its march to the sea.

On November 21, Major General John G. Foster, commanding the District of the South, reported to Major General Henry W. Halleck at the War Department that he was "now in a condition, in case of need, to draw from each district one or two regiments to . . . constitute a small force to attack the enemy.[32] An opportunity of this kind may shortly occur, if, as appears from the late rebel papers, General Sherman really be upon the march from Atlanta to Savannah or Charleston." Writing to Halleck the next day, Foster continued in this vein:

> General Hardee has left Charleston, with his staff, to meet Sherman. He is collecting every man to defend the State. He has withdrawn considerably from the force guarding the Savannah and Charleston Railroad. I do not consider that my orders to stand strictly on the defensive were intended to prevent my taking advantage of such a favorable opportunity, and I shall therefore scrape together a small force of 3,000 men and attack and capture, if possible, some point on the mainland.

That same day, after his note to Halleck had been dispatched, Foster received a letter from "Old Brains" dated November 13. In it, Halleck said: "Should Sherman come to the Atlantic coast, which I think most probable, he expects to reach there the early part of December, and wishes you, if possible, to cut the Charles-

31. Fox, *Record of the Service*, p. 37.
32. The Department of the South was divided into four districts—Beaufort, Hilton Head, Florida, and a Northern District made up of the garrisons on Morris and Folly islands.

ton and Savannah Railroad near Pocotaligo about that time. At all events a demonstration on that road will be of advantge."[33]

The force that Foster actually assembled for this operation was about twice the 3,000 he had first estimated. By his own accounting it amounted to "5,000 infantry, cavalry, and artillery, with 500 sailors and marines."[34] While his possession of key posts along the Atlantic Coast gave Foster the mobility necessary for a movement of this type, the fact that his command had not yet functioned as a single task force made it difficult, if not impossible, to effectively carry out his movement.

The units assigned to this expedition were organized into three brigades, which in turn made up a "Coast Division" that was commanded in the field by Brigadier General John P. Hatch. The First Brigade was led by Brigadier General Edward E. Potter, the Second by Colonel Alfred S. Hartwell, and the Naval Brigade by Commander George H. Preble. The 55th served in Hartwell's brigade, a unit that also included the 54th Massachusetts, the 56th New York, as well as the 34th, 35th and 102nd USCT.[35]

Foster's plan was to move his force up the Broad River from Hilton Head, land it at a place on the left bank called Boyd's Neck, and from there strike quickly for Grahamville and the railroad some seven miles to the west. His assumption that the Confederates defending this region were few and far between was correct, but lacking the ability to have his plan executed promptly, he allowed his opponent what proved to be a fatal advantage of adequate reaction time.

Problems for this operation began almost at once. Foster's men sailed from Hilton Head on time on the night of November 28, and ran right into a thick fog that slowed the vessels and scattered them. Several of the ships got lost, others went aground, and it was not until well into the afternoon of November 29 that all the troops were safely ashore. Once on land operational control passed to General Hatch, whose luck was no better than Foster's. He set off at once, but a combination of bad maps and unhelpful guides led him on a weary tramp to nowhere. Not until the early morn-

33. *OR*, Volume 44, pp. 517, 525, 591. *OR*, Volume 35, Part 2, p. 328.
34. *OR*, Volume 44, p. 420.
35. The 34th USCT was formerly the 2nd South Carolina (Colored) Regiment, and the 35th USCT was formerly the 1st North Carolina (Colored) Regiment.

ing of November 30 did his footsore columns correctly identify the road near Bolan Church that led to Grahamville.[36]

Hatch's leading elements had been in contact with the enemy from the moment the landings had begun on the morning of November 29, so word of his coming had passed quickly up the Confederate chain of command. According to Confederate accounts, only a small detachment of the 3rd South Carolina Cavalry was on hand to oppose the initial Yankee landing at Boyd's Neck. But by the next morning Colonel C.J. Colcock, the district commander, along with the South Carolina cavalrymen who had first spread the alarm, had been able to pull together about 1,400 men drawn from Georgia militia units and a few regular Confederate regiments, as well as cannon from three batteries. Colcock put his men into a previously prepared position along a small ridge known as Honey Hill, located about halfway between Grahamville and Bolan Church.[37]

This defensive position had been well sited. Not only were its flanks resting in nearly impassable swampy ground and its front shielded by a creek that had been filled with cut-down trees, but the approach road made two sharp turns before reaching it so that the Union troops were almost on top of the entrenched line before they got their first good look at it. According to a post-war speech by Confederate Colonel Charles C. Jones:

> As the head of the Federal column appeared at a curve in the Honey-Hill road, less than two hundred yards in advance of the field works occupied by the Confederates, it encountered a murderous fire of artillery and musketry before which it recoiled.[38]

The time was now about 11:00 A.M. According to General Hatch's after action report:

> Potter's brigade was quickly formed in line of battle, parallel to that of the enemy. . . . The left of Potter's brigade—re-enforced by two companies of the Fifty-fourth Massachusetts Volunteers and part of the Fifty-

36. OR, Volume 44, p. 420.
37. Charles C. Jones, The Battle of Honey Hill (Georgia, 1885), pp. 11-15.
38. Jones, Battle of Honey Hill, p. 14.

fifth Massachusetts Volunteers, . . .—made two desperate attacks on the main work of the enemy. . . . They were repulsed with severe loss. The Fifty-fifth Massachusetts Volunteers were rallied, and, with the Marine Battalion, sent to . . . turn the left flank of the enemy. They advanced gallantly, but were unable to carry the intrenchments.[39]

By 2:00 P.M. the worst of the fighting was over. A standoff ensued for the rest of the daylight hours; the Federals were unwilling to renew the attack and the Confederates were too weak to undertake any offensive action of their own. At dusk, General Hatch's troops began a slow retreat to Boyd's Neck, where they took up a defensive position under the protective umbrella of the Federal gunboats that had accompanied the transports from Hilton Head. According to the Record of Events for the 55th, the regiment lost eight commissioned officers and 140 enlisted men killed and wounded, though a post-war accounting by one of the 55th's officers puts the loss that day at 29 killed and 108 wounded, total 137. Among those killed was the young farmer from Vincennes, Indiana, John Posey. According to the inventory of his belongings as reported by his company commander on March 19, John Posey left behind "no effects." Also seriously wounded in this action was Colonel Hartwell, the 55th's former commander, who had led the Second Brigade in this action. Lieutenant Colonel Charles B. Fox now took charge of the regiment.[40]

While most of the other units involved in this expedition were soon posted elsewhere, the Boyd's Neck position was fortified and held by the 55th until the new year arrived. On December 21, Federal troops under Sherman entered Savannah, and on January 11 orders came for the 55th to proceed there for garrison duty. It took two days' travel and when the 55th landed at Fort Thunderbolt on January 13, Sherman's soldiers lined the roads to see them —the first African American infantrymen they had ever met. According to the history of the 55th Massachusetts: "The feeling of

39. OR, Volume 44, p. 423.
40. National Archives: Compiled Service Records, 55th Massachusetts. Charles C. Soule, "Battle of Honey Hill," (in "Annals of the War"), The Philadelphia Weekly Times, May 17, 1884. OR, Volume 44, p. 591.

Sherman's army against colored troops occasionally made itself manifest in words, but in no other way."[41]

The 55th remained in the Savannah area performing mostly fatigue duties until early February, when it was shipped to Hilton Head, arriving just in time to take part in an inland raid commanded by General Potter. Then it was back to Folly Island. Almost at once the 55th was assigned to an expedition under General Schimmelfenning to James Island. A combination of bad weather, poor planning, and the usual faulty overall coordination stretched the pointless operation out for several days. The 55th led a charge on February 10 that carried a stubbornly defended Rebel line—an engagement that marked the last combat in the Charleston campaign. On February 19, word came that the city had been evacuated by its Rebel defenders.[42]

The Union troops were immediately organized into a triumphal column and, on February 21, the 55th led the way into the city that had defied Federal attempts to take it for more than three years. As one of the officers in the regiment would remember: "Words would fail to describe the scene which those who witnessed it will never forget,—the welcome given to a regiment of colored troops by their people redeemed from slavery." Hardly had the 55th passed through Charleston when it was ordered out on another expedition into the interior under General Potter. This one took the 55th on a roundabout march that kept it in the field until March 10, when it returned to Charleston. The 55th was posted there for several days until a garrison assignment spread detachments of the regiment across James Island. Here the regiment remained until April 5 when it was sent out in company with the 54th New York to support a larger column of troops that had marched from Georgetown, South Carolina, to wreck the railroad lines around Camden. By April 12 the 55th had completed this duty and gone into bivouac near Charleston. Here the officers and men learned of the fall of Richmond and Lee's surrender at Appomattox Court House. Also here, on April 19, came the tragic news of Lincoln's assassination. "Even the rebel population united in condemnation of so cowardly a murder," noted the regimental history, "and scarcely a colored person could be

41. Fox, *Record of the Service*, pp. 48-49.
42. Fox, *Record of the Service*, pp. 51-53, 55-56.

met in the streets, who had not assumed, in some form or other, the badge of mourning."[43]

On April 20, the 55th Massachusetts moved out to take up occupation duties at St. Andrews. In May it marched to Orangeburg, where nearly a thousand former slaves flocked to see the "Black Yankees." Finally, on August 24, the 55th broke camp to begin the long journey home. The men boarded railroad cars that took them into Charleston, where they transferred to the steamers *Karnac* and *Ben Deford*. Storms delayed the latter, which did not land its cargo in Boston until September 20, seven days after the *Karnac* had arrived. On September 23, 1865, the 55th Massachusetts was paid off and discharged from the service of the United States.[44]

The history of the regiment closes its own narrative of service with this accounting: "32 commissioned officers and 822 enlisted men were mustered out, of these, 18 officers and 653 men had left Readville in 1863, and had served with the regiment from its organization." A total of 175 enlisted men had died while in service with the 55th—54 of them were killed or mortally wounded in action. There were 30 who deserted the regiment and 121 who passed away from disease or other causes. The regiment lost five officers in the course of the war, two of them at Honey Hill. The 55th Massachusetts had not only played its part in the great historical saga that was the American Civil War, but by the record of service of its African American enlisted men, the 55th Massachusetts (Colored) Volunteers had itself made history.[45]

43. Fox, *Record of the Service*, pp. 56, 64, 74.
44. Fox, *Record of the Service*, p. 80.
45. Fox, *Record of the Service*, pp. 84, 111.

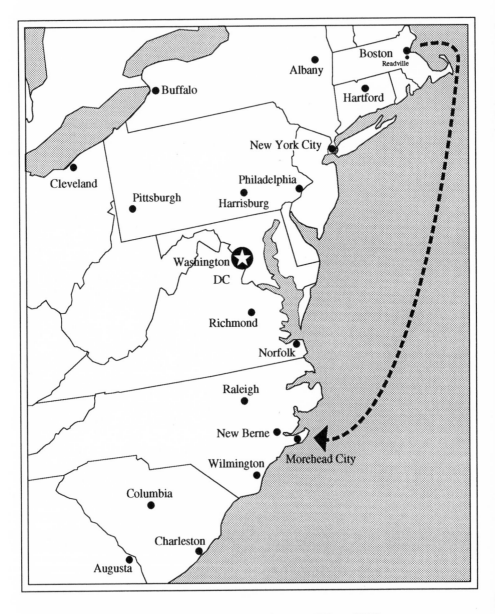

The 55th Massachusetts Goes to War: 1863

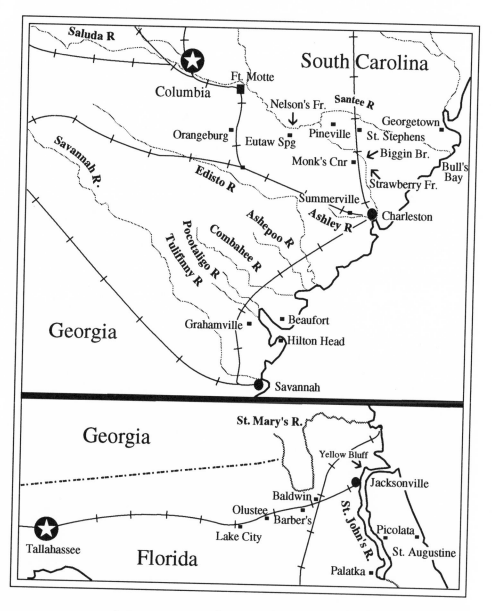

Area of Operations, 55th Massachusetts: 1863-1865

Part One

"In defense of my race and country."

May 1863 through January 1864

Massachusetts—North Carolina— South Carolina

The 55th Massachusetts (Colored) Volunteers took shape in Camp Meigs, Readville, Massachusetts, between May 12 and July 21, 1863. During that period it received recruits from around the country, with the heaviest concentration coming from the Mid-West. By war's end, the 55th would have taken in a total of 97 members from the state of Indiana. One of these, a farmer from Vincennes named John Posey, arrived in camp on June 20 and joined Company D, which had been activated less than a month earlier.

In many ways, John Posey was no different than most of the 800 other enlisted men in the regiment. The record of his service, as reflected in the bimonthly company muster rolls, shows him to have been a dependable soldier with no marks against him. One way in which John Posey differed from his comrades was the small but solid trail he left in the form of a series of letters to home written throughout his service. These are modest missives, concerned with family matters for the most part, and tight-lipped on many of the great questions of the time that confronted African American soldiers in the U.S. Army. The first Posey letter that has survived was written before the 55th Massachusetts left Camp Meigs for the front.

[Camp Meigs, Readville,] July the 11, 1863[1]

Dear Cousin
   It is with the greatest of pleasure [that] I do take my pen in

1. This letter is from the collection of Robert Younger. The unedited version can be found on page 235 in Appendix Four. It evidently took Posey several days to complete since some of the events it refers to clearly took place after July 11.

33

hand to inform [you] that I am well at present and I hope when these few lines come to hand, [they] may find you [enjoying] the the same [blessing].

We had a hard rain here last night and this morning [learned] we are not going as was reported. We were to go two weeks ago [but did not] because of a great disturbance in Boston, and we are a-going to stay [here] till the [troubles] resisting [the] draft [end]. There [was] a white regiment here and they went in once or twice there [on] July 17 and they have killed 18 or twenty of them.[2] They are all Irish and have [carried out] colored executions [there], and also in New York.

Give Jo Sheen one of the coppers. Let me tell you I am a-going to send some money home in a few days and what so ever I write to do with [it], I wish you will carefully do and respectably do. I expect it will be in next week by express at Vincennes.

One of the soldiers an Irish lieutenant today at twelve o'clock knocked him down. They put him in [the] guard house.[3]

Take good care [of] the old woman, no more at [present.] John Posey [to] Joseph [W. Embry] [PAGE TEAR]
rest until I tell you the time I started home. You might suppose that I acted quite presumptuous and so do I, but forgive me for I was very heavy, so heavy that I was like [to have] passed [going] home.

No more at present. Answer as soon as [you] can.

John Posey to Joseph W. Embry

———————— •◦• ————————

John Posey was not the only soldier in the ranks of the 55th writing home at this time. What makes this next letter of especial interest is the fact that it was written during the relatively brief period that the regiment was in North Carolina. According to the regimental Compiled Service Record:

"The Regt left Boston July 21, 1863, on steamer Cahawba, *landed at Morehead City, N.C., July 25, 1863, and proceeded at once by rail—reported the same evening to Brig. Genl. E. A. Wild*

2. On the evening of July 14 a mob estimated at 5,000 attacked Boston's Cooper Street armory. Troops fired into the crowd with rifles and cannon, killing a number of people.
3. A portion of this letter is torn out and lost, and the handwriting much cramped in places, so the next few lines are fragmentary and incomplete.

34

at Newberne, N.C. [sic] & bivouacked on river bank near Ft. Spinola; on the ground where the camp was next day established. July 30 the Regt embarked for Charleston, S.C. in light marching order."

July the 26, 1863[4]

North Carolina Fort Spinola

Friend Hannibal

Having just arrived at this place on Saturday night the 25th I take my position this morning behind my knapsack in the sun to address you a few lines to inform you that I & all the rest of the boys are in good health. The Rebels are within 12 miles of us, where we are encamped now. We are 50,000 strong. We are expecting a fight before long & I am glad of it. They have Bill Givins standing on a barrel nearly every day for bad behavior.[5] It is too hot to write much to day. Hannibal, I wish you would see mother [and find out] if she got that money I sent her. Read this to mother. When you direct your letter to the 55th regt, direct it to Co. F in care of Capt. [Sigourney] Wales. Give my love to every body. Tell mother & all of our people I would like to have some of their pictures. They promised to send me some of their ugly mugs. Nothing more this time.

Yours respectfully,
Jordan R. Burton,[6] Co. F
55th Mass. Regt., North Carolina Fort
Spinola in care of Capt. Wales

———◆•◆———

Newspapers were important to soldiers of the Civil War. Often, they were the only timely source of accurate information available to the men regarding the course of the war and events at home. Soldiers in the east had relatively little trouble obtaining copies of the major dailies from New York, Boston or Philadel-

4. Jordan R. Burton Pension File, National Archives.
5. There is no one in the 55th Massachusetts with this name. Probably this refers to an acquaintance in a nearby regiment.
6. Jordan R. Burton was a nineteen-year-old farmer from Lewiston, Pennsylvania. He would die on Folly Island on June 27, 1864, from what is noted in the regimental history roster as "consumption."

phia. Several could be purchased directly from the news agents that accompanied the armies or from sutlers, while others came through the post from friends or benevolent associations. Writing from the Petersburg front in September 1864, a Michigan soldier noted: "We now get the Washington Chronicle, Philadelphia Enquirer, *and the* New York Herald. *Through the mail we get the* Detroit Tribune *and* Free Press *and the* New York World."[7]

The newspapers did an excellent job of covering the military campaigns, and most treated actions involving black troops no differently from those operations undertaken solely by white units. There also existed two nationally distributed newspapers published by Americans of color that sought to speak to and for black soldiers. The New York based Weekly Anglo-African *had been founded in 1859 by editors Thomas and Robert Hamilton. Beginning in 1861 it regularly gave column space to letters from African Americans serving with U.S. forces, as well as reporting on the activities of the various "colored" units. The following is the earliest letter from the 55th to appear in its pages.*

Newbern, N.C., July 27, 1863[8]

Mr. Editor:

Thinking you would like to hear from the 55th, I will embrace the present opportunity of telling of our trip from Boston to this place. On Tuesday morning [July 21], at 7½ o'clock we broke up camp and took up a line of march for the depot. After waiting there for half an hour the cars came down from Boston, and in half an hour we were ready to start. The cars began to move; the crowd began to cheer, and the men to sing. After half an hour's ride we arrived in Boston. The crowd at the depot was very great. We then formed a line and marched through a few of the principal streets. When we arrived at the State House the crowd was very great—women and children were crowded on the steps to see the 55th pass. We there halted and presented arms, and afterwards took a line of march to the steamer. After a long and weary march, we embarked on the *Cahawba*. At 1 o'clock every man was on board. The colored people were collected in great

7. Boston, William. *The Civil War Diary of William Boston,* (Michigan, 1937), p. 62.
8. *Weekly Anglo-African,* August 22, 1863, Houghton Library, Harvard University.

36

crowds, outside of the wharf, to see the 55th off; but there being a guard of police to keep out the people, and the soldiers in, it was 1 o'clock before they were permitted to come inside. At 2 o'clock we left the wharf, amid a heavy rain.

On Wednesday morning [July 22] nearly all the men were sea-sick. Nothing occurred worthy of note during the voyage. On Friday morning [July 24] every person was well, and our sea-sick men were as hungry as wolves. On Saturday [July 25], at 4 o'clock in the morning, we came in sight of land, and at 5 dropped anchor and fired a gun. In an hour a pilot came on board, but could not get in the harbor on account of low tide; but at 10 we weighed anchor, ran in [to] port at Morehead City, and landed at the depot. We then marched about a mile and encamped until the cars should come down to Newbern [*sic*]. After having ate our dinner and rested, we took the cars for Newbern. At 8 o'clock we arrived within one mile of the city; we then formed a line and marched in front of it, where the First North Carolina Colored Regiment is encamped. Here we were supplied with a quart of coffee and hard tack, which was as much as any man wanted. After supper we encamped out in an open field.

Next morning (Sunday) [July 26] we were up at 4½ o'clock and began to fix for encamping. We received our tents, but did not make much progress in putting them up at first, but now we have them all up, and it looks like a camp. On Sunday evening we went out to fire blank cartridges. I am very sorry to say that the First North Carolina done better firing than the 55th, and as for drilling, I never saw a regiment, white or black, drill better, and they have been organized only since the 1st of May. Many may wonder that this North Carolina regiment is so well drilled. They take more pains to learn, and go through with every movement as though their very lives depended on the manner in which it is executed. They are raising another regiment of blacks, and it is nearly full. It is called the Second North Carolina. None of the Sergeants can read or write, except the 1st Sergants of Companies A and G. They are very intelligent men. Their wives come from Newbern every day with pics[9] and cakes to sell. Our boys buy them as fast as they fetch them, for we all have got tired eating

9. A reference to picnic, which in this context means a portion of food meant to be eaten out of doors.

hard tack and salt pork.

The health of our regiment is very good. We have had but one death since we came here.[10] The water does not agree with our men, it is very poor and scarce at that.

A very serious affair occurred to-day over at the camp of the First North Carolina Regiment. The 1st Sergeant of Co. H, I think, was down in a little town about a mile from the camp, when he and a colored citizen got into a quarrel about a woman, which resulted in the citizen cutting him in the left side. He is at present very low, and not expected to live. When they arrested him and brought him up to put in the guard-house, the soldiers, as soon as they learned the particulars, rushed to the guard-house, and would have taken him out had not the guards charged bayonets on them. They all say the first time he is seen out, they will kill him. We may stay here some time, and I will let you know all the news from our regiment.

H.C.P.[11]

<hr />

While at New Berne the 55th Massachusetts was made part of Edward A. Wild's "African Brigade," which otherwise consisted of the 1st North Carolina Colored and portions of the 2nd and 3rd N.C.C. On July 30, 1863, the Brigade was moved to the barrier islands outside Charleston, where U.S. forces confronted the City's defenders.

The next letter from the 55th was published in the other national African American newspaper, the Christian Recorder *of Philadelphia. This paper had been established in 1853 as the official organ of the African Methodist Episcopal (AME) Church. Although its focus was primarily religious, it too began to print letters from black soldiers. The following is the first from the 55th to appear in its pages.*

10. Joseph Rodman, a twenty-two-year-old farmer from Pike County, Ohio, who died on July 26. The listed cause is "measles."
11. There is no one on the rolls of the 55th Massachusetts with the initials "H.C.P." Possible candidates for this honor are: Henry Pulpress (Company B), Henry D. Perkins (Company C), Hampton Phoenix (Company G), and Harrison Peril (Company K). Based solely on the fact that the overwhelming majority of enlisted men soldier-correspondents came from non-commissioned ranks, Hampton Phoenix, a sergeant from Wilkes Barre, Pennsylvania, becomes the leading contender.

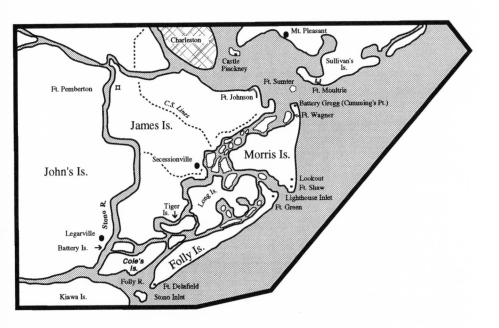

Charleston Harbor and Nearby Islands

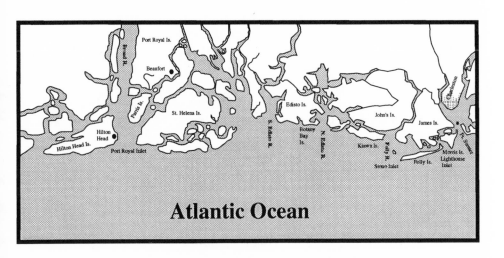

Hilton Head to Charleston Coastline

Folly Island, S.C., October 15, 1863[12]

Dear Brother in Christ:

Yours of the 5th came safely to hand, which found me quite well indeed. I was happy to get hold of the *Christian Recorder* once more. It is true, I never subscribed for it. I have read it frequently, and have found it a paper worthy of notice; and it is fraught with importance. I read it carefully the columns of which contained something about Wilberforce[13] that did me as much good as though I were there to enjoy hearing of so many going from all parts, or I might change the above and say, coming from the East and West, North and South.

I rejoice that the white man has not had much of a hand in the matter. Thank God for that. They have been working hard to obtain that fine place; but they had their largest guns elevated too high; consequently missed the University.[14]

I have nothing very interesting at this time but what you perhaps have heard long since. I will mention a little about the 55th Massachusetts Regiment. They seem to be in good health at present, and are desirous of making a bold dash upon the enemy. I pray God the time will soon come when we, as soldiers of God, and of our race and country, may face the enemy with boldness. For my part, I feel willing to suffer all privations incidental to a Christian and a soldier.

This is the calmest day that I have witnessed on the Island. Since here I have been for some four weeks or more in bombarding the enemy's forts. Thank God, we have silenced their batteries. Brother Weaver,[15] I stood upon the parapets surrounding the "Swamp Angel,"[16] and saw men fall around me like hail-stones. I stood fast and kept the men that were working upon them together as much as possible. The enemy fired shell and grape into us like hot cakes, but we kept at our work like men of God. In

12. *Christian Recorder*, October 24, 1863. Edwin Redkey collection.
13. Wilberforce College in Ohio, the first college to be run by African Americans.
14. The AME took over Wilberforce College in 1863.
15. The Reverend Elisha Weaver, editor of the *Christian Recorder*.
16. Nickname given to an eight-inch, 200-pounder Parrott rifled cannon emplaced by orders of General Gillmore in a Morris Island marsh to target Charleston with incendiary shells. Putting this massive gun into position required that a 2½ mile trestle be laid over the swamp, and the gun position itself needed 800 tons of sand and pilings sunk twenty feet into the ooze to make it a firm enough platform for the gun to fire. The "Swamp Angel" fired its first shot at Charleston at 1:30 A.M., August 22.

conclusion, let me say, if I fall in the battle anticipated, remember, I fall in defense of my race and country. Some of my friends thought it very wrong in me setting aside the work of the Lord to take up arms against our enemy. Certainly I can with as much grace as taking a drink out of Wilberforce spring. Another excuse or reason they offered was, that it is wrong to take that which you cannot restore, but I am fully able to answer all questions pertaining to rebels. If taking lives will restore the country to what it once was, then God help me to slay them on every hand.

May God bless your efforts; may His choice blessings rest upon Wilberforce. In soliciting subscribers for your paper, please inform me in your next missive what is the price per quarter.

I remain yours truly,
I.H. Welch
Orderly Sgt.[17]

The muster roll for Company D for the period from September through December, 1863, shows that the unit was stationed on Folly Island during that time. The only comment for the period under "Record of Events," is the one made in the September-October report: "Constant fatigue duty."

[Folly Island, S.C.] November the 18, 1863[18]
To My Cousin [Mathias Embry]

It is with the greatest of pleasure that I take my pen in hand to inform you that I am well at present and seriously hope these few [lines] may find [you] enjoying the same blessing.

I have been deeply interested in the welfare of my dear kindreds at home, and to my surprise and sorrow, [I was] rather thinking that you all, [were torn] up so instantly, without terribly good luck, [and that it] has created great losses. If [I] write you should write [me] anything you expect to take place or that you are a-going to do. If it should not take place or is not done, you

17. First Sergeant Isaiah H. Welch was a twenty-one-year-old farmer from Bellfont, Pennsylvania.
18. This letter is from the collection of Robert Younger. The unedited version can be found on pages 235-36 of Appendix Four.

should write [me] immediately; if the case be certified the next day you should [write] as soon as the nature of [the] case would admit. So if it were [a] surprise, our minds would not be so long frustrated with it. I can tell you that [you] cannot write too often, for I have wrote several letters and was sadly disappointed in hopes of getting answers.

[I] give you to know that a letter from home is quite consoling to a soldier that cannot get the news of the day. As for Uncle James I have not received the scratch of a pen, though I honored him with two [letters], and Aunt Sarah [says she] wrote three, but I never got one of them—so I was informed by Louise Embry. I got one of Mary and Ellen Embry. I [would] like to get one from home and like [to] get it before I get to Boston. [But as] I had not wrote a letter, she did not precisely know where I was.

The Captain said this morning that Charles Newton is now in Virginia, [this] was the first of my knowing where he was since he wrote to me from North Carolina. I [had] heard he was gone there, but it was disputed though I supposed it so, and I expect he is faring better than we are. There are several others [there] with him that have got [on] well, and they have nothing to do but have fun. [Here] they drill us till we cannot rest; sometimes several of the behive got sick and had to leave the ranks, and some fainted and fell, but this old horse [has] never been fazed. I was sick, which I thought was about [to] wrestle me down to the foot of the hill.[19] I am about right now, though I have not drilled for six weeks.

Take good care of the girls. There have been no real movements here since I wrote last, only there has been [a] great [deal] of fortifying and mounting gun mortars. They think that some of them will throw a ball 400 pound in weight. The [enemy] show[s] no great sign of fight—6 colored regiments here, the 55th, 54th, First and Second South Carolina, 3rd Pennsylvania [and] Second North Carolina is here.[20] I have nothing to drink worth

19. Possibly, Posey is saying here that he feared he was going to die.
20. For the period ending December 31, 1863, the following black units were stationed on Morris or Folly Island: 54th and 55th Massachusetts, 1st North Carolina, 2nd South Carolina, and 3rd USCT. Posey's reference to the 3rd Pennsylvania is likely the 3rd USCT, which was organized at Camp William Penn, near Philadelphia. He probably means the 1st North Carolina for the "Second." Since the 1st South Carolina was posted at Hilton Head, South Carolina at this time, Posey's mention of the "First and Second" must mean only the 2nd, which

speaking of. The quartermaster gives us a little when we come [in] from work at night, though we have moved camp and now we can [LETTER ENDS HERE]

The worst enemy facing the 55th Massachusetts during its first tour of Morris and Folly islands was disease. From August, 1863, to November, the regiment lost 32 through causes as varied as: "dysentery," "typhoid fever," "chronic diarrhea," "consumption," "general debility," and 'inflammation of the brain." The biggest killer was typhoid fever, which would eventually account for 33 of the 121 non-combat fatalities in the regiment. Especially poignant was the passing away, on September 26, of two brothers, David U. and Jonathan King of Mt. Pleasant, Ohio. The cause of both deaths was the fever.[21] Most often deaths were merely noted in the regimental records, but every now and then the accomplishments of an individual merited a more public tribute.

Headquarters 55th Mass. Vols.,
White House, Folly Island, S.C.,

November 25, 1863[22]

At a meeting of the non-commissioned officers of this regiment to take into consideration the death of Sergeant S.P. Thomas of Company A, the following preamble and resolutions were adopted:

Whereas, it has pleased Almightly Providence in His infinite wisdom to remove from our midst, our beloved brother and companion in arms, Sergeant S.P. Thomas of Co. A;

Resolved, That while we bow in humble submission unto the rod of affliction, we deeply mourn the loss of the deceased whose bravery, displayed while under a daily fire from the rebel forts; whose patience while afflicted by a severe disease and whose exemplary, soldierly conduct on all occasions won our highest admiration.

may have had a detachment from the 3rd with it. See: *Official Records,* Volume 28, Part 2, pp. 137-138.
21. Fox, Charles B. *Record of the Service of the Fifty-fifth Regiment of Massachusetts Volunteer Infantry* (Boston, 1868), pp. 110-144.
22. *Weekly Anglo-African,* December 26, 1863. *Christian Recorder,* January 2, 1864. Edwin Redkey Collection.

Resolved, That by his death the country loses a brave and faithful soldier, the regiment to which he belonged one of its best noncommissioned officers, and his bereaved parents a dutiful son; and that we deeply sympathize with his relations and friends.

Resolved, That a copy of these resolutions be sent to his family, a copy to the *Anglo-African* of New York city, and one to *The Christian Recorder* of Philadelphia.

Sergeant J.H. Walker, Co. B, President

[Sergeant Major] James M. Trotter, Secretary[23]

———————— ◆◆◆ ————————

The men who joined the 55th Massachusetts did so with the understanding that they were to be paid the same as white men serving in other Federal regiments. Massachusetts officials from Governor Andrew down believed this to be the case, as did the recruiters and officers for the regiment. At first the actions of the U.S. Government bore them out; payments made in early 1863 to the 1st South Carolina Colored and the Louisiana Native Guards were at the standard rate, thirteen dollars a month to a private. But on June 4, 1863, the War Department announced that it considered all "colored" regiments to fall under the Militia Act of July 17, 1862, which specified the pay to black privates to be ten dollars per month, three of which was set aside for clothing.

The merits (however dubious) of this judicial rendering aside, the new Government policy cast a terrible shadow over the African American men serving in infantry regiments. It quickly became the topic that dominated many of the letters written to public forums such as the black newspapers. This one came from a soldier in the 55th who identified himself only as "Wolverine."

Folly Island, S.C., December, 1863[24]

. . . We don't wish you to look upon us as being inclined to be

23. Sergeant Samuel P. Thomas was eighteen years old when he joined the regiment. The Madison County, Ohio native listed his occupation as "laborer." Sergeant Joseph H. Walker, 34, was a cook from Lewiston, Pennsylvania, while Sergeant Major James M. Trotter was a school teacher from Cincinnati.
24. *Christian Recorder*, January 2, 1864. Reprinted in Edwin S. Redkey, *A Grand Army of Black Men: Letters from African American Soldiers in the Union Army, 1861-1865.* (Cambridge University Press, 1992)

Parade Ground

Camp Layout of the 55th Massachusetts, Folly Island: November, 1863

Road

Co. K

Co. A

Co. C

Co. B

Co. G

Colonel's
Street

Co. D

Co. H

Co. E

Co. I

Co. F

Well
Well
Well
Well
Well

Guard
House

Sutler

Qr Master

Ordnance
Tents

Stable

Asst. Surg.
Asst. Surg.
Qr Master
Lt. Col.
Colonel
Adjutant
Major
Sur & con
Chaplain

Hospital
Tents

Field & Staff
Servants' Tents

Company Kitchens &
Officers' Servants

Company Officer's Tents

Tents of different
companies, 10 each
side of Street facing
in

45

a little stubborn; we were told that we would be accepted by the U.S. Government on the same terms as her other Regiments, and do you call the same terms reducing pay, and receiving part pay from Mass[achusetts], and a part from the government at the same?[25] If you look at it in that way, you don't look at it as we do. Massachusetts has always been first to open the door to the poor colored man; was first to send two colored regiments in the field to extinguish the last spark of a most infamous rebellion—one that will figure largely in the annals of history for centuries to come. You sit at your firesides and just study a little what the poor soldier is suffering. You have no idea, and just you fight and slay the rebels that are at our backs, or we will fight them that are in front of us, or fight in Congress for our rights, and we will fight here for yours. I feel proud, and so does every other man that belongs to the 55th, to think that they stand so well upon the principles which they came here to fight for. Our pride has won us a name amongst the white regiments around us; they call us the Independent Colored Regiment, and say to us, You do the work that we ought to share in, and they don't want to pay you anything for it. Do you want to break that spirit of pride! I hope not; and as you say that we have proved ourselves worthy of approbation, don't put our principle upon the grindstone. We love this government, and will sacrifice our lives to maintain it. Just think for a moment, reflect deeply, that there is good for you to gain by it; our lives we value just as highly as you do yours; but without a stimulant, our exertions would not be worth anything. Let our faces be black, but our hearts be true, you will find us true and loyal and obedient, and all qualities pertaining to a soldier. A true and rather singular idea for a colored man to wish to be placed on equal footing with a white man! Why not? Can't we fight just as well? We showed our qualities at Port Gibson and Wagner.[26] Now, if there is not pluck, just fall in some big hole, and we will guarantee to pull you out without blacking your hands; fall down and we will pick you up; we won't pass by and

25. Even as he lobbied Washington to reverse this decision, Governor Andrew went to his state legislature, which agreed to appropriate funds to make up the difference in pay for the men of the 54th and 55th. But, as Wolverine makes clear, this solution did not resolve the deep insult to the principle of equality represented by the Government pay policy.
26. Reference, partly incorrect, to widely publicized actions in 1863 involving black troops in combat. Both were assaults against fortified positions, and both

perhaps give you a kick or a cuff, but pick you up, carry you home to your good wife, and won't ask of you your daughter for compensation; all the compensation that we ask is to give us our rights, and don't be dodging around every corner as if you owed us something, and your conscience is getting the upper hand of you. . . . Our motto: "Liberty and Equality."

Wolverine

———————————◆•◆•◆———————————

This next letter from the 55th by John Posey is both fragmentary (the first page or pages are missing) and undated. The envelope shows a postmark of December; that and other internal references to the weather would tend to confirm that this letter comes from December 1863.

[Folly Island, S.C., December, 1863][27]
[Joseph W. Embry]

. . . did write and tell me them doggone negroes was married before this time. You could have sent a word too as Miss Thomas did to her brother. God bless her dear soul for thinking so much of him. I am just a-getting out of humor about it, for you knew [that] I wanted to know when that happened, if not before. I suppose I must not consider Mr. George Parker a company keeper of mine any longer, but rather consider him my cousin, and I expect she made her bed, as she would be [still] waiting if she [were] young. Now she is taken out of the family; keep that wharf rat out [for] the redeemer's sake, nor let Ellen keep [him] company.

If you are doing well send me some money. I loaned and spent all that I had and the paymaster has not come to pay us as yet, but they say he will be around in about three months. If he comes I will [pay] my bill, [which] will be over one hundred dol-

failed in a military sense, but succeeded in the political sphere by demonstrating that African American soldiers would fight. The charge at Port Hudson, May 27, involved Louisiana black regiments, while that at Fort Wagner, July 18, was by the 54th Massachusetts.

27. This letter is from the collection of Robert Younger. The unedited version can be found on pages 236-38 of Appendix Four.

lars, and I am a-going to send it home to Vincennes by express and I want you to get it. Pay strict attention to the office and [do] not let it get lost, for if I lose that I had as well be dead. But if possible send me five dollars and I will the[e] re-pay by half the amount, which is 50 [per]cents interest.

I will now state and inquire of something else. We are all doing well, we have a good time and good captain and nothing is [causing us] distress, and as for caring [for] anything, we do not. We do not [much] as [care about the] pesky rebels, for we had just as soon get as many of them as not. They are still a-bombarding yet, and it's not cold here yet. We have only had one day or two that [was] a little cold, but [not] so much what we could [bear] in a camp without any fire and not be cold. The worst times we have is a-going on picket and on camp guard. The short stay of us here [now] appears to be a very long one, but as we have stayed so [far], I had rather stay [here] until spring than go north or east on the account of the cold weather, though we may leave and go north and have to bear it.

We wanted to go [to Virginia before] this, but we do not want to go now, though it is several hundred miles closer home. There is where I expect to get my furlough, and then you all had better look wild, especially if [I] should come.

[A PAGE OR PAGES APPEAR TO BE MISSING HERE]

. . . to hear how about Uncle Elias Case, and whether he was much [worse] or not, and if you all have not sold it, it is no use to sell until you get what your property is worth. When you wrote to me and said you was a-going away and I got a letter from Louise Embry. She stated that they were a-going to leave the next Wednesday, this being wrote on the 1st of September, and I never got [word] until the 1st of August [October?], in which time I supposed you were gone and I wrote to Sims Embry and sent a small note in his letter. I told [him] if [you] were there to give it to you. I am sorry that there was ever such a mistake. You will get the run of this letter by the number at the top.[28]

28. Given the vagaries of the postal system at that time, it was not uncommon for letters to be delivered and received well out of the order in which they were written. To remedy this problem, many took to numbering their letters sequentially and would refer to letters received and sent by number rather than date.

I did not think I would write so much, but I suppose [all the] marrying going on at home, and me in South Carolina, makes a great difference. I have no more [to write] at present.

Give my love to all the inquiring friends.

John Posey
Co. D, 55th Mass. Regt.
Morris Island, near Charleston

During the Second World War the U.S. government produced a series of films designed to explain to the civilian turned soldier why he or she was fighting. It was a question very much on the minds of African Americans since there were some voices among them that argued it was a White Man's War, not a Black Man's affair.

Answering the question of why they were fighting is part of the message in this letter from the 55th.

Camp, 55th Mass.
Folly Island, S.C., December 2, 1863[29]

Brother Weaver:

I have nothing very interesting to which your attention is invited, only concerning your important paper and other matters of minor importance. I noticed by the reading thereof, the valuable work that is being performed by our people of the North, which will, I pray, result in official good when accomplished. Sir, while watching with interest the onward move of my race, I cannot avoid harboring the thought but that our people will in a short period become a nation worthy of the applause of others. Mr. Editor, they have undoubtedly labored faithfully amid prejudice and oppression, to the accomplishment of a work now partially done; if a moment be spent in reflecting upon our past condition, which was comparatively helpless, we would certainly

29. *Christian Recorder*, December 19, 1863. Edwin Redkey collection.

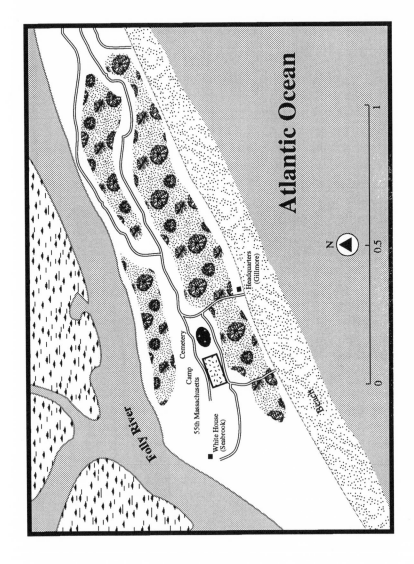

Camp Location of the 55th Massachusetts, Folly Island: November, 1863

50

say the Lord of grace and glory has been with us. Very few think as the writer upon the subject they murmur in consequence of the war. Sir, there is a medium through which God is helping us: it is certainly true it takes life; but will we shrink from that, knowing there are so many being freed thereby? Be it understood, wherever the Stars and Stripes float, there is liberty, and where it was once said the black man should not learn the alphabet, there he is being taught to read the divine word of God.

Sir, I am truly glad to learn that the friends are organizing societies for the purpose of meeting the absolute wants of those families whose husbands and sons are now on the battle-field. I earnestly and sincerely hope they will not allow a single case to pass unnoticed. I would say for the encouragement of wives, mothers, and beloved ones, to grieve not if you hear of the fall of those whom you cherish; bear in mind they fall, not in cause disgraced, but honorable and just. Parents, if it takes from you your favorite son, let him go and fight and die, if need be, for his race and country.

Sir, I am proud to speak of the colored troops in this department; they have shown themselves worthy of being called gallant men of the North, and those of the South evince by their efforts and labor, a willingness to die in defence of their race. Sir, they speak as did Nehemiah, should such as I flee; no suggestion of mine can add anything to its completeness. May they who have come to this condition live long to fight the battles of their noble country, and may we as soldiers of our race and country agree upon one fundamental principle, "sink or swim, survive or perish —give me liberty or give me death."

Yours most respectfully,

I.H. Welch
Orderly Sgt.

Dear Brother,

I receive my paper very regularly indeed, and you should receive the thanks of every soldier in the army of color, for your services in the preparation and publication of this truly valuable paper, and I certainly feel indebted to my father for sending it.

It would seem that the month of December found many members of the 55th Massachusetts with more time on their hands than had been the case in September and October. There was a reduction in the amount and duration of fatigue assignments, one direct result being, in the words of the regimental history, "the general health of the regiment greatly improved." In the letter John Posey of Company D wrote that month, he expressed something of his frustration with the lack of news from home—something that was very important for all soldiers, North and South.

[Folly Island, S.C.] December the 2, 1863[30]

To My Cousin [Mathias Embry]

I take my pen in hand to inform you that I am well at present and I [hope] these lines may find you enjoying the same blessing.

You all appear to be dead, and whether you be [so] or no, I can not tell. If you are not dead you are very careless about either friends or relations, and for writing you do not give a damn whether you all write or not, though I might write often, which I do every two or three days, and sometimes every [day], and to get [a letter] once a month—I care not [for] it. [It] looks as though you might [write] once in a while every three or four months, and I would get a letter now and then, but you all [won't] write at all or almost never. I want you to write for I won't or will not be home before or under six or seven months. I do not want to come before the last of August, and perhaps by that [time] we will be closer to home, and if not, I do not know when I will be home. If [I] have any more such reports as I have I do not expect I will come at all. One more move like this heretofore takes place and I start and get in ten miles of home and [before] I hear of it, I take a little tack and tack right back and catch the old gray goose by the hind [leg]; then it will be flip flop old mother huckle backmamy dog bait, if I ain't gone. E.O. and I will eat somebodys for it, if [I] don't I will not get no Indiana wedding cake. I see you are all trying to get married because I have gone [to] war to eat rebels and take blue pills.

30. This letter is from the collection of Robert Younger. The unedited version can be found on pages 238-39 of Appendix Four.

Never mind my time [for furlough] is coming and I will catch some of you a-napping, but all I ask of you is not to do no more, for my time must be next, if not, I will stay here among the rebels while I live. And I would not have thought to have gone up your way, for I would have given 2 five dollar bills to have seen George marry. If I was to come I would come and have fun. I wonder if old Charles Allen was there, if he was, I know him and Mathias and Jos. P. Hapeen had plenty of fun and if [you] had been [there] you would [have] had fun.

Just got the word yesterday, and I thought if perhaps if I would wrote today I might get some of the cake, for I know Fern[?] has got some and I want a piece of it, if it has to be five years old; and I dare another of my cousins to get married without me there, or unless I die or the rebels feeds me too heavy; than if they will, [they can] go on as such against my orders, they will have to, but Mathias must not marry until I come home—for I intend to have all of my connections to my wedding. And tell if you can you devil, if you got something good to eat—all of that good 'possum, coon, rabbit, black squirrel. And I heard rooster crow yesterday morning and just below here they have plenty of good deer and turkey and dem dar great big fat hogs, and don't you know that I will have good times. 25 of our boys was down in the woods [the] other day and [the] rebels got after them, and they got to an intrenchment and fired on the rebels and they took the wings of morning in retreat[ing] and they got out of [the] intrenchment, and the rebels seeing that there was not many of them, and [so] they come again. The [Union] captain, seeing a gunboat which was making its way to them, the captain run a little distance back, gave the gunboat [a] sign, and she opened fire on them and [they were obliged] to retreat for something.

Give my love to all of the friends, don't give the secesch an inch, but John Howard has a word on them.

No more at present.

John Posey to Mathias Embry
Write to me soon again to Folly Island, South Carolina
John Posey, Company D, Mass. 55th Regiment, in care of Captain Nutt, who is a good father to us.

The next letter John Posey wrote that December is much longer and far more difficult to decipher. Highlights are presented here in lieu of any attempt to represent the whole.

[Folly Island, S.C.] December the 27, 1863[31]

Mathias Embry

Write as soon as possible.

My Dear Cousin

It is with greatest of pleasure that I take my pen in hand to inform you that I am well at present and I hope when these few lines come to hand they may find you enjoying the same blessing.

Andy Hill, Co. G,[32] has come to the regiment and has fit right in to a great extent. You would not know him, he has an entire appearance of a man.

Elijah Cox has got well and [is] able to [do] duty, but he is not the man he used to be in health. Thornton Larmont is lame and is gone to Beaufort, South Carolina [to] the hospital. Charles Newton is gone to Portsmouth, Virginia, somewhere near Fortress Monroe and I [have] not seen him since the last of July and have not heard of him since the 16th of September, and he was well at that time, and I did not receive his letter and [I] suppose [I] thought [he was] done [for] it and would not write any more. I wrote a letter to him yesterday stating the reports from home which I got in letters and sent it by a colored soldier. William Larmont is ill but will be getting better. Samuel Graves is the same, as for myself I [am] well and getting better.[33]

❋ ❋ ❋

31. This letter is from the collection of Robert Younger. The unedited version has been omitted.
32. This is supposition on my part. The only "Andrew" from Vincennes in the 55th is Andy Hill of Company G. Almost all the soldiers in the regiment that are mentioned by Posey came from Vincinnes.
33. These all appear to be fellow members of the 55th. Thirty-two-year-old private Elijah Cox (Company C), a farmer from Busron P.O., Indiana, is shown on the regimental records as having been discharged September 15 for "disability." Thornton Larmont (Company C), another thirty-two-year-old private, was a teamster from Vincennes. Private Charles Newton (Company C) was a twenty-one-year-old farmer from Vincennes. William Larmont (Company C) was a twenty-year-old farmer from Vincinnes and was perhaps related to Thornton Larmont. Twenty-eight-year-old Samuel Graves (Company D), was a miller from Knox County, Indiana.

As for our Christmas it [was] taken first by going down on the sea shore and firing several rounds after which we came into camp and put away our guns and fell in for dinner which was beefsteak and mutton chops and it was the best time I ever had. . . . We are all very well satisfied [thus] far. I forgot to state I was arrested Christmas morning for the first time for my laziness not being present [at] roll call and [had] to take my knapsack, gun and go and stand before the Captain's tent from an hour before day until day light, and it [was] about as cold a morning as we have here, though nothing to be compared with the weather at home for the flies is as common here to day as they are in August. . . . Last Sunday we was taken down on the sea shore on review and about 25 officers exclusive of ours rode around us just as [you'll] see pictured in the New York Ledger, on them great big old horses and they marched us some time until I got tired. Not thinking about us a being on foot and them on horses they [ordered] us around about like mice. . . . No more in this. John Posey of the 55th Massachusetts Co. D. Captain William Nutt company Commander.

———————◆•◆———————

Pride within a regiment is one important measurement of the morale and condition of that unit. This next letter suggests that the 55th was a proud regiment indeed. It also makes clear that the issue regarding the pay of the regiment was still one of serious concern.

Camp 55th Mass. Vols., Folly
Island, S.C., Jan. 12, 1864[34]

Mr. Editor:

Thinking that a line for one of the soldiers in the regiment to which I belong might not prove unacceptable to your readers, and that by so doing I may, in a slight manner, lay open to the Northern colored people, a few of the sentiments cherished by a portion of their representatives in the army, I crave a small portion of your valuable space, hoping that a knowledge of our

34. *Weekly Anglo-African*, January 30, 1864. Houghton Library, Harvard University.

thoughts and feelings upon subjects vital to us as a people, may not be uninteresting. At the same time I wish to give a concise account of the duties which we have been called upon to perform, and to say a word or two in defence of my gallant comrades, as, I have been credibly informed that some individuals, North, are engaged in praising our brothers of the 54th and in vilifying us.

I am not aware, Mr. Editor, that you have a correspondent in our regiment, and, therefore, infer that you are not very well informed of our opinions upon matters which have been discussed again and again, as affairs in which our sister regiment, the 54th Mass., was alone concerned. But, sir, allow me to say, that although we may, heretofore, have been silent upon the probabilities of the U.S. government treating us as soldiers and men, I assure you we have been none the less careful in choosing what we consider our proper line of conduct.

The 55th Massachusetts landed on Folly Island on the 2d day of August, 1863, and encamped on the North end of the island, about a quarter of a mile from Lighthouse Inlet, which divides this from Morris Island. Immediately upon our arrival, large details were made from our brigade (consisting of ours, the 1st North Carolina Volunteers, and detachments of the 2d North Carolina Vols., and the 2nd U.S. Colored Troops)[35] for fatigue duty before Wagner and Gregg.[36] Our men were but poorly drilled, and had not been in the service long enough to become acquainted with military discipline; had never been into action, and were thus immediately exposed, with such manifest disadvantages, to the most dangerous and disagreeable duty that a soldier is ever called upon to perform. I do not hesitate to assert, sir, that it requires a higher standard of courage to perform fatigue duty under fire, than to go into battle. When men are exposed to a galling fire of artillery and sharpshooters, with no means of returning it and bear themselves in a cool and soldierly manner, doing their duty without a complaint, and when that duty is forced upon them, both day and night, for weeks without intermission, they may

35. The 2nd USCT never served in South Carolina. According to the August 31, 1863, list of troops in the Department of the South, Wild's "African Brigade" consisted of the 55th Massachusetts, the 1st North Carolina (Colored), a detachment of the 2nd North Carolina (Colored), and one company from the 3rd North Carolina (Colored). Probably the 3rd USCT is the one referred to here.
36. Fort (or Battery) Wagner and Battery Gregg were the two principal Confederate entrenched positions on the northern end of Morris Island.

justly lay claim to some credit. And this was the manner in which the 55th Mass. and 1st N.C. Colored Volunteers, were initiated into the duties of soldiers in active service in the field, by being subjected to hard labor under a heavy cross fire of solid shot and shell, without any other means of showing to their unseen foes their determination, than what would be, and ultimately was, shown, by the result of their patient and faithful labor—the fall of Wagner and Gregg.[37]

Do not understand me, sir, to lay claims for our brigade to *all* the fame earned by colored soldiers at that well known siege. Far from it; I only wish to claim our proper share of it, and when we get that we will be content. I do not wish to imitate a certain corporal of the 3d U.S. Colored Troops, who claimed (through the columns of the *Christian Recorder*) the capture of Wagner and Gregg, for the 3d U.S., the 54th Mass., and the 2d South Carolina.[38] No, sir, we of the 55th are not quite so anxious to obtain military glory as to grasp, not only that belonging to us, but that belonging to our companions in arms in other regiments. I believe I am correct when I state that we were before the rebel works for fully three weeks before the 3d U.S. came into the department, and done as much hard service as any other regiment in the field did in the same length of time. I can appreciate the sentiment which led the gallant corporal to praise his regiment so highly and I can imagine and do admire his feeling of soldierly pride in belonging to so noble a regiment as the 3d U.S.; but I *cannot* imagine what could induce him to claim, so absurdly, the entire reduction of such formidable works, to the utter disregard of thousands of brave men by whom he was surrounded.

The attention of our men is now almost entirely engrossed by the subject of pay. Will or will not the United States government pay us the same as she does her white troops? We enlisted with as purely patriotic motives as actuated *any white* soldiers; and our highest military authorities have here stated that the duties we have performed are as valuable to the government as any done by

37. Following his failure to storm Fort Wagner in a direct assault on July 18, General Gillmore began siege operations against the position that pushed Union trenches to the very walls of the entrenchment. On the night of September 6, Confederates began an evacuation that was successfully completed before dawn. Union troops then occupied the fort without opposition.
38. These units formed a brigade under the command of Colonel James Montgomery.

white troops. We will not take the paltry sum of $7 per month; we consider ourselves as manly and as soldierly as any other troops *of our experience, and therefore their equals,* and will only be content with an equal amount of pay. We did not enlist for the pay. Any man would be foolish to risk his life for from $18 to $21 per month. We enlisted because we considered it our duty, and all we ask is to be treated as men should be. True, Massachusetts has guaranteed to us the amount which would be required in addition to $7 per month, to make our pay the same as that of white troops; but *that is not what we want* and is not what is justly due to us. While we are in the greatest degree grateful to Massachusetts for fulfilling her promise of giving us or guaranteeing us the same pay as her other troops receive, we must most respectfully and yet firmly reject her generous offer, knowing that should we accept it, we would place ourselves in the same relation to the U.S. government as we would have been had we been enlisted as contraband troops. Our position would not be altered from that of $7 soldiers, and we would be considered as second class troops, which does not at all accord with our opinions and wishes. When Major [James] Sturgis, Paymaster for the State of Massachusetts, came to us, and offered the money which the State so generously *donated* to us, we respectfully declined receiving it, as we considered it beneath our manly dignity to thus virtually acknowledge ourselves the inferiors of our white comrades in arms, and thus by our own actions, destroy the very fabric we originally intended to erect. Rather than thus disgrace ourselves and those whose interests we came to advocate and defend, we will serve our term of three years without pay.

We have understood that a bill has been brought forward in Congress, which will, if passed, raise the pay of all troops, and will make our pay the same as that of others. If that bill does does pass, the U.S. government will never regret it, for then the colored troops in this service will have something to fight and *hope* for, and will not prove recreant to the trust that is placed in them. But now we are expected to do wonders with every influence working against us. We are subject to the most disagreeable drudgery, deprived of our rightful pay, debarred from promotion, and yet are expected to do as good service and as much of it, as those who have all possible inducements and advantages extended to them. Yet should we, when brought into the presence of the enemy, show the least hesitation, or should we refuse to do duty under existing circumstances, as has been the case with white troops in more than one instance, it would immediately be brought forward as evidence that we are unfit to be soldiers, and were unequal to the responsibilities which must devolve upon us as troops in active service in the field.

Our circumstances have been improving somewhat in course of a month or so past; our regiment, which was divided into half a dozen detachments, has been ordered into Winter quarters, and the detachments recalled. We had detachments on Botany Bay Island, Morris, St. Helens and Long Islands, and no less than three on this Island, which left us with about 100 men for duty in camp. I think we are indebted for the advantageous change in our condition, to the influence exercised by our able and excellent brigade commander, Col. M.S. Littlefield,[39] who has shown himself to be uncommonly solicitous of our welfare, and has exerted himself in our favor at all times since he has commanded us. If all who have connection with colored troops, were as impartial, as manly, and as unprejudiced as our noble brigadier, we would have nothing to fear and would defy any troops to surpass us.[40]

We are anxiously waiting to see what action the rebels will take in regard to our (colored) prisoners now in their possession. We are interested, particularly as two of our men, Sergeant R. Johnson and Private E. Logan of Co. "F," are now in their hands,[41] having been captured at Botany Bay when our detachment was there. Should the rebels consent to exchange, as is usual with prisoners of war, all will be well; but should Jeff. Davis enforce

39. Colonel Milton S. Littlefield, who had commanded the 54th Massachusetts following the death of Colonel Shaw, took over Wild's "African Brigade" on November 6, 1863.
40. Ironically, right after the war, Alfred S. Hartwell compiled a sizable dossier on Colonel Littlefield, intending to prove that Littlefield had diverted to himself portions of the bounty money the government provided for black enlisted men. Though the evidence put together by Hartwell was compelling, the case was never taken up by the government.
41. According to Record of the Service of the Fifty-Fifth Regiment of Massachusetts Volunteer Infantry, "Sergt. Johnson and Private Logan of Company F obtained permission to go for oysters along the creek, and venturing too far, and being unarmed, were taken, as was afterwards ascertained from a rebel surgeon, by a boat-party in search of oranges for the Rebel hospitals. When first captured, the men narrowly escaped being killed, but were finally taken to Charleston, where they were imprisoned, but not treated with very unusual severity. When Charleston was evacuated, they were removed to Salisbury, N.C., where, after many hardships, Sergt. Johnson died, Dec. 12, 1864. Logan was afterward exchanged."

his threat of treating us as servile insurgents, there will be but little quarter shown to rebels who fall into *our* hands; every man shall die who has not the power to defend himself, and then we will hear what Jeff. has to say about enslaving or butchering black soldiers. It must be one thing or the other—liberty or death.

There is considerable speculation among the men now, arising from rumors of the two regiments (54th and 55th) being recalled to Massachusetts and disbanded. It has been said that the State will be forced to recall us, if we stay out nine months without pay, and muster us out as State Militia. I am unable to say whether this report be true, but the majority of our men seem to be placing great confidence in it. As far as I am concerned, I do not wish to be discharged while the war lasts. If the United States government *chooses to act honorably and justly,* and acknowledge us as *soldiers and men* and show us an *equal chance* with others, I am willing, under those circumstances, to resign my life without a murmur, fighting for a cause that would be beneficial to *all*; but I am not content to throw away my life to support a government that seems to have done, and be still doing, all it can to crush us.

Our chaplain, Rev. William Jackson of New Bedford, Mass., has, I understand, got into a difficulty and is about to resign. What the cause of his resignation is I am unable to say positively, but have heard from good authority that there have been some disputes between him and some of the men about the mail—he being the mail officer of the regiment, which at last culminated in an open quarrel, and a threat from the chaplain to shoot one of our sergeants, and the actual drawing of a revolver upon the latter with intention of executing the threat. The result was that the sergeant reported to the colonel, and the chaplain offered his resignation. I think that better course for him could not have been pursued, as he was never popular with the men, and for some time past they have been murmuring against him, as he never held service, and is considered of little worth amongst us —this last act arousing a feeling of bitter animosity. Mr. Jackson is, I doubt not, a valuable member of society, and excellent minister of the Gospel in civic life; but is certainly unfit to be chaplain of a regiment.[42]

42. William Jackson resigned January 14, 1864. He was replaced as chaplain on March 27, 1864, by John R. Bowles.

I must conclude, Mr. Editor, by earnestly regretting that your journal has not a more extensive circulation in our regiment. We consider it the most efficient exponent of our ideas, and defender of our rights now in circulation. The reason why it has not more recipients here is our great cause of complaint—non-receipt of pay. Should we receive pay, I have no doubt but you will receive numerous calls from our men for your paper; but they are averse to subscribing when they know not by what means they can pay you. But should I find any who are able and willing, I will send you their names.

A Soldier of the 55th Massachusetts Volunteers

———————— •◦• ————————

With the ringing editorial declaration: "I am in earnest—and I will not equivocate—I will not excuse—I will not retreat a single inch—and I will be heard," a young activist and printer named William Lloyd Garrison, on January 1, 1831, launched his abolitionist journal, The Liberator.

The paper and its editor soon became widely known and, in the South, widely hated for their uncompromising stand against slavery. Although primarily a journal of opinion, the white-edited Liberator *did publish occasional letters from black soldiers at the front. One of the timely matters discussed in this letter is a familiar one, while it also touches upon something that would become an increasing concern to the black rank and file as the units went through the inevitable personnel changes.*

Folly Island, S.C., January 18, 1864[43]

Sir:

After an absence of several months in the field, I feel it my duty to inform you of some facts in regard to our regiment. We are here on Folly Island as you will see from my heading. Since we have been here our duty has been fatigue, almost continuously.

The first thing that suggests itself to me is the kindness of the State of Massachusetts in offering to make up to us the amount

43. *The Liberator,* January 29, 1864. Edwin Redkey Collection.

which we enlisted for, and which is withheld from us by the United States. We earnestly hope that it will not be thought by the state of Massachusetts that we returned the money for any motive other than that we desire at this crisis, the recognition of our rights as men and as soldiers. Sorry am I to say, that we have been considered incapable of acting for ourselves long enough and as it stands, we are even now not equated with other troops in the field—as is seen in the taking of officers, or rather sergeants from white regiments and making them captains, lieutenants, &c over us, when there are large numbers of our men who are more capable even in every regiment to be commissioned officers than those, or a great portion of those who are coming in continually. I do not state this as mere hearsay, for I know it to be a fact, and, sir, we think and hope that these matters, however small they may appear to some, will be looked into. We, as a race, have been trodden down long enough. Are we, who have come into the field of bloody conflict, and left our quiet homes the same as white men, for the sake of our country, and to beat down the rebellion—are we to be put down lower than these, many of whom have not enlisted with as good motives as we have? If we have men in our regiments who are capable of being officers, why not let them be promoted the same as other soldiers?[44]

I hope sir, that you will urge this matter, as I am well aware that you are on our side, and always have done for us all in your power to help our race.

I remain, yours
S.J.R.[45]

———————————— •●• ————————————

This memorial notice reminds us that African Americans of this

44. In the early period of black enlistment, the Federal government sought to migrate a white blacklash by placing only white officers in charge of the units. Although several appointments of men of color were made in 1864, most black officers assigned to combat units did not have those ranks confirmed until 1865. Three African American members of the 55th Massachusetts eventually received the rank of lieutenant: William H. Dupree (commissioned May 30, 1864, but not mustered until July 1, 1865), John F. Shorter (commissioned March 24, 1864, but not mustered until July 1, 1865), and James M. Trotter (commissioned April 10, 1864, but not mustered until July 1, 1865).
45. Most likely Samuel J. Robinson, a twenty-two-year-old 1st Sergeant in Company D.

period were as likely to seek and enjoy membership in fraternal organizations as their white counterparts.

Folly Island, S.C., Jan. 22d, 1864[46]
Camp of the 55th Mass. Vols.

At a meeting of the Masons of the 55th Massachusetts Volunteers, and 1st North Carolina Colored Volunteers, to deplore the loss, and adopt measures to carry out, the last request of Brother John Bird, a sergeant in this regiment, who, about an hour previous to his death, requested Brother David W. Johnson, that his remains be forward to his home, and there be interred by the fraternity, the following resolution were adopted:

Whereas, it has pleased the Supreme Architect of the Universe to remove from our midst our worthy and well beloved brother, Sergeant John Bird, and that in his death we have lost a kind friend and true brother, our sacred and ancient institution, a noble and worthy member, whose charity knew no bounds to a friend and brother in distress, and whose love for his fellow-man were among his many virtues.

Resolved, In his death the nation has been deprived of a brave and noble soldier, a true patriot, and one who would freely have sacrificed his life for freedom and the Union.

Resolved, That in accordance with his dying request we forward his remains to his Lodge in Ypsilanti, Michigan, that he may be there interred with Masonic honors.

Resolved, That while we mourn his loss as a friend, a Mason, and fellow-soldier, we sympathize deeply with his bereaved family and friends, assuring them that he died at his post of duty, serving his God, his race, and his country.

Resolved, That a copy of these resolutions be sent to his family, to the Lodge of which he was a member, and that they be also published in the *Anglo-African* and in *The Christian Recorder*.

David W. Johnson, Chairman
Rev. Wm. Jackson, Secretary[47]

————————— •◆• —————————

46. *Weekly Anglo-African*, February 20, 1864. *Christian Recorder*, February 20, 1864. Edwin Redkey Collection.
47. Sergeant John Bird was twenty-four years old when he joined the regiment. The Ypsilanti, Michigan, native listed his occupation as "barber." David H. Johnson was a member of the 1st North Carolina, while William Jackson was the chaplain of the 55th, who had turned in his resignation on January 14.

On February 13, 1864, the 55th Massachusetts left Folly Island to take part in the Florida expedition. This letter was written before that departure.

Camp near White House
Folly Island, S.C., January 27, 1864[48]

Mr. Editor:

After an absence of some eight or nine months in the field, I feel it my duty to write you a few lines to inform you how the Fifty-fifth Regiment is getting along. The men are generally well at this time, quite as much so as could be expected under the circumstances which surround us. We have been worked almost to death since we came here. When our regiment first landed here, we were used for fatigue duty on Morris and Folly Islands; but since the fortifications have been completed on these islands, we get along much better. I suppose you would like to hear how we are getting along for money, as you well know that we have not been paid yet. We have very hard times to get such things as we need; but, by hard work and contrivance, we manage to get along about as well as our neighbors. I think we have great reason to be thankful for the many blessings we have received since we came here. Though we have suffered a great deal since we came here, yet we have seen such rapid changes in our favor, that I feel richly paid for all that I have or may suffer. When we first landed on this island, we were liable to be insulted by any of the white soldiers. But, thank God, that is about played out, and they have come to see that they are bound to treat us as men and soldiers, fighting for the same common cause, if not directly, indirectly. When I read the columns of your excellent paper, it makes me rejoice to think we have such an able advocate for our rights. I wish you great success in all of your undertakings, and also pray God that the day will soon come when every chain shall be broken and every slave freed and allowed to worship God according to the dictates of his or their own conscience, where none dare molest or make them afraid.

48. *Christian Recorder*, February 4, 1864. Edwin Redkey Collection.

Nothing more at this time. Please publish, and oblige yours, respectfully,

R.W.W.[49]

Part Two

"Under the guns of prejudice and hate"
February 1864 through April 1864
Florida

The prospect of action at last loomed for the men of the 55th when, beginning February 13, they began to board transports that would take them south to Florida where a large-scale Union operation was getting underway. John Posey's company, Company D, embarked on the steamer Collins *on February 14, arriving at Jacksonville the next day.*

[Baldwin, Florida], February the 20, 1864[1]

Dear Cousin

It is with the greatest of pleasure that I take my pen in hand to inform you that I am well at present and do hope when these few lines come to hand, [they] may find you enjoying the same blessing.

We have left Charles Newton behind again. We have left the sandy shores of South Carolina and today finds us in the State of Florida and we are once more on the entire [i.e., main] land. It is a new and big thing for [us to have] the privilege of somewhere [new] to go, [though the destination came as a surprise] to us. We left Folly Island on the 12th [14th] about noon and landed in Jacksonville, Florida, on the 13th [15th] about 5 o'clock in the afternoon, and I was one of the first [to be put] on guard, and went on post immediately [after] landing.

The country here reminds to me more of home than any place else I have seen in the south. It is as level as ever I saw, the weather is in growing order, peach and cherry [trees] have put forth their blooms, there is a-plenty of hogs and chickens here, the boys are a-fairing well and having plenty of fun.

1. This letter is from the collection of Robert Younger. The unedited version can be found on pages 239-40 of Appendix Four.

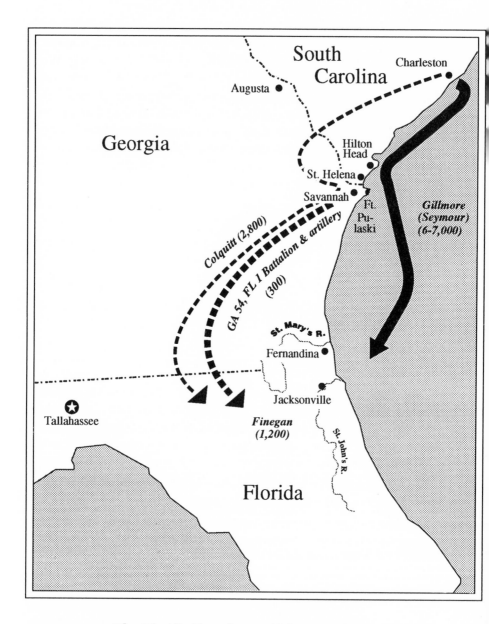

The Florida Expedition: February 1864

Charles Newton was well, but about the time he left Virginia, some of the boys had the small pox and they said there was a great danger [of] them [all] having it, and he was left [behind] until the fact was ascertained that there is no danger.[2]

We have been on an expedition: last Saturday and Sunday we ventured about 30 miles west on the Jacksonville & the Gainesville railroad. We got a nest of hornets, but did not stay long. We went there like old sober men, but when we came back, we came back like gay and well-trained men. When we started, we did not get any orders to close up [with the enemy] but never mind. We will get behind them some of these days. The troops are a-moving back toward them again, and this time we are a-going to get them before us, and then we will show them how to shoot.[3]

No more at present. Write again soon to the 55th Massachusetts, John Posey, Company D only. I can not write any more for I am in a hurry. Mathias Embry, Florida. You need not write to any certain place, only 55th Massachusetts, in care of Captain William Nutt, Company D. We have forty miles of the railroad in our possession.

———————————◆•◆———————————

The 55th Massachusetts saw no combat action in the Florida campaign. Instead, the regiment was again assigned to provide details for outpost and fatigue duties as the defeated Federals built up a defensive pocket around Jacksonville and the upper east coast of the state. On March 11 portions of the regiment were posted to the town of Palatka, up the St. John's River from Jacksonville.

2. According to the regimental history, "On leaving Folly Island, a number of men who had been exposed [while on detached service] in Virginia to the smallpox were left behind; but the precaution nearly proved unavailing, as several cases were found among the troops which had preceded them in Florida."
3. Posey is slightly off in his chronology. Six companies of the 55th left Jacksonville and marched toward Baldwin on February 19, a Friday. The next day the 55th units continued westward to Barber's Station, though Captain William Nutt's company was left at Baldwin. Nutt's men were ordered forward later in the day, even as the bulk of the 55th reached Barber's and learned about the defeat at Olustee. It is likely that Posey wrote this note while waiting at Baldwin.

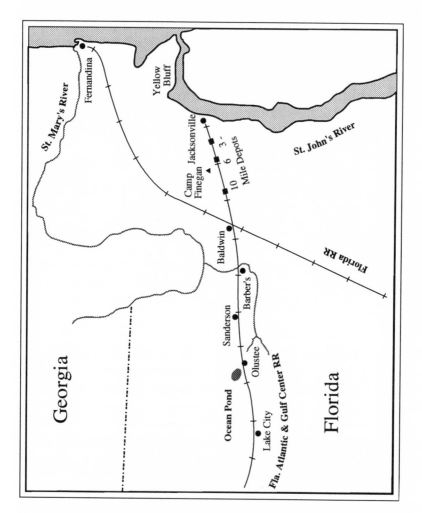

Eastern Florida, 1864

Edward W. Kinsley was a prominent Bostonian, a friend of Governor Andrew, and an ardent supporter of Massachusetts' black regiments.

Camp of the 55th Mass. Vols.
Palatka, Putnam Co. Fla.
March 13th, 1864[4]

Mr. Edward W. Kinsley, Esq.
Boston, Massachusetts

Honored Sir:

"Ingratitude is a dark crime," but I am happy in saying that the soldiers of the 55th, cherishing a recollection of the pleasant visit you favored them with at Folly Island, the kind interest you manifested in their welfare by your words of cheer, knowing how unceasingly you have advocated their cause in order that they might receive the same pay and treatment as other soldiers of their country, and by this means obtain, what is dearer to them than life without it, *the recognition of their manhood,* and lastly, receiving yesterday the large box of things so necessary to their comfort in camp, all this, dear sir, has made them love you, and I assure you that they are not guilty of indifference to friends so noble as yourself; to thank you from our hearts for such kindness as you have shown the men of the 55th is my excuse for this, uninvited, addressing you. Our white friends of Mass. God bless them and their Noble Governor, is the prayer of every soldier of the 55th, [you] may rest assured that it shall be our constant aim to add naught to the growing fame of Massachusetts but new laurels won by devotion to her interests and that of our whole country and I would add that since our entry into the service it is hoped that our conduct has been such as have increased the interest our friends at first felt for us.

That the American Congress should regard us so indifferently makes us sometimes sad. Could we feel otherwise under the circumstances? But we do not fear for the final result while we have such distinguished advocates on our side as those I have alluded

4. Edward W. Kinsley Papers. Duke University Special Collections.

to. Yes, Sir, the men are not discouragged though often sad when thinking of the necessities of a dear wife and little ones and other beloved ones at home whom they have not power to relieve. Can you account for this great manifestation of *patience*? I say 'tis an inspiration given them by the great Jehovah, who will not suffer this war to end until every trace of Slavery is gone.

Sir, will you tell all our friends how deep is our regard for them and that we shall continue to deserve theirs?

> With wishes for your health and
> happiness, I remain very Respectfully,
> Your obedient Servant
>
> James M. Trotter
> Sergeant Major 55th Mass. Vols.

--------•◦•--------

Although written more than a month after the 55th Massachusetts arrived in Florida, this letter from R.W.W. (likely Commissary Sergeant Richard W. White) provides a vivid account of the regiment's movement from South Carolina.

Palatka, Florida, March 14, 1864[5]
Head Quarters, 55th Reg. Mass. Vol. Inf.

Mr. Editor:

Thinking that some of the many readers of your most worthy paper might be somewhat interested in an account of our journey from Folly Island, S. C., to this place, I will proceed to give the details in as brief a form as possible.

It was, I think, on the 12th of Feb., that orders came for the 55th Reg. Massachusetts Infantry, then on Folly Island, S.C., to report at Jacksonville, Florida, to Brig. Gen. [Truman] Seymour, as soon as it was possible for us to do so. It is not worth my while to say, whether we obeyed the order or not; but supposing my readers have some idea how things are carried on in the army, I will leave it for them to judge. As I said, it was on the 12th inst.

5. *Christian Recorder*, April 2, 1864. Kathy Dhalle Collection.

that our Col. received orders for the 55th to break up our then very pleasant camp on Folly Island. We were not in the least sorry, I assure you; for the ever memorable 54th Reg. Mass. Infantry, had left some time before for the same place; and as we are so much alike in disposition, and both being from the same state, it is natural to suppose we would hail with joy the time when we should join them. The camp was soon broken up, and everything scattered hither and thither, resembling the western country after one of those awful storms that sometimes recur. This was not all; there not being transportation enough for all the regiment, everyone was anxious to know if he or some else was to go. But that matter was soon settled by a small man, generally known as the Colonel [Alfred S. Hartwell], who ordered three companies, A, C, and I, under the gallant leadership of Lt. Col. [Charles B.] Fox, to get ready to embark on the U.S. transport, Peconic, then at Pawnee Landing, these, with our brigade commander, J[ames] C. Beecher, Col. of the 1st N[orth] C[arolina] Regt., and his staff officers, composed the cargo on board of the above named transport.

After we were all safe on board, we expected to be off, when we received the sad news from the captain of the boat that we would not leave before the next morning; so we made up our minds to spend the time as agreeably as possible by engaging in the following amusements; some playing cards, and some telling stories, &c., &c.

Before we bid adieu to Folly Island, there is one thing more worthy of a place in my story. While we were waiting with patience for the long looked for morning to dawn, some of the men got to rambling about, as is common among all soldiers, when one of them happened either by chance or otherwise, to get a little too near one of those men, contemptible scamps, notable for no greater crime than having burned the colored Orphan Asylum, in the city of New York, less than a year ago,[6] who took on himself the prerogative of calling one of our men a nigger: this not going down well with the soldier, he was for using the stock of his gun over Pat's head. But Pat, being very sensible of his danger, soon found his way to the hull of a ship that lay near the dock. The

6. Reference to the New York draft riot of July 1863. Among the buildings destroyed by the white mobs was the Colored Orphan Asylum.

73

soldier, having one more way by which he could get justice, lost no time in resorting to it. He well knew that if he reported the case to Col. Fox, that he would see that he got justice, for Col. Fox is not one of those men who let his men be run over by a lot of mobocrats, who better deserve to die than live. As soon as the news reached Col. Fox, he hurried to the place where the men were gathered in groups discussing the impropriety of such a man calling a soldier a nigger, but when the Colonel commanded silence, and assured them that he would have the scamp attended to, they soon all became quiet. Co. Fox ordered Pat to come out and give a reason why he should call a soldier a nigger, but, not being able to satisfy the Col., he ordered him under arrest, and sent him, accompanied by at least two files of good brave colored soldiers, to report to the Provost guard. A few cases like this will teach these fellows to attend to their own business and let other folks alone.

At daylight the order was given for all to come on board, and we were off. As we steamed down the river, I could see the many forts and batteries our men had helped to build since they had been on the island. There was one thing more I saw, as the boat glided down that beautiful stream, which caused me to take a hurried glance over the past. I think I hear someone asking, what was that? I will tell you. As I passed near the place of the regimental graveyard, I could not help thinking how many of our number we were leaving behind, whom we would never more see on this earth; those who had left their homes and home comforts at the same time that I did, the young, the noble, and the brave, to fight for their country, and to avenge the country's wrongs. While reflecting on this subject, these lines of the poet crossed my mind.

> Strange voices ever hum to me,
>   The deepest, sweetest, mystic lays,
> As sad as ever sigh'd the sea,
>   Or like the plaint of Autumn days.
>
> They sing sweet tunes in muffled lanes,
>   Where piles of runnet leaves are strewn,
> Or pierce my soul with nameless pains,
>   Of carol sweet as birds of June.

74

I listen to them in the night,
    The melancholy moon above,
White-veiled priestess, star bright,
    Presiding in the courts of love.

And then like lutes by fairies play'd,
    They soothe my mood to gentle dreams,
In which my willing feet have strayed
    In dangerous paths, [WORD OBSCURED] streams.

And even in the garish day,
    I listen to these voices sweet,
Until gaunt care is charmed away,
    And flowers spring up in the street.

The Summer's breath, or Winter's blast
    These tuneful messages do bear,
And in their balm or ice, is cast
    The germ to me of smile or tear.

I find my warnings in the roar
    Of deep-voiced thunder, ere the showers;
And hear God's sermons o'er and o'er
    From tiny lips of simple flowers.

So these strange songs of love, to me
    Ring out from every way-side cell,
And call me on the moaning sea,
    And in the templed groves as well.

I call them voices of the dead,
    For those we lov'd on earth so well,
By love's attractions still are led,
    To throb us with their spirit bells.

        Yours respectfully,

        R.W.W.

Jacksonville: 1864

76

This letter provides another account of the regiment's move-ment to Florida and its subsequent actions. It also makes clear the differing stresses and conditions to which the members of the 55th Massachusetts were sometimes subjected. (Although the author of this letter is not identified beyond his nom-de-plume, according to the regimental Record of Events for March and April, 1864, the only company of the 55th present in Jacksonville was Com-pany F. The 1st Sergeant of this company was James D. Ruffin, a barber from Boston.)

Jacksonville, Fla., March 18, 1864[7]

Mr. Editor:

Some time has elapsed since I last wrote to you, and I now seize the opportunity offered by a few minutes leisure, to drop you a few more lines. When I wrote before, we were on Morris Island, S.C., but it has pleased Gen. [Quincy] Gillmore[8] to re-move us to this place, where we will have more active work be-fore us.

We arrived at Jacksonville on Monday, Feb. 15th, and in a day or two were ordered front; but probably Gen. [Truman] Seymour[9] thought we could be used to better advantage as fatigue hands, so, on the day after we marched to Camp Finegan,[10] we were ordered back, and back accordingly we came. Then came a day or two of fa-tigue on Redoubt Fribley (an earthwork on the West side of town, named after Col. Fribley of the gallant 8th),[11] and forward is again the word. Six companies of our regiment were ordered front to reinforce the troops which had gone before, and under command of Col. [Alfred S.] Hartwell we commenced our march

7. *Weekly Anglo-African*, April 9, 1864. Houghton Library, Harvard University.
8. The Florida Campaign of 1864 took place within the limits of the Federal Military district known as the Department of the South, which was commanded at that time by Major General Quincy Adams Gillmore.
9. Although General Gillmore was in command of the overall Florida operation, field control of the units actually posted there was the responsibility of Brigadier General Truman Seymour.
10. Located about eight miles west of Jacksonville, Camp Finegan was a fortified encampment for Confederate troops defending the Jacksonville area. It was evacu-ated on February 8 in the face of the Union advance from Jacksonville.
11. Colonel Charles W. Fribley, commanding the 8th U.S.C.T., was killed at Olustee on February 20.

77

for Lake City. Soon followed the sanguinary affair at Olustee, in which we did not participate, as we could not get up there in time, although we "double-quicked" several miles to reach the field, but reached Barber's Station in time to cover the retreat.[12] Terrible fighting had been done in the few hours that the battle raged, and our colored regiments had done their part nobly, as is proved by the manner in which the 8th United States and the First North Carolina Colored Volunteers, were cut up. The loss of the 54th Massachusetts was comparatively slight, although they were in action for more than an hour.[13] Then came the retreat, hurried in the extreme, everything that could not readily be removed was burnt or broken up, and the whole force fell back upon Jacksonville, and commenced intrenchinig the town.

There are still, it seems, unbelievers in the efficiency of colored troops, or, if not unbelievers, those who render themselves willful slanderers. Our colored soldiers behaved in an unflinching and dauntless manner in the late battle, eliciting the praise of not only our own troops, but those of the enemy who shouted to our boys, "Fight! you d--d black Yankees, fight!"—thereby showing that their attention was drawn fully as much to the blacks as it was to the whites, as the former evidently annoyed them the most. And notwithstanding that the praise showered upon our regiments by their commanding officers, and the majority of officers and soldiers of other regiments, and the severe loss suffered by the 8th United States and 1st North Carolina Volunteers amply prove to the contrary, there are some who (to shield themselves, doubtless) persist in willfully slandering us. Such a one is Lieut. Eddy, of the 3d Rhode Island Artillery who, after deserting his guns in the recent fight, now attempts to exculpate himself and throw the blame upon the colored troops, thinking, doubtless, that we are the weakest and least likely to complain when slandered. The assertion of Lieut. Eddy that his guns were

12. General Seymour's expeditionary force of approximately 5,500 was moving west along the Florida Atlantic and Gulf Railroad when it was met, on February 20, near the station stop of Olustee by a Confederate force of almost equal size. The next principal depot past Olustee was Lake City, while to the east along the line were stations at Sanderson and Barbers.
13. Federal casualties at Olustee were 1,861 killed, wounded or missing. Some of the greatest losses were suffered by the 8th U.S.C.T., which lost 310. Not far behind was the 1st North Carolina Colored Volunteers which suffered 230 men killed, wounded or missing. The 54th Massachusetts reported combined losses of 86. (*Official Record*, Volume 35, Part 1, p. 298.)

lost by the running of a colored regiment, is a deliberate false-hood, and unworthy [of] anyone who pretends to be a gentle-man. But although an officer is expected to be a gentleman, we find many, very many, who positively disgrace the uniform they wear in many different ways, but nothing in my opinion renders a person, whether he be officer, private or civilian, as thoroughly contemptible, as a low, mean falsehood, and especially when such is intended to heap opprobrium upon an already de-fenseless individual, or a race of such.[14]

Things are going on rather smoothly in Jacksonville now; for since the retreat our men have been engaged in intrenching the town, and three sides of it are now protected by breastworks, with three or four batteries and redoubts. Three of these field works are garrisoned by colored troops: Redoubt Fribley by a detach-ment of 55th Massachusetts Volunteers, and Redoubts Reed and Sammons by detachments of the 3d U.S. Colored Troops. These batteries are erected on little eminences around the town, and command the face of the country (which is remarkably level) for some distance in all directions.

Jacksonville has, to all appearances, been a very handsome town in days or years gone by, but really it is a most woeful-look-ing place at present. Higginson and Montgomery left in legible characters the record of their visit in February, 1863.[15] All through the place, on every street, are the ruins of houses which were burnt at that time, and in many places there are tall weeds, re-sembling young trees, growing where one short year ago were splendid mansions. The finest looking house in town is occupied by Gen. Seymour as his headquarters; it is a large, red, brick man-sion, and evidently belonged to a man of wealth and importance. The most of the houses around the town which are worth oc-cupying are occupied by officers, some as headquarters of divi-

14. First published in the Province *Journal,* and picked up by a number of other papers (including the Boston *Evening Transcript* of February 29, 1864), Lieu-tenant George O. Eddy's letter included this statement: "It was our misfortune to have for supports a negro regiment, who by running, caused us to lose our pieces."
15. Jacksonville had been occupied (for the third time in the war) on March 3, 1863, by a combined force of black and white troops. Among the African Ameri-can units involved was the 1st South Carolina Volunteers (Colored) commanded by Colonel Thomas Higginson, and the 2nd South Carolina Volunteers (Colored) under Colonel James Montgomery. Higginson's men had engaged in a series of raids up the St. Mary's River in late January and early February of that same year.

sions and brigades, and some as boarding places, while not a few very comfortable and pleasantly situated houses are used as hospitals for the wounded in the late campaign.

The streets of Jacksonville are lined with trees, and give the town, at a distance, the appearance of a thick forest; and indeed coming from the Westward, along the Florida Central Railroad, there is nothing which resembles a town to be seen save two church spires, the tops of which can be seen peeping over the thick foliage. Looking along under the low branches toward the St. John's, one can see the fierce-looking Pawnee, with her six long, black guns protruded from her ports on one side, while just above her lies another smaller gunboat, the name of which I have not ascertained. What with the batteries around the town, the light artillery, and the gunboats, I think we can hold our friend, Finegan,[16] at bay for more than one hour, should he be foolish enough to attack us. But these fellows are too wary, and will not venture to attack us in our intrenchments.

We are being reinforced pretty heavily now, as the re-enlisted veterans are coming down to rejoin their regiments. One or two colored regiments have arrived this week; the 7th U.S., I have understood is one of them. I think from appearances, that we will have some active operations ere long, and, perhaps, may be successful, but more probably will be butchered, as at Olustee. Our officers and men place but little confidence in the Commanding General, and among troops of all arms can be heard expressions of distrust regarding him. He has never been successful, and has, in different instances, been the means of having men uselessly slaughtered; but we earnestly hope that his next offensive operations will be attended with different results.

A Soldier of the 55th Mass.

———————————— ✦•✦ ————————————

While in Florida, the 55th Massachusetts was split up, with detachments assigned to various Union strong points scattered about the eastern portion of the state. Yellow Bluff was about halfway between Jacksonville and the mouth of the St. John's River.

16. Brigadier General Joseph Finegan commanded the Confederate military district of the Department of Middle and Eastern Florida and led the troops that defeated Seymour at Olustee.

Detachment 55th Regt. Massachusetts Vols.
Yellow Bluff, Fla., March 26, 1864[17]

Mr. Editor:

Will you please let us know what action has been taken in Congress in relation to our pay.

Eleven months have now passed away and still we are without pay. How our families are to live and pay house-rent I know not. Uncle Sam has long wind, and expects as much of us as any soldiers in the field; but if we cannot get any pay what have we to stimulate us?

To work the way this regiment has for days, weeks—nay months, and yet to get no money to send to our wives, children and mothers, who are now suffering, would cause the blush of shame to mantle the cheek of a cannibal, were he our paymaster.

But we will suffer all the days of our appointed time with patience, only let us know that we are doing some good, make manifest too that we are making men (and women) of our race —let us know that prejudice, the curse of the North as slavery is the curse of the South, is breaking, slowly, but surely; then we will suffer more, work faster, fight harder, and stand firmer than before.

Our regiment is present at Paltaka, about 80 miles above Jacksonville, and our detachment consists of Co. B, Capt. Charles E. Grant, the favorite of the regiment; Co. K. Capt. [Charles C.] Soule; Co. I, Capt. J[ohn] Gordon, and last though not least, Co. E, Capt. [William H.] Torrey.

We have our Lieut. Col. [Charles B.] Fox with us, a man, to all intents and purposes, and pity is it that there are not more like him in the service.

We lost a fine officer last Wednesday, shot accidently by one of our captains. I pity both. The captain would as soon have shot his mother as Lieut. Jones, of Co. I.[18]

17. *Weekly Anglo-African*, April 16, 1864. Houghton Library, Harvard University.
18. According to the regimental history of the 55th: "At Yellow Bluff an accident deprived the regiment of one of its most promising young officers, Lieut. Dennis H. Jones, of Company I. He had gone with a scouting party down the river, landed from the creek, and proceeded a short distance inland, to a house where boats were reported concealed. An alarm being raised that the rebels were approaching, caused by the firing of a party in search of cattle, they hurried to

The weather is fine. Your poor frozen people ought to see us in our glory, some bare footed and some bare-headed.

We are now situated 12 miles below Jacksonville, and have built two block-houses and one signal station. We can give John H. (new name for rebel) all he wants should he come in force. We feel secure, perhaps too much so, but fear is a stranger to our boys. We never will suffer ourselves to be surprised, and will sell our lives dearly.

We are pleased to see that some of your street railways are learning to treat our people correctly. This is another proof that our cause is making progress.[19]

Joseph H. Walker
Sergt. Co. B, 55th Massachusetts Vols.[20]

The importance to the soldiers of news from home is made clear in this incomplete fragment from a John Posey letter, presumably written during the regiment's tour of duty in Florida.

[Palatka, Florida? April, 1864][21]

I want you to know that I have not got any letters [from] you or your mother since the 10 of March. More than that, I have not had more than 5 letters from the whole family. I think it is the height of contempt.

I will [give] you one month more to write and if you do not; when I write [I will] tell you how things is. You will write [and] tell all the friends to write, and when you write to my dear mother, tell her I am well and doing [LETTER FRAGMENT ENDS]

---

their boat, which had been drawn up on the marsh; but in the endeavor to launch it, a revolver was accidentally discharged, the ball passing directly through the heart of Lieut. Jones, and instantly killing him." Although not identified in the official regimental history, the officer whose gun accidently killed Lieutenant Jones was Captain Soule.

19. According to James M. McPherson in *The Negro's Civil War,* "in New York City, Negroes were subject to occasional discrimination on some of the streetcar lines, and were required to ride in a Jim Crow car on the Sixth Avenue line . . . the Jim Crow policy was abandoned in New York . . . in 1864."

20. Thirty-four-year-old Joseph H. Walker was a cook from Lewiston, Pennsylvania.

21. This letter is from the collection of Robert Younger. The unedited version can be found on page 240 of Appendix Four.

Another detachment from the 55th is heard from here, with more comments on the pay issue.

Headquarters 55th Regt. Mass. Vols.,
Palatka, Fla., April 4, 1864[22]

Mr. Editor:

It is about three weeks since we were ordered here from Jacksonville. Palatka is quite a small town. It has every appearance of having been a great business place before the war began, but it, like many other towns and cities in the sunny South, has suffered greatly from the ravages of a long and tedious warfare. When we left Jacksonville we expected to find, on landing here, some of the Southern chivalry, who would welcome us to their kind of hospitalities; but, to our sad disappointment, we found they had got word we were coming, and had cleared out without waiting to test the right of possession with us.

At present our brigade is having a little rest from fatigue duty, the town being pretty well fortified, at least so much so that we are not afraid of the rebs driving us out until we get good and ready to leave.

We are at present in Col. Barton's brigade. He appears to be a very fine man, and I think he tries to do justice by all of his troops, whether white or colored. We all like him very much and only wish we had more like him.[23]

Now a few words respecting the pay of our regiment. It is true, and I say it with same to the government and all concerned, that although we have been in the service ten months we have not received one cent of pay, and many of our families are suffering for the aid we might render them if we could only get our hard-earned and just dues. It is also true we have been twice insulted by having the paltry sum of seven dollars per month offered us. But I thank God that we did not take it; for if we had our children would blush with shame to think their fathers would ac-

22. *Weekly Anglo-African*, April 30, 1864. Houghton Library, Harvard University.
23. On March 9, Colonel William B. Barton, commanding a force consisting of the 47th and 48th New York, five companies of the 55th Massachusetts, two sections of Captain Martin S. James's 3rd Rhode Island Heavy Artillery and some cavalry, received orders to occupy Palatka. The occupation was accomplished the next day.

knowledge their inferiority by taking inferior pay to that of other soldiers, and the whole civilized world would look on us as being a parcel of fools, not fit to enjoy our freedom.

I hope, Mr. Editor, you will urge this matter through your paper as much as possible, and oblige your friends who are fighting for justice and liberty.

De Waltigo

—————◆ •◆• ◆—————

Among the changes in the 55th Massachusetts that took place in Florida was the arrival of its new chaplain, John R. Bowles. Summing up the events of this period, the regimental history stated: "A skirmish or two with the pickets and several alarms occurred; but the enemy kept usually out of sight."

Co. D, 55th Mass.
Palatka, Florida, April 6, 1864[24]

Mr. Editor:

Permit me to write a few lines to your excellent paper, hoping that you will excuse all mistakes, it being my first attempt. Thinking that a word from this part of the country might be interesting to some of your readers, I seat myself to feebly try to tell you how matters are progressing in our regiment.

The health of the regiment is generally good, and, under existing circumstances, the men are in good spirits. There has been no fighting here since we have been here, worth speaking of, though we have been called out and formed in line several times since we have been at this place, with the expectation of meeting the enemy; but he has not dared to approach the range of our guns. There have been quite a number of rebels captured by the pickets and scouting parties since we have been at this place. Although our regiment has not, as yet, been able to distinguish itself for bravery on the battle-field, yet we feel that the time is not far distant when our actions must accomplish, for the ele-

24. *Christian Recorder*, April 30, 1864. Edwin Redkey Collection.

vation of our race, something that will tell louder than a daring charge on some rebel work.

We have not, as yet, received any pay from the Government, nor do we know how soon we will; but we hope that something may be done, for the regiment in this particular. Excuse the length of time.

With respect, yours,

J.F.S., Co. D.[25]

On April 16 the various detachments of the 55th Massachusetts received orders to proceed to Folly Island, but transportatioon was not available until the next day. This is one of two letters from the 55th to the Anglo-African *written just before the regiment ended its stay in Florida.*

Headquarters 55th Reg. Mass. Infantry,
Palatka, Fla., April 10, 1864[26]

Mr. Editor:

This Regiment was mustered into the United States service about the 18th or 20 of June, 1863, consequently we have been ten months working for Uncle Sam, not taking into account the time when some of us were sworn in.

The only thing that engrosses our mind now, is the old and troublesome subject of pay.

We have been promised that we would be paid, and a paymaster came (last November) to pay us. He offered us $7 per month. We enlisted for $13 per month, with the promise (and I wish the public to keep this fact before them, to see how these promises are being fulfilled) that we should be treated in all respects like white soldiers, our bounty, rations, and emoluments being the same. The same inducements were held out to us as to all Massachusetts volunteers.

25. Likely 1st Sergeant John F. Shorter, a twenty-one-year-old carpenter from Ohio.
26. *Weekly Anglo-African*, April 30, 1864. Houghton Library, Harvard University.

You, sir, no doubt, have copies of the circulars that were distributed through the country to encourage enlistments. By whose authority this was done I cannot say; but I know that his Excellency John A. Andrew's, Governor of Massachusetts, name was on them.

Mr. Editor, we wish to be plain, and state the exact truth, and this we shall do regardless of whomsoever we may offend.

We do not look upon Massachusetts as being responsible for our sufferings; but upon the government of the United States, and how a government with such a lofty reputation can so act, is beyond our conception or comprehension. We know, and the world knows that had we been white men the whole land would have been in a blaze of indignation in regard to the great injustice done us.

How the authorities expect our families to live without the means to buy bread, pay house rent, and meet the other incidental expenses of living in these terrible times, we know not; but if it does not exert its well known power it certainly will not be held guiltless in this matter.

Are our parents, wives, children and sisters to suffer, while we, their natural protectors, are fighting the battles of the nation? We leave the government and Congress to answer.

That they *do* suffer we have abundant evidence.

I have seen a letter from a wife in Illinois to her husband, stating that she had been sick for six months, and begging him to send her the sum of *fifty cents*. Was it any wonder that the tears rolled in floods from that stout-hearted man's eyes?

How can it be expected that men will do their duty consistently with a soldier's training, under such circumstances?

Patience has an end, and with us will soon cease to be a virtue. We would be contented and happy could we but receive our pay.

I have been asked by officers, not connected with our Regiment, why we did not take our pay when we could get it. My answer was that our pay has never been sent to us. True, money has been sent here, but it was not our pay. When the United States authorities shall send us $13 per month, which is our just due, we will take it, *and not until then, will we take one cent.*

We cannot accept pay from the Old Bay State while we are working for the United States; for we do not want two paymasters. One will answer, provided he be the right one.

We have waited long for our just dues, but many have waited and many will wait in vain.

The battle-field and grief are doing their work, and many a poor fellow will sleep his last sleep ere the adjusting time shall come. We begin to think that that time will never come *as long as we stay in the field.*

There is evidently something wrong about this business. The United States government says nothing about it, and Gov. Andrew never comes to see us! Does it not seem strange? The presence of Gov. Andrew here would inspire us with renewed confidence, and send a thrill of great joy through our victimized regiments.

Money has been sent us through different channels which we have refused, and which we must continue to refuse. To accept our pay in this way would degrade us, and mark us as inferior soldiers, and would be a complete annihilation of every vestige of our manhood.

The United States knows our value as soldiers too well to suppose that we will sacrifice the position that we have gained by most arduous labor, and we, thoroughly comprehending our relation to the past glorious history of our race, and the verdict that must fall upon us in the future if we falter; will stand up for our rights, come what may.

As regard the question whether we are equal in value as soldiers to white troops, we have only to say that if Port Hudson, Milliken's Bend, Pocotaligo, Fort Wagner, Olustee, and Fort Pillow,[27] do not settle it in our favor, then it is because our enemies *will not* have it settled in that way.

But it is a matter of indifference to us now how they settle it; we, by God's help, will settle it for ourselves before this war is over, *and settle it right too, or die in the attempt.*

It is glorious to see how our noble fellows stand up under their trials. Pride has kept them where they are to-day, and they certainly deserve to be respected.

But you, sir, were not aware of the fact that we have passed

27. References to engagements involving black troops: Port Hudson (May 27, 1863), Milliken's Bend (June 7, 1863), Fort Wagner (July 18, 1863), Olustee (February 20, 1864) and Fort Pillow (April 12 1864). It is unclear what the reference to Pocotaligo, South Carolina, is, as there were no black troops involved in actions there in 1862, 1863, or early 1864.

into an Holy (holey) and hungry order—but it is true. The boys pantaloons are at this time flapping about their legs trying to whip them to death; while the "vacuum" *within is calling* for something to assuage the gnawing. Scarce rations have been our luck since we came to the department.

Our men, as a general thing, are obedient, and the detachment now at Yellow Bluff, Fla., under Col. [Charles B.] Fox, and which has been there since February 28, are the ones to whom I allude as being so ragged. Yet only one of these men has been punished for disobedience.

We have been silent in regard to our wrongs hitherto, but it will not do to be so any longer. Agitation and legislation must do what silence has failed to accomplish.

We have been tried in the fire both of affliction and of the rebels, and nothing remains but pure metal. We took our first lesson at Forts Wagner and Gregg, and our last we are now taking in the field of want, and under the guns of prejudice and hate.

We should like to know whether we belong to Massachusetts or Uncle Sam; for we are tossed about from pillar to post, one saying come here, and another saying go there, and we come and go like dogs, and this has been the case ever since we went to Folly Island.

Promises have no weight with us now, until the past and present is fulfilled—future ones we will not heed.

Three years cannot pass in this way. Some change must come.

The words of cheer that we once received from our mothers, wives and sisters, are becoming fainter and fainter, and their cries of want stronger and stronger with each revolving day. Is the picture of our desolate house-holds, and the gaunt figures of our friends now suffering almost the pangs of starvation, to haunt us by day and night in our camp? Is this dread sight to hang between us and our starry flag upon the battle-field?

Oh, God! most bitter is the cup presented to our lips; but that others may live we will drink it even to the dregs.

Our debasement is most complete. No chances for promotion, no money for our families, and we little better than an armed band of laborers with rusty muskets and bright spades, what is our incentive to duty? Yet God has put it into our hearts to believe that we will survive or perish with the liberty of our country. If she lives, we live; if she dies we will sleep with her, even as our brave comrades now sleep with Col. Shaw within the walls of Wagner.

More anon,

Bay State

———————•◦•————————

This letter, though written on the same day as the one previous, appeared almost two weeks later in the Anglo-African. *The reason may have been an editorial one, as the paper was making heavy reference to the pay issue in April. This contribution provides a different side of life in the 55th.*

Headquarters 55th Reg. Mass. Infantry,
Palatka, Fla., April 10, 1864[28]

Mr. Editor:

The lady from Canada West wanted to know why the non-commissioned officers did not write. She will not ask soon again. The boys have just waked up. We waited for the angel to trouble the waters; our sails are set; we intend to keep them in full trim. The rest of the advantage is ours. Our course is up not down, but shoals, bars, and quicksands lie through the channel.

I understand Sergt. Walker, Co. B,[29] was out scouting last Friday, Saturday and Sunday, and went within ten miles of Jacksonville. He got into reb lines. This was, certainly, a bold, saucy, daring adventure, to go so far with only three men and himself, 22 miles from his camp, through a strange country and new roads; but it showed of what material he was made. He went to a house where he was sure secesh were in the habit of coming. Madam Brewer met him at the door. Sergt Walker (bringing his musket down to arm), "Good day, madam." "Good day, sir." Walker (looking savage enough to eat a man, let alone a weaker vessel)— "Whose place is this, madam?" "It belongs to me" (looking very

28. *Weekly Anglo-African*, May 14, 1864. Houghton Library, Harvard University.
29. Joseph H. Walker was made sergeant on September 29, 1863. His service record shows that he was reduced in rank on May 13, 1865.

shy and timid, trying to affect modesty). Sergt. Walker—"Can you inform me where Dun's Creek is" (he knew). Mrs. B. (pointing her finger to the left)—"About three miles." Sergt. Walker—"What creek is this?" (a stream that he and his men had just forded.) Madam B.—"Cedar Creek." Sergt. Walker—"How far is it to Jacksonville?" Madam B.—"Ten miles." Sergt. Walker—"Whose quarters are those over the road?" (meaning the slaves). Madam B.—"They belong to me." Sergt. Walker—"Where are your slaves?" Madam B.—"I do not know." (Lie No. 1.) Sergt. Walker—"Do you live inside of the Union or rebel lines?" Madam B.—"Well, I am here." Sergt. Walker (angrily)—"I know you are here. I did not ask you that, I ask you again do you live in the Federal lines or not?" Madam B. (woman-like drawing herself out large. Southern blood could not stand such questions)—"I claim the protection of your commander." Sergt. Walker—"If you are a Union woman you do not need protection." Sergt. Walker, happening to see a fair saddle and an oil-cloth blanket, and a set of equipments, asked, "Whose equipments are those?" Madam B.—"They belong to my old colored man." (I do not think the old chivalry ever said "colored" before in her life.) Sergt. Walker—"Where is your colored man?" Madam B.—"I do not know." (Lie No. 2) Sergt. Walker—"Where are all the male members of your family?" Madam B.—"I do not know." (Lie No. 3. She has two sons in the rebel ranks.) Sergt. Walker—"Where is your husband?" Madam B.—"He is old and sick and is in the interior." (It was known that he was in the woods, so I had to put that down as lie No. 4.) At this time the old woman thought it her time to ask a few questions: Madam B.—"Where did you come from?" Sergt. Walker (sharp enough to detect she wanted information)—"I came from camp." Madam B.—"Where are you going?" Sergt. Walker—"I am lost, and want to find my way back to Dun's Creek, then I can get where I intend to go." Madam B.—"Are you going to Jacksonville?" Sergt. Walker—"I shall go to my regiment when I leave your house." You ought to have seen her eyes. They lost their glad eagerness when he said "regiment." He thought she had some company to Sunday dinner.

While this conversation was going on in front, two of his men went in search of articles contraband of war. The search revealed lard, butter, sweet potatoes, cotton cloths, cotton gins, to gin cotton by hand, and leather looms—everything to make a man happy. The things I have just mentioned were in houses outside of the mansion. The boys then went into the dining-room. Lo and behold! six plates, cups and saucers on the table; the coffee was warm, the eggs were warm, and the day was warm (March 27), and, to tell the truth, Sergt. Walker found himself in a close place. He had only seen the female; but there were six rebel cavalry men in the house. He smelt danger; now then to get out of it.

He told his men to fall in and get down to the company, and not keep them waiting in the woods all day. By the way, the company he meant was 24 miles away from him at Yellow Bluff. The scouts that went out after Walker came in and said that besides the six men there were three females in the house. He is a large man, but had to back out that time; but he done well, he not having orders to take prisoners, and not force enough. I think he showed his bravery by retreating with his men, which he did, coming in safe and sound with his small force.

The exchange of colored prisoners. Will the government fulfill its promise made us that we shall be exchanged if captured? As far as this regiment is concerned we will ask no quarter, and rest satisfied that we will give none. Where is the wounded that fell into the enemy's hands at the battle of Olustee? Echo answers, "where?" We will never forget the cry of "Kill the G--d d--n s--s of b--s," when the 54th Massachusetts Volunteers went into the fight, neither the well-aimed shot that made a rebel officer bite the dust before he had time to draw his sword. We are compelled to take this in our own hands. The Johnny Reb will find out that niggers won't die so fast.

Brig. Gen. Seymour has gone, and there was no tears shed when he left. He may be a good man and soldier, but there is room for reformation; and for that flag of truce that was sent over to find out the welfare of our colored prisoners, I think that our folks have seen and had dealing enough with Johnny to know that he would not tell what he does with his prisoners of color.[30]

30. There is strong evidence that some wounded black soldiers left on the Olustee battlefield were murdered instead of being taken prisoner. In a letter he wrote nearly a month later to the commander of the 1st North Carolina Colored, General Seymour declared, "I may assure you, I believe, that the colored soldiers and their officers are treated by the Confederates precisely as are those of white Regiments." (Archibald Bogle file in Record Group 94, The Adjutant General's Office, Compiled Service Records of Volunteer Union Soldiers, National Archives.)

Part Three

"What becomes of the colored soldiers?"

April 1864 through November 1864

South Carolina

Carried on the transports Sentinel *and* Neptune, *the 55th Massachusetts returned to the barrier islands outside of Charleston. The first companies arrived at Folly Island on April 18, followed by the remainder of the regiment on April 20.*

There were changes. Many of the encampments were now empty, as the troops occupying them were transferred to Virginia to take part in operations there under the command of Major General Benjamin F. Butler. But, as this letter indicates, other things had not changed.

Folly Island, S.C., April 23, 1864[1]

Mr. Editor:

I am greatly interested about the pay of our regiment (the Fifty-fifth Massachusetts.) Eleven months have nearly passed, and we have not received any pay yet. We have fatigue in drawing cannons and mortars from Morris Island to defend the stars and stripes, upon half rations. We work with great vigor and patience. We expected to receive our pay in December last. The pay was to have reached Morris Island. The Fifty-fourth [Massachusetts] Regiment were offered ten dollars per month; but they refused it like men. A few days after, the Paymaster came to Folly Island and offered the same amount to the Fifty-fifth Regiment; but they also refused it, saying: "We will stay our three years out, and then go home like men to our homes, and go to work."

On the 14th of March the Fifty-fifth had orders to go to Jacksonville, Fla., to reinforce General Seymour. The Fifty-fifth reached

1. *Christian Recorder*, May 21, 1864. Edwin Redkey Collection.

there on the 15 of March.[2] We marched out and went into camp. On the 19th the bugle sounded for us to strike tents to go up front to see Jim Finigin[3] and his boys. The Fifty-fourth got to Olustee, near Lake City. There they met Johnny Reb, and fought like heroes. They re-captured the First North Carolina flag three times, and saved it for them.[4] They reached Barbour's plantation on the 20th, and when they heard that Johnny had defeated the brave boys, they all wished that they had been there.

The question is this: What is the reason Congress will not pay the gallant and brave boys of the Fifty-fourth and Fifty-fifth Massachusetts Volunteers their thirteen dollars per month? They cannot say that they are not good fighting soldiers in the field. I rather think that it is the color and quality and citizenship of the United States that is the reason they want us to take ten dollars per month, and three deducted for clothing. No, never will I take it. You may sever my head from my body first. Give us our rights, and we will die under the stars and stripes for the glorious old Union.

"Union forever! hurrah, boys, hurrah!"

From a Soldier

There was a dispiriting force eating at the soul and morale of the 55th Massachusetts. Questions of racism and equality, and, in the parlance of the 19th Century, of manhood—all were focused on the pay issue. That the spirit of the men was being affected is only too clear in this next letter from the 55th.

55th Mass. Regt.
Folly Island, S.C., April 26 1864[5]

Mr. Editor—Dear Sir:

A long time has elapsed since you have heard from me; and I shall try and let you know how we are, and how we are getting

---

2. "Soldier" has his month wrong. The first elements of the 55th left Folly Island for Florida on February 13, with the remainder leaving the following day.
3. Reference to Confederate General Joseph Finegan.
4. Pure camp rumor. Luis F. Emilio, in his history of the 54th Massachusetts, makes no mention of saving the flag of the 1st North Carolina Colored.
5. *Christian Recorder*, May 7, 1864. Edwin Redkey Collection.

along: we have been here and there, and I hardly know where.

There is a great deal of uneasiness among the men, and they attribute the fault to the innocent. Let me say one word to the different members of my regiment, the 55th. For soldierly and manly conduct, there is hardly her equal, not to flatter her and throw other regiments in the dark. There are both good and bad soldiers here, and so there are in every regiment in the field, none excepted; for, as any common sense man may know, the world would be too heavenly if all men were good; but for all that, I say let us all improve ourselves; let us all act like Christian brothers, and always remember the passage of scripture, "Whatsoever you would that men should do unto you, do yet even so unto them."

Soldiers of the 54th and 55th, just think what a change there is in the policy of the government since 1861! Is not that enough to warrant you of success in time! It is the policy of this government to move slowly; we cannot expect to be raised to the highest pinnacle of honor in three years. Did you ever hear of a people being placed on ground equal with the nation, which has held them under foot in the short space of one year?

Hereafter, do not look upon your officers as being the men who cause you trouble: if they do not suit you, make application for their removal, but respect them as much as possible, for there never was heart so proud and haughty but that it could be made to blend and swell from kindness. Look out, when you make selections, that you do not make your position worse instead of better, now let me tell you, you will never feel the good of these officers, until you lose them. Who would you find to fill the positions of the F.F. of Mass? A finer and more military set of men cannot be found! Major G.L. Sterns resigned on your account[6] —he feels like myself—but remember that old motto, "Patience and perseverance conquer in the end."

If the government is so mean that it will not fulfill its promises,

6. In October, 1863, George L. Sterns, the recruiter who had played such a large role in the formation of the 55th, began to work in Nashville as "Commissioner for the Organization of United States Colored Troops." He was given the rank of major with the powers of an assistant adjutant general. He was outspoken in his opposition to the extensive use of black troops for fatigue duty, and fought against local government officials who sought to restrict the numbers of African Americans recruited. After the War Department failed to support Sterns in his actions, he resigned his commission in December, 1863.

let us show the government that we can be, and are men, and that we will suffer death before dishonor. We must remember that we are neither 782 nor 350 dollar soldiers, but volunteers! We responded to the first call, and would have done the same in 1861, if we had been allowed! Remember, keep cool! This government will either pay us or take us out of the field: she will never allow herself to be disgraced in such a manner. Let your motto be Patience and Perseverance.

Wolverine

———————— •◦• ————————

It is almost axiomatic that the perspective of a footsoldier is limited only to that coming under his immediate view. Yet after the smoke of the battle had settled, and the soldiers had an opportunity to compare notes with others in their unit and in companion units, many were able to piece together a remarkably cohesive and correct account of the larger action in which they played a (usually) small part.

Camp of the 55th Mass. Vols.,
Folly Island, S.C., April 27, 1864[7]

Dear Anglo:

Some time ago, a lady, writing in your useful paper, administered to the sergeants of this regiment a mild, but as this letter will prove, an effective rebuke, because we did not write oftener through THE ANGLO to our friends.

The lady in question has, ere this, smiled with satisfaction as several letters from the 55th have met her eyes as she unfolded the neat and racy organ of colored men's rights—THE ANGLO-AFRICAN.

Well, Mr. Editor, to please you, this dear lady, and your many readers, and because I feel it to be my duty, I send these lines, hoping they may prove interesting.

We have returned to Folly Island—sickly, torrid Folly—where, last Summer, we buried beneath its sands not less than sixty of

7. *Weekly Anglo-African*, May 21, 1864. Houghton Library, Harvard University.

our brave comrades, who fell victims to most arduous fatigue duty, continued through the night as well as day, together with this miasmatic climate.

But shall we weep for the sleeping braves who, turning their backs upon the alluring charms of home life, went forth at the call of country and race, and died, noble martyrs to the cause of liberty? 'Tis noble to *live* for freedom, but is it not nobler far to *die* that those coming after you may enjoy it?

> Dear is the spot where Christians weep,
>   Sweet are the strains which angels pour;
> O! why should we in anguish weep?
>   they are not lost, but gone before.

You have heard of the expedition to Florida, the sad reverse at Olustee, the culpable sacrifice of brave officers and men there by Seymour, and of the matchless bravery displayed in the awful contest by the 54th Massachusetts, 1st North Carolina, and 8th U.S. Colored Troops.

Where was the 55th? Having been ordered to Barbour's [Barber's], 18 miles this side of Olustee, we moved in heavy marching order, from Jacksonville the day previous to the battle, scarcely halting for rest, and arrived at Barbour's an hour or two after the fight was over. Had we been ordered to the front a half-day earlier, we, too, to-day, would remember many of our number as those who sleep in a soldier's grave. So say all who were engaged in the unequal contest.

The rebs outnumbered the Union forces as three is to one, and, as the papers say, it was only the distinguished valor of the colored troops that saved our little band from destruction. But enough of dark Olustee.

So far, little has been gained to government by the expedition to Florida. A part of this, with five other regiments, were sent, about two months since, to occupy Palatka, Fla., a village situated on the left bank of the River St. John's, and distant about 50 miles South of Jacksonville. After, by hard labor, fortifying the place, to avoid its being taken from us by the Rebs (and we never heard of more than 200 of them being nearer than 50 miles to us) we have been ordered to evacuate.

The fruits of this expensive little expedition were two miniature worn-out steamers, captured near Lake Dunnes, with their crews and a few dollars worth of cotton and turpentine, a few horses, and about twenty-five contrabands. These acquisitions cost our government the loss of two of its finest transports, the *Maple Leaf* first, and then the *General Hunter*, said to be the swiftest steamer of her kind, were blown almost to atoms by torpedoes, placed in the river by the barbarous rebels, while passing between Palatka and Jacksonville. Very fortunately, no great number of troops were on board at the time of these explosions, else the destruction of life would have been terrible.[8] On the *Maple Leaf* three firemen were lost, and a quartermaster was instantly killed on board the *Hunter*. What a narrow escape for 4,000 troops, who, only a few hours before the *Hunter* struck the infernal torpedo, had passed over the same channel from Palatka to Jacksonville. The aggregate cost of these two steamers was about $130,000.

So much for the Palatka occupation. How we all did hate to come back to Folly Island. The beautiful orange groves, with the great luscious fruit, mockingbibrds warbling sweetly from every tree in the day time, and even continuing their harmonious confusion of songs far into the night, the delightful healthy climate and pure water, rather spoiled us, and we are not in a way to appreciate this barren, sandy isle. But soldiers necessarily have worlds of patience, and would government only treat her colored soldiers as well as she does her white ones, we would not murmur.

Just think of it, Mr. Editor, nearly a year has passed since the government at Washington authorized Gov. Andrew to enlist this regiment, assuring him that we should receive the same pay as other Massachusetts soldiers, and still we are *slaves*; still that precious principle—manhood—for the attainment of which we consider no hardship too great to be borne, is withheld from us. But aside from the recognition of our title to equal rights with the white soldier, who suffers no more for his country than ourselves, have they no care for the heart-rending appeals of the wives, children, and other relations, to the soldiers, for aid in their suffering—yes, in some cases, starving condition? Is it not perfectly delightful to hear your wife and darling babies crying

8. Two officers of the 55th were onboard the *Maple Leaf*: Major Sigourney Wales and Lieutenant George T. Garrison (son of the abolitionist editor William Lloyd Garrison). Neither was injured.

to you for the necessaries of life, while you are so confined that you cannot help them? Every mail brings news from home to the soldier, telling of destitution that well nigh distracts him. Let me speak of one case out of many similar ones. A few days ago some soldiers talking of the dear ones at home and of the fidelity of their wives, one of them, full of confidence, offered to wager his life that although his wife might be suffering for bread she would, notwithstanding, be proof against any temptation that might present itself. Alas! poor man. In a day or two after, he received a letter telling him that she whom he loved as he did his life, and who had always been a dutiful, affectionate wife, had been driven by want and the cries of her children for bread, to yield to the tempter.

These are very pleasant reflections for soldiers to have while enduring a thousand other privations. But what means this cruel, aye, barbarous treatment? Every two months the white soldiers in camps next to ours, are paid $26, and we nothing. Why?

White and colored soldiers went together into battle at Olustee, the former a recognized man, knowing that should he fall his wife and children would receive a pension; the latter knowing—what? That he was outraged. And yet bravely he fought; and when hundreds had fallen bleeding and dying to the earth, those same proscribed men had "saved the little army from rout." Government will have an eye to the widows and orphans of the white-soldiers that fell, but what becomes of the colored soldiers? "O well, 'tis your own fault that you are not paid. Government offered you pay and you refused it." True, and government may offer to *degrade* us with $7 per month a thousand times, and our friends and ourselves may perish for want of money, but never— no, by the Eternal! never will we take it.

MANHOOD IS OUR MOTTO. 'TIS WRITTEN IN OUR EVERY PURPOSE AND SEALED IN OUR HEART OF HEARTS.

In conclusion, dear ANGLO (I hope you will excuse the length of this letter. If I write again I will not write so long), I trust that you will occasionally refer, in your valuable paper, to the treatment of the 54th and 55th Massachusetts Volunteers, as well as other colored troops, are receiving at the hands of this government, and that you will recommend that the attention of soldier's

99

aid societies be given more to the families of soldiers than to the latter. Yours, for freedom and colored soldiers' rights.

Mon

———————— •••• ————————

It appears that some of the soldier correspondents of the 55th Massachusetts tried to give equal time to each of the two national black newspapers. In this letter to the Weekly Anglo-African, *the writer who called himself* Wolverine *picked up the thread of unrest that he had presented in a letter written just four days earlier and sent to the* Christian Recorder.

Folly Island, S.C., April 30, 1864[9]

Mr. Editor:

There has been considerable uneasiness in the two Massachusetts Regiments on the point of their position with other regiments in the field, and I am sorry to think that they attribute the fault to their officers, for a more generous, open-hearted and faultless set of men cannot be found on the Continent of America. They do for the men what others refused to do one year ago. They fill the places for no other object than the elevation of the colored race, and they have done their duty faithfully. They have, I am certain, sacrificed a great many pleasures, and [had] to endure hardships they have even show their willingness by enduring them with us.

Let us look to what constitutes military discipline. What fault can we find there? The officers are bound by a solemn oath to perform their duty, and I will do all in my power to sustain them in it. I have been sworn in the service thirteen months, and will be willing to serve twice as long if the government does according to agreement. When I look back to '61 and '62 it makes me stronger in my belief that time brings all things right. If I should stop and allow my feelings to govern I would soon be void of reason. The harder my duties the more cheerful I try to be. What is thirteen months in the army! To stop at that short period, and

9. *Weekly Anglo-African,* May 14, 1864. Houghton Library, Harvard University.

because I am not made a man from the word go, I must despond and let foolishness run away with my brains. This reminds me of falling in love, and because you cannot consummate your object, wish to commit violence on your own person, and thereby spite yourself by cutting off your own nose. Just remember that respect commences at home first. If you will only remember the ten commandments and have forethought enough to put them in their proper place, you need never anticipate trouble, for good and bad will never mix equally. We cannot expect to have sunshine and kid gloves in the army. All that we ask is good men, and them we have got. There is one thing more. Let the good wives at home show their love by suffering with us. Don't write such down-hearted letters to the soldiers. Tell them of something that will make them happy and contented. Every heart-burning letter makes us less contented and gives us a very bad disposition. I wish every member of the 55th to remember that the disposition that is growing among them will not only condemn them, but the whole African race. Their elevation either rises or falls with their conduct. Let it be honorable and such as will call for a page in the history of the American rebellion. Let our motto be Patience and Perseverance.

Wolverine

———————————◆•◆———————————

Black soldiers in the Civil War were truly fighting on two fronts: the Confederate enemy before them, and Northern racism behind them. How so many continued to serve in the face of all this with such a high level of dedication and sacrifice, is one of the glories of African American participation in the war. How heavily the great social and racial questions of the day wore on the minds of the men of the 55th is made clear in this next letter.

Headquarters 55th Regt. Mass. Vols.
Folly Island, S.C., May 1, 1864[10]
Mr. Editor:

This is Sabbath day, but how very different—how unlike a

10. *Weekly Anglo-African,* June 4, 1864. Houghton Library, Harvard University.

Sabbath in your crowded city. Instead of a Sabbath school we have a general review. Yet how beautiful God, in his infinite wisdom, has planned all things. Nature here shows herself in her most sublime colors. The ocean is in her highest glory, throwing her briny spray from wave to wave until it reaches the shore. Oh! how magnificently these billows roll! And the tall, beautiful pine trees, and little flowers that occasionally show their tiny heads on this desolate island, show us that God still lives and takes care of all things. I cannot help admiring the wisdom of the Creator—how He has planned the most simple of His creation that we may, if so disposed, learn an instructive lesson from them. Even here, on this island, where one might suppose there would be none of Nature's works to teach man that there is a God, we have only to study Nature and it will teach us that He lives and rules the universe, and that He is the same today He was six thousand years ago, when He said, "Let there be light," and there was light. He will care for us the same as He did for our fathers of the Revolution, if we only trust His power. For if their cause was just, ours is surely as much so. If they were justified in taking up arms against their mother country to resist a three pence tax on tea, are we not justified in resorting to arms to gain our freedom, and will not God protect us in so doing, and lead us through this bloody war successfully?

Then why are we discouraged? Is it because we have not been paid the thirteen dollars promised us at the time we enlisted? No! It is because we have not been treated like men and soldiers belonging to the army of the United States. We feel this outrage on us as men and soldiers of the United States, and this is why we are not satisfied. We did not leave our homes and friends for the sake of the money, but in order that our suffering might work out a great good for ourselves and friends, no matter what had been their former conditions. In part, we have accomplished this, but much remains yet to be done, and if we can be treated as other soldiers from the State of Massachusetts, that is, get the pay, clothing, rations, bounty, and be eligible to the same positions as are her other troops, we will then be willing to suffer on to the end, if, by so doing we can, in the end, gain our own freedom and that of three million and a half slaves, who have been for the last two hundred years enslaved by the government and religion of this country. I say religion, for the Christianity of the nation has done more to uphold slavery than any other one thing. I hope by this I will not be understood as opposing true religion, for I have as high reverence for Christianity as any one, so long as it accords with justice, reason, and common sense; but when it fails to do this I abhor it as I do the devil and the pits of hell, as every true reformer should do. I think we may be of good cheer for a while yet, although the work of reconstruction is not progressing as fast as we would wish. Still it moves slowly, and it is to be hoped, surely, for we see by reading history that reforms never go back, but is always onward and upward. Then may we not hope for better times in this country for the oppressed and down-trodden, if we are but true to the cause of justice and liberty?

Now, friends and soldiers, let us take new courage. Let us determine to fight on, fight ever, until the last fetter is broken from off the limbs of the slave. When this is done, if we do not get our reward on earth we will in Heaven received the blest plaudit, "Well done then good and faithful servants, ye have broken every yoke and let my people go free; enter into the joys of your Lord." Do not think I am over zealous in the work; for I think I can see a bright future opening up to our people and I am determined to fight and do all in my power to hasten the day of universal freedom, that the present generation may behold its light and rejoice to see the fruits of their labor—a free country to leave as an inheritance to their children, where no slave clanks his chains, and no mother weeps for her babe forever doomed to slavery's hell.

Then let us go on believing. God will bless and crown us for what we have or may do in this great work of freedom.

R.W.W.[11]

————— ◆•◆ —————

There is a difference in tone, subject, and emphasis between soldier letters written for newspaper consumption, and those

11. Previously identified tentatively as Richard W. White, commissary sergeant in the 55th.

addressed to home. That both are reflections of similar issues and concerns is made clear in this next missive from the pen of Private John Posey.

[Folly Island, S.C.] May the 16th, 1864[12]

Dear Cousin

It is with the greatest of pleasure that [I] do take [my] pen in hand to inform you that I am well at present and I hope when these lines come to hand, [they] may find you enjoying the same blessing.

I lay down last night and laughed pretty near all night and got up this morning with a double-stamp resolution, and feel as happy as a nightingale 16 degrees above the sky. Times are good here. I expect we will be paid off in a few days and of course what little I get will be sent home as soon as I get it. You must do the best you can. I can not be with you, although you are dear to me and [the] sight of you all will [mean a] great [deal] to me. You must be satisfied for I am all right. If I had my choice today, [to] stay here or go home, under the circumstances I give you the honor of a friend, I would prefer staying. I am better satisfied now, and have been so ever since I left home than ever I was for three years previously. I am in better health now than I have been for nearly five years. I am out of one thing and into another and I am glad that I am away from home and in the regiment.

I am a soldier for Uncle Sam and I will obey and stay with his men as long as it suits me, [even] if that is till I am gray. I used to come home but found that was not making the thing gay. I call myself a rebel router, and in the Confederate country I stay. Use my girl tender if you please, and be sure you do it as well as I would treat [them] or ought to treat myself.

Remember we are a nation [of people] that have been greatly oppressed and our kind President is making slow but a sure effort to open up the way for us, and, my dear cousin, it is a glorious blessing and a great many others are engaged in this glorious undertaking, and all people of our color ought to be happy and

12. This letter is from the collection of Robert Younger. The unedited version can be found on pages 240-42 of Appendix Four.

give our noble President all the praise that the tongue could express and [to] every individual that is now engaged in [our] cause.

You are supposed to be up and a-doing [things], not idle and waste time and I am certain you will not waste your money. Your friends are watching for your appearance of improvement. You all must move [ahead], there is no excuse for you whatever.

The White people said the colored people could not drill; now we have proven it: that we can drill as good as any other nation on the globe. Now prove to them that you can [im]prove and show them something else.

We are yet on Folly Island.

The boys are all well and doing well. Give my love to the friends as soon as you get this and see this report. You must give three cheers for the fortune that happened in our regimental, our Sergeant John F. Shorter of Ohio is promoted Second Lieutenant —hurrah, hurrah, hurrah.

No more at present.

John Posey of the 55th Massachusetts regiment. Company great big D.

To Mathias Embry

———————— ◆•◆ ————————

Another review of the regiment's activities from July 1863 to May 1864.

55th Mass. Regt.
Folly Island, S.C., May 29, 1864[13]

. . . A soldier's life, take it what way you will, is a hard one. I have seen a good bit of it. Being the steward of an officer on the Potomac, I had a chance of seeing and learning a great deal of how a soldier ought to be treated. Now I am going to address myself to the public, and shall endeavor to be as brief as possible. I shall not add, but rather diminish.

The 54th, our brother regiment, came to this department last summer, and made that gallant charge on Fort Wagner on Morris Island, where many a brave man fell; I will not say soldiers,

13. *Christian Recorder*, July 9, 1864. Reprinted in *A Grand Army of Black Men.*

for in these two regiments we are only soldiers for the time being.

Shortly after this charge we landed on Folly Island, and soon after fatiguing duties began. We went to the front every night and day for six or eight weeks in a stretch, mounting cannon, pulling cannon, throwing up batteries, when I would much rather have taken my position in line of battle; for the seizing of Morris Island, preparatory to the siege of Charleston, was anything but a pleasant undertaking; so we fatigued from that time until the 13th of February, when we embarked for Florida. The 54th being several days in advance from Jacksonville, we marched out to Barber's Station, en route to assist in making the attack at Olustee. Arriving at Barber's Station, and finding our troops on the retreat, we concluded to encamp there for the night.

The next morning found us retreating back on Jacksonville, where we were immediately set to work throwing up entrenchments and erecting batteries, building forts, and so on, which were all successfully completed. After remaining there a few days we were detached, part going to Palatka and part to Yellow Bluff, where fatigue duty commenced. When we go through there, we were ordered to South Carolina, leaving the 8th Pennsylvania [USCT] regiment to enjoy the fruits of our labor, as we had done for other regiments.

So we entered South Carolina once more, and it was intimated by some prominent officers that by promising to do double duty, we would be allowed to land, but not otherwise. However, we landed and commenced picket duty, each man coming off and going on the next day. This kept up for some time. We were then taken off that duty and put on fatigue duty on Saturday—all this going on, and we not receiving a cent of remuneration, after having been in the service for one year. . . .

Sergeant

————————◆•◆————————

Another letter from the 55th addressed to its strong supporter, Edward W. Kinsley.

Head Quarters 55th Mass. Vols.
Folly Island, S.C., June 2d, 1864[14]

14. Edward W. Kinsley Papers. Duke University Special Collections.

Devoted Friend:

You most cheering letter of the 22d ult was received last night and caused within me feelings of the most pleasant emotions. I read it over 3 times with unflagging interest, handed it to our noble Colonel and determined that a thing so good should be enjoyed by all, and also knowing that you meant it for all, I started it on its mission of cheer around among the sergeants of the Regiment. While I write, it is being read, and I feel sure that from its perusal a *contagion* will spread—a contagion that will produce cheerfulness and a grateful remembrances of its kind author, whom many God bless for the interest taken in men never so vilely treated as they have been by a government for whose safety they have left all, given all, and are still willing to peril all, say all the boys of the 55th. I was much pained to learn that the noble Gov. Andrew had been led to think that we had lost confidence in thinking that he did not care for us, &c. Indeed I never had any thing that has occurred in our circumstances dark as they have been, to cause me so much trouble of mind as the above, and I assure you, Mr. Kinsley, that in possessing these sentiments of regret that our eminent and chief friend should allow himself for a moment to suppose his "colored boys" unmindful of the untiring zeal with which he has *labored* for their *elevation*, I am shared in by nearly all the Regiment, *all of those who are capable of judging.*

I do trust and feverently pray that "Our" magnanimous "Governor," nobler than whom lives not, will be kind enough to observe in looking at this matter that a man of the 54th ('twas not written from the 55th) who wrote a letter charging upon him all the blame because we were not paid must have been either an *ignoramus* or a scoundrel—most probably the former. No sensible man can feel towards the Gov. otherwise than most grateful. I thank him a thousand times (and O how I wish that he could know how many in this Regiment and out of it feel the same) because when no other man *dared* to, he boldly stepped forth upon ground occupied by no other Governor, and, regardless of the opinions of proslavery wicked men, regardless, aye, insensible to, public frowns, dared to do Right, dared to invite and aid the oppressed colored man to take into his hands the wrong—avenging and freedom—securing musket, and point to him the way to

Elevation. True, a year has passed without our having been paid. But we do not lose sight of the great changes that are continually occurring in our favor and full well do we know that the privations, sufferings, wounds and deaths of the colored soldier are resulting gloriously for the *race*. We also recognize the important fact that the passage of a bill equalizing the pay of soldiers is a "big thing," not because it is more than our rights, but because belongs to it a great Principle, that for the attainment of which we gladly peril our lives—Manhood & Equality.

True, we have been disheartened on account of the long delay, cruel and unnecessary of the *government at Washington*, some more so than others. You know how hard it must be for a husband and father to retain his evenness of mind and spirits when he knows that his loved ones suffer for his aid while he is so bound that he cannot give it. This circumstance has impelled many to grow disheartened, and others losing patience on account of government's refusing to accord to them the rights that they *knew* they had so dearly earned, and feeling that they were treated as slaves, have almost given over hoping. O, Mr. Kinsley, we have *all* been blue, very blue at times. Still there is at present a most cheerful state of feeling and your glorious letter has helped to cause it.

God grant that soon, very soon, the dark clouds in sky may soon disappear, to give place to the bright sunshine of Equality and Manhood.

All the sergeants send grateful remembrances to you and all those disinterested friends that have taken such a noble stand for our rights. Truly, as you say, we need not fear for the result when we have so noble advocates. I have told a good many that you would be pleased to get letters from them and from present indications I predict that somebody will fail to get replies for you will have a good many letters from the Regiment.

The health of the Regiment is good at present. We have lost two men by disease since our return from Florida. Our men are going night and day; guard, picket and fatigue duty. While I write there is not a man in camp who is well. The others are all on duty.

About two weeks ago about 250 men of this Regiment, with Col. [Alfred S.] Hartwell, went on a reconnaissance to James I[slan]d. They landed safely and drove the Rebels in double quick time from their first line of intrenchments. So hasty was their departure they left a good warm breakfast; save coffee, which our boys very readily appropriated after the fight was over. After retreating about a mile or two to their 2d line of works the rebels made a stand and prepared to give battle. This was very acceptable to the Union boys, and after a sharp fight "Johnny Reb" retreated behind their works, having lost several killed and wounded, beside several Springfield rifles, marked "U.S.," and our forces only one man slightly wounded. The Col., having accomplished his purpose and not having force enough to advance further among the Rebel batteries withdrew his men safely and when he got home he made a little speech to them praising them for their cool bravery and saying that he was proud of them &c. I knew that for he never stepped more proudly than when on his return.[15]

Sergeant [John F.] Shorter, who was commissioned by his Excellency—the Gov[ernor's] commission—has been refused his discharge papers by Genl [John P.] Hatch on the ground, as he says, that he (Shorter) is of African descent, and therefore cannot be commissioned and mustered as an officer. In conclusion, Respected Sir, I would say that Our Band is beaming to be the pride of the Regiment so finely do they perform. Yesterday a beautiful set of caps arrived for them through the kindness of Adjutant [Leonard B.] Perry, they are very pretty. The Band have a very poor set of instruments. I wish that you would see our Drum Corps. They excel all others in the two islands in martial music and soldierly bearing. Indeed we are proud of the little fellows and so are they of themselves. You are such a good friend of the Regiment, Mr. Kinsley, that I am tempted to ask you if there is any way by which a nicer uniform than that which they now wear can be got for them. It is a delicate question, sir, but I have I fear got myself into trouble by promising the Drum Major that I would suggest this matter to some of our kind friends in Boston.

[unsigned][16]

---

15. A reference to a reconnaissance undertaken on May 21 by four companies and detachments from two other companies of the 55th and the 103rd New York. According to the 55th's regimental history, "The expedition was under the immediate command of Major Morrison of the One-hundred-and-third New York. Col. Hartwell accompanied it as a volunteer."
16. The tenor of this note and its references to all the other sergeants suggest that

This is the last letter from John Posey we have. The reference to the "fight we had," must be to the May 21 action, though the casualty figures Posey provides can only be attributed to camp rumor. According to Major Joseph Morrison's official report of this demonstration, casualties at the end of the operation were "9 men wounded and 2 missing."

[Folly Island, S.C.] June the 3rd, 1864[17]

Dear Sir

It is with the greatest of pleasure that I do take my pen in hand to inform you that I am well at present and I hope when these lines come to hand, [they] may find you enjoying the same blessing.

The boys are all well and doing well. Times are pleasant here, the mule still remains contented. I wish to tell you of the fight we had, though perhaps you have heard [of the] three or five [accounts] I wrote since, but not having a correct report of affairs, as we have heard different [accounts], and all confidence [is] to believe it is so that there was 18 killed and 30 wounded.

I have not time to write to you as I wish, but will [truthfully] say I have had no letters from [you] or your mother since the 10th of March and, as everybody else are a-getting letters, I think it must be from your neglect. I think I will have to continue [my letter writing] in the field where I am the most respected.

No more at present. Give my love to all friends and write soon again.

John Posey of the 55th Massachusetts regiment, Company D, S.C., Folly Island.

———————————— ◆·●·◆ ————————————

There were occasions when a letter from a soldier in one of several units involved in an action would comment upon the

its author might well be Sergeant Major James M. Trotter.
17. This letter is from the collection of Robert Younger. The unedited version can be found on page 242 of Appendix Four.

*actions of another unit and, in turn, spur a response. Here first is
an excerpts from a letter by "G.E.S." (most likely Sergeant George
E. Stephens of the 54th) that commented upon the conduct of
the 55th in the May 21 reconnaissance, followed by the rejoinder
from the 55th.*

Folly Island, S.C., May 26, 1864[18]

Mr. Editor:

. . . The soldiers of the 54th and 55th are as good as you usually
find. . . . An officer told me to my face that the non-commissioned
officers were not as good as they are in white regiments. I suppose
he thought that could be no insult to me. The question of pay
has caused some little trouble, but the regiments are just as efficient as they ever were if there is any fighting to do. As an
evidence of this, on the 22d inst., Gen. [Alexander] Schimmelfennig sent out an expedition to James Island, just opposite Long
Island, to take a rebel battery which could be seen from the distance. Its appearance was formidable. It had a towering magazine,
brazen guns, and bristling abatis. The expedition consisted of
detachments from the 54th N.Y., 74th Pa., 103d N.Y., and nearly
the whole of the 55th Massachusetts Vols., who were the storming party. They thought of deadly assault, of gaping wounds and
of victory in the midst of death. The landing was effected just at
day at two points, one above and the other below the battery.
They had to pass through a marsh waist deep. Col. [Alfred S.]
Hartwell led the storming party, and forbade any man to discharge his piece, until ordered. As soon as they landed the rebels
opened fire. On they steadily advanced until they reached terra
firma, which, as soon as they did, they opened with cheers, the
rebels turned and ran, and did not make any stand whatever,
and what was their astonishment when they reached this famous
work they found it empty—not a rebel to be seen. The magazine
contained sticks and stones, the brazen guns were made of wood,
and the bristling abatis was rotten, a mere sham. Gen. Shimmel-
fennig demolished it in very short order. There is no doubt the
55th would have acquitted themselves nobly had they met "foe-

18. *Weekly Anglo-African*, June 18, 1864. Houghton Library, Harvard University.

men worthy of their steel." Col. [Leopold] Von Gilsa also complimented them for their promptitude and anxiety to be led into action Col. Hartwell told them they did all that could be expected from men. Said he, "not a man has flinched from duty." This was different from some of the men from one of the New York regiments. Capt. [William] Nutt of the 55th and some of his men found one of its Captains hid in the bushes. His excuse was, that he gave out, and could not keep up with his company.

Folly Island, S.C., June 30, 1864[19]

Mr. Editor:

It is at last understood among us that the Committee of Conference in Congress has settled the vexed question in regard to the pay and emoluments of colored troops, and by so doing considered, doubtless, that the public mind will be satisfied, their consciences eased, the troops contented, and the whole disgraceful squabble hushed up most effectually. But in rendering their decision, the honorable delegation made it evident to the world that the American politician has yet a need of a few more pounds of rebel bullets before he can arrive in safety at the standard of justice, and conclude to deal honorably and uprightly with all men, regardless of creed or color. Let Lee exert himself a little and beat back the National forces from before Richmond; let us meet with a few more reverses like that of Banks in the West,[20] and we will find our legislators trying some new method of crushing out the rebellion which has so long been gnawing away the vitals of the Great Republic.

In the event of such circumstances, we would not be surprised to hear of the Secretary of War authorizing the appointment of such officers for colored troops as would inspire them with most confidence, viz: men from their own ranks, and not disgrace as loyal and faithful men and soldiers as the world ever saw, by placing them under command of vagabonds and upstarts, who

19. *Weekly Anglo-African*, July 30, 1864. Houghton Library, Harvard University.
20. References to the Overland Campaign in Virginia, May-June 1864, and the Red River Campaign in Louisiana, March-April 1864.

have passed most of their civil life in bar-rooms and gambling halls, and nearly all of their military life in the guard house, or undergoing other punishments.

Many of the officers of the U.S. Colored Troops are of the above description, and who have, by reputation (or otherwise) as "sporting characters" become ingratiated into favor with some members of Congress, who have forthwith procured them appointments in regiments of colored troops, to the utter exclusion of intelligent soldiers (both white and colored, whose capacity no one can for one moment doubt. Why is it that so many officers who have passed the famous Board of Examination of Casey are now going about begging appointments?[21] and why is it that so many of the places which they should occupy are now filled by street-loafers and grog-shop rowdies from New York, Philadelphia and elsewhere? I have it from intelligent men in a certain colored regiment now down here, that some of their subaltern officers openly boast of having been active participants in the New York riots of last Summer, and take as much delight in picturing the suffering of their unfortunate victims, as though they had been engaged in some laudable enterprise. Such are the men, or brutes, who are chosen by the Executive to command men who are in every respect—physically, intellectually and morally—their superiors. Why is not justice done?

We had a most unfortunate and sorrowful scene to witness a few days since, in the execution, by martial law, of one of the men of our regiment for mutiny, in disobeying the orders and violent assaulting and maltreating his superior officer.[22] We were marched down the beach about two miles, and back into an open space of ground, where the grave was already dug and yawning for its victim. All the troops on the Island were present. Such scenes are of too frequent occurrence, and have been depicted too often to need any description here, so we will be contented with saying that the prisoner, Private Wallace Baker, Co. I, displayed the most unflinching courage, and met his death with

21. In May, 1863, to deal with the issues arising from the large number of United States Colored Troops regiments being raised, the War Department created the Bureau of Colored Troops. The Bureau in turn set up boards of examination to test prospective USCT officer candidates for general knowledge and understanding of military tactics and proceedures. Major General Silas Casey, author of a tactical manual used by USCT units, sat on the Washington Board of Examination.
22. Private Wallace Baker, executed June 18, 1864.

113

stoical indifference. The firing party was from our regiment; seven bullets struck the doomed man, and he died instantly, without a struggle. This had been the first execution of the kind in ours, and I sincerely hope it will be the last.

We have many men, not only Copperheads at home, but dough-faces and puppies in the army, who are continually doing their utmost to pander and show their subservience to the Confederacy. An instance of this occurred a few days since on Coles Island, just opposite here, across Folly River, where a detachment of our regiment, commanded by one of our captains, was doing picket duty. A rebel officer came down with a flag of truce to our advanced posts, and upon being met by our Captain, bluntly refeused to treat with an officer of colored troops. Our officer immediately reported the case to Lieut.-Col. Meitzel, 74th Pennsylvania Vol., commanding the island, who servilely sent an officer of *white* troops to treat with the rebel; thus accepting and endorsing the policy dictated by him: that not only were colored troops inferior, but that their officers were not entitled to enough respect to enable them to receive a flag. So it goes: officers and men are alike treated as dogs, and put in arrest if we complain. What will be the end of all this double working.

In THE ANGLO of the 18th inst. appeared a letter over the signature of "G.E.S." which has attracted a good deal of attention in our regiment, both for the excellence of one portion, and the apparent jealousy and inconsistency of the other. The writer, after citing quotations from speeches from different orators, repeating the Dred Scott decision, and giving a concise history of the great Reformation—all with very great effect—branches off suddenly, and commences a very vigorous attack upon a certain correspondent of yours in this regiment, directly, and our whole regiment indirectly, the cause of the attack, ostensibly, an article written by the correspondent aforesaid.

Following up his attack upon "Wolverine," Mr. "G.E.S." proceeded to give an account of the reconnaissance upon James Island, last month, in which a portion of our regiment participated; and I must say that his remarks were touched with that petty jealousy which distinguishes so many letters from his regiment, and were decidedly incorrect, and ungentlemanly in the extreme. In fact, Mr. "G.E.S." appears to be travelling two roads at once —praising the anxiety of the 55th to be led into action, and at the

114

same time ridiculing them for charging upon an empty battery, known by them (according to "G. E. S.") to be empty. He proceeds to admit the possibility of the 55th behaving well had the enemy stood their ground, and finishes by intimating that the 55th knew at first that they would find the fort empty, *which was the cause of their anxiety* to be led forward. This whole statement of "G.E.S." is grossly incorrect, in that the 55th knew nothing of an empty battery; that the rebels did make a stand, and a firm one, until they were flanked by Capt. Nutt, of the 55th, inflicting some loss on our men, and suffering (according to deserters, etc.) rather severely themselves; and that so far from their intrenchments being empty, the rebels stayed behind them until they were forced out, and in danger of being cut off from their reserves. If there was no danger, and the coast was clear, what need was there of a captain of a New York regiment hiding in the bushes from cowardice?

The story concocted by "G.E.S." is inconsistent—very—and when he wishes another to embellish his correspondence, and make it amusing at the expense of regiments other than his own, we advise him to make it a little less glaring, or his veracity may be impeached. Standing, as he does, at the head of all the correspondents of his regiment, it was thought that he would not fall into the common error of his fellows—detracting from the good name of other troops, thinking, doubtless, that they will gain thereby, and fearing that another regiment might eclipse theirs. But it seems that in order to prove that man is fallible, "G.E.S." has plunged headlong into the same course, and has indulged in drawing the ridicule of the public to his delight and satisfaction. Could not the worthy correspondent and representative of the noble 54th for a moment take into consideration that we are all here as brothers in one common cause, striving for our rights and country, and that we have enough to vilify us without adding ourselves to the number of our enemies. The colored man who will wantonly attempt to misrepresent his fellow-soldier, is a greater enemy than any rebel in Secessia. I am sorry to say that there are some of the 54th who often give false coloring to the actions of their comrades in other regiments, as was their representation of the 1st North Carolina and 8th U.S. Colored Troops after Olustee, when all know that there are not more daring men in the field than those in the two regiments just named. Copperheads and rebels, are doubtless, happy to know that so much jealousy exists among some of our colored troops, but I am confident that every true lover of liberty and advocate of human rights must view the contemptible feelings in a very unfavorable light.

Again, in a former part of his letter he proceeds to ask, "Why shall we not rise in open mutiny, as white troops have done or would do?" I would ask "G.E.S.," or any other how would we be benefited thereby? Would a mutiny, attended as it would be by a profuse shedding of the blood of our officers and men, in any way add to the already glorious reputation of the 54th? or would it add to the splendid discipline which characterizes this regiment? Would it alleviate the sufferings of our wives and children at home, or increase or hasten our chances of relieving them? Finally, would it elevate us either mentally, morally or socially, or hasten the time when we shall get our rights under this government? I suppose "G.E.S." will think that I, also, am making "a bid for official favor"; but if so, I can only reply that it is the duty of all soldiers to suppress *all* insubordinations; and if by so doing one renders himself worthy a favor, it is not less honorably or less dangerously won, than if it were won at Wagner or Olustee.

Picket.

The months of June and July were especially tense ones in the ranks of the 55th Massachusetts. According to the regimental history, "On the 13th and 14th of July, two partial combinations among the enlisted men to refuse duty took place. . . ." This petition, from John Posey's company, is dated two days after those incidents of unrest.

To the President of the United States
Folly Island, South Carolina, July 16th, 1864[23]

23. Office of the Adjutant General, Colored Troop Division Letters Received. National Archives. This letter has been edited for clarity.

Sir:

We, the members of Co. D of the 55th Massachusetts Vol. call the attention of your excellency to our case.

1st. We were enlisted under the act of Congress of July 1861 placing the officers, non-commissioned officers & privates of the volunteer forces in all respects as to pay on the footing of similar corps of the Regular Army. 2nd. We have been in the field now thirteen months & a great many longer. We have received no pay & have been offered only seven dollars per month, which the Paymaster has said was all he had been authorized to pay colored troops. This was not according to our enlistment. Consequently we refused the money. The Commonwealth of Massachusetts then passed an act to make up all deficiencies which the general Government refused to pay, but this we could not receive as the troops in the general service are not paid partly by Government and partly by State. 3rd. That to us money is no object. We came to fight for liberty, justice & equality. These are gifts we prize more highly than gold. For these we left our homes, our families, friends & relatives most dear to take as it were our lives in our hands to do battle for God & Liberty.

4th. After the elapse of over thirteen months spent cheerfully & willingly doing our duty most faithfully in the trenches, fatigue duty in camp, and conspicuous valor & endurance in battle as our past history will show.

5th. Therefore we deem these sufficient reasons for demanding our pay from the date of our enlistment & our immediate discharge, having been enlisted under false pretence as the past history of the company will prove.

6th. Be it further resolved that if immediate steps are not taken to relieve us, we will resort to more stringent measures.

We have the honor to remain your obedient servants.

The members of Co. D.

Sergts	John M. Jones
	Frank Webb
John F. Shorter	John Brown
Eli Lett	William Wright
Armsted M. Jones	George P. Smith

Pierson Fountain*
Austin R. Lewis†
Corp. George W. Taylor†
Matthew Johnson
Simon Douglass
Thornton Parker
Simon Peter Shorter
Matthew McFarlin*
Basil Henry*
Charles Edwards
Samuel Graves
David M.P. Kenny
John Taylor
Robert Wilson
Charles H. Holmes
Thomas Holland
Charles Johnson
Gilbert Butler
Elijah Dericks*
William H. Griffin†
George Robinson
Lyne S. Brown†
Nelson Adams
Dennis Wilkinson
Nathan Lane
Trotman Sarmons†
John Q. A. Crosby
Charles H. Stafford†
Stephen Ward†
Frank Brown
E. A. Highwarden
James Riley*
William J. Peel†

Samuel Taylor
John W. Highwarden
George B. Lewis
S.J. Robinson
Emery Allen†
Lewis Gaskins
Samuel Jobe
William Cephas
William Crainshaw*
Richard Crockett
Wallace Glaspy†
James Lewis
Paul Crowder*
James H. Dixon
Stephen W. Pediford
James Johnson
Thomas H. Fitzgerald*
Ellis McGerry
James H. Simpson
Frank McCoglin
Nelson Mills
John Posey†
Joseph Jones
Frederick Hall*
Robert Burke†
Bolden Tanner
William Hill
Alexander Scott
Jeremiah Sanders
Weston Johnson
G. W. Whyte
Elijah Revels
William Cazy[24]

† Killed in action.　　* Wounded in action.

---

24. For the original spelling of this petition, see: FREEDOM: A Documentary History of Emancipation, Series II The Black Military Experience, pages 401-402.

On the evening of July 1, 1864, the 55th Massachusetts left Folly Island as part of an expedition to test the defenses of James Island. The result was the most severe combat to date for the regiment. The following war-time letters provide details on this engagement from the perspective of the 55th. Also included are several postwar letters from soldiers of the 55th regarding this action.

Folly Island, S.C.
July 18, 1864[25]

My Dear Friend [Edward W. Kinsley],

I have read both of your last letters. They came to me just after the short but active and I may say bloody campaign on James Island, of which you have ere this heard. We were *lying in the dirt* behind our breast works when your kind and very interesting favors were handed me. I found no way of replying then, although I wanted to reciprocate your kind[ness] very much. Since our return to camp I have entered upon the duties of Lieutenant, having been for 3 days on picket duty on Long Island. All these things, dear and honored friend, have prevented me from writing until now, and I trust that I will not be thought hard if I waited until I could reply to both.

While we were on James Island and the next day or two after the Charge, and when all of the men were out of and suffering for tobacco, with no way whatever of getting any, what should come but a *great heap* of the very article, a quarter of a plug to each man. My Dear Sir, could you have been a witness to the complete joy had you seen the beaming countenances and active mouths after this tobacco was distributed. I know you and the firm would have been happier than if you had sold it at $5.00 per plug. The two splendid horns have also arrived, and this morning after I came off duty I went out to Guard Mounting and heard Prof. Moore and his first asst. Smith perform the "Cottage by the Sea" most delightfully. Moore & Pete are tickled to death and so are we all, and we say God bless noble hearted Mr. Kinsley and all our dear Massachusetts friends.

25. Edward W. Kinsley Papers. Duke University Special Collections.

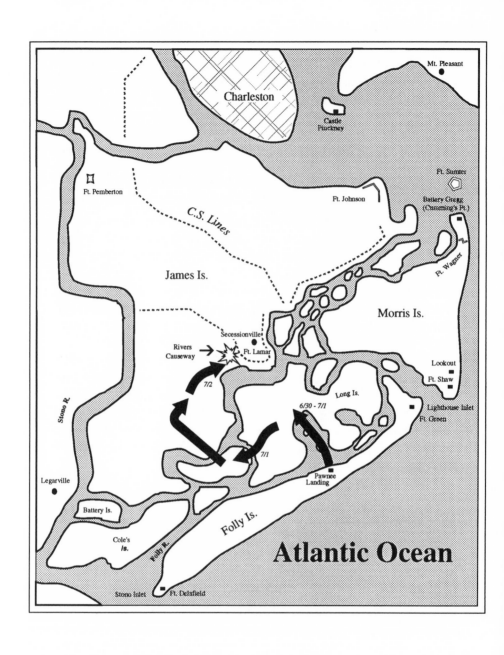

James Island Skirmish: July 2, 1864
120

I will tell you now about the expedition. On the night of July first, the 55th, 103rd N.Y. and 33rd U.S.[C.T.] crossed in small boats from Folly to Long Island, marched to the south end of the latter and again quietly taking boats, crossed another stream to Tiger's Island. On our way to James our landing was disputed only by the mud and some of the men sunk nearly up to their necks in the mire at the landing. However we were at last all safely in Rebel Territory, and although much fatigued and all wet and muddy began our march toward the enemy and his numerous forts on James Island. We soon found natural difficulties before us in the shape of a swamp across which we had to pass in order to get on further. But we were not to be discouraged, and plunging, wading and part of the time almost swimming, we got on firm ground. (I forgot to say that our brigade was commanded by Col. [Alfred S.] Hartwell.) The 103rd N.Y. was now deployed forward as skirmishers and very soon the sharp crack of the rifle was heard, shot after shot exchanged, so we knew that the Rebel Pickets had been encountered. We moved forward briskly, day was just beginning to break, and just as we were emerging from a narrow wood, we were opened upon by the enemy from a battery at River Causeway Landing, hitherto unknown to exist to us on Folly, and at first they threw solid ball and shell among the advancing brigade, doing great damage. Still on they pressed. Very soon the Rebels ceased throwing every thing but grape and canister. This they hurled among us like hail scattering death and destruction all around. At this time the 103rd N.Y. & 33rd U.S. [C.T.], who were in the advance and on the right of us, became panic-stricken and could not be restrained by their officers and Col. Hartwell from retreating pell mell. This emboldened the Rebel gunners and infantry in the fort and they poured a deadly fire into them. The Reserve, 55th, Lt. Col. [Charles B.] Fox, was now appealed to save the Brigade. We numbered 350 men and 9 officers. Col. Hartwell cried "Bring forward the 55th"! We were already advancing on the double-quick bayonets at a charge, and the men cheering, shouting, and the battle cry "Fort Pillow" came forth from many a throat. The behavior of the other two reg[imen]ts had no other effect upon our men than to inspire them with a daring determination to capture the fort. The enemy seeing the right fleeing and our little band advancing steadily now turned their whole attention to the latter, pouring the grape with deadly effect. The ground over which we were advancing had previously been rendered most impassable by the Rebels by cutting down and crossing trees. The ground was also very marshy and we had a hard road to travel and no friends at the end of it. This gave Johnny a great advantage over us, as we could only advance very slowly and men were continually sinking in the marsh. Rapidly they discharged their cannon and our brave boys were falling all along the way. But onward we plunged getting nearer and nearer the battery and very soon the enemy seemed to get confused seeing that we were determined on their destruction or capture and their aim became inaccurate, their shots going over our heads. We had now got beyond the jungle, was within 200 yards of the battery, when we made a desperate rush, yelling unearthly. Here the Rebels broke, jumped on their waiting horses and by the time we had gained the parapet were far down the road leading to Secessionville. O how they did fly! They left behind two pieces of cannon, which as soon as we had gained the fort our artillery company, "F," faced about and sent two discharges, which they had not time to fire, after them, killing several. We had been out two days and nights wading through the mud and water and were too tired to pursue the enemy, besides, we had no support, the other Reg[imen]ts having failed us.

In the charge our loss was 9 killed and 19 wounded, which considering the circumstances we think was miraculously small. Capt. Frank Goodwin of Co. "E" was severely wounded in both thighs while bravely leading his company. We lost also two of our best Sergeants, [Alonzo] Boon of Boston and [William J.] Stedman of P[ennsylvani]a. Well, you may imagine how proud we felt when we found ourselves masters of "Johnny's" fort and with what satisfaction we looked upon *our* pieces of cannon which now looked innocent enough but which a few minutes before had dealt death to so many our brave fellows. We captured one prisoner only in the fort, and he fell on his knees and begged most earnestly for his life. The wounded were all conveyed to camp. Two have had their arms amputated and you will probably see them when discharged. All the wounded have been removed to Beaufort. We brought the cannon to our camp and they are on the hill at Head Quarters. Our men fought bravely, we have achieved quite a name in the department.

The loss in the 3 Regts of this Brigade is about one hundred killed and wounded, ours being 28 killed and wounded.

We hear since Col. [Norwood P.] Hallowell announce that the question is justly settled and that our paymaster is at Hilton Head preparing to come. I pray that soon all will be all right.

Mr. Kinsley, what do you think will be done about the *muster matter?* Three of us have been commissioned by the Gov[ernor] but have not been discharged and mustered; yet, our discharge papers have been sent in but we have not heard from them yet. Sometimes I doubt our getting justice. What do you think will be done? This *acting* Lieutenant business is not all pleasant when you reflect that no other thing stands in the way but our *color*. We, of course, have bought no uniforms yet because we do not know how it will end.

But I must close by wishing you health and happiness and hoping that I may have the pleasure of hearing from you again.

Respectfully, your obedient servant,

James M. Trotter[26]

———— ♦•♦ ————

Camp 55th Mass. Vols.[27]
Folly Island, S.C., July 24, 1864

Mr. Editor:

I wish you and the many fair ladies and other friends who have so generously given their money to send THE ANGLO to the soldiers, could know what genuine comfort and solid benefit it imparts to them. Then you would be more than paid for whatever labor and expense it costs you. When the mail arrives we inquire as earnestly for "MY ANGLO" as for "my letter from home," or almost, not quite, of course, as for my letter from "dearest Mollie." This is as sure an evidence of its value to the

26. James Monroe Trotter was a teacher when he enlisted with the 55th. Born in Grand Gulf, Mississippi, he was recruited in Cincinnati, Ohio. He enlisted as a private in Company K and became its First Sergeant on June 11, 1863.
27. *Weekly Anglo-African*, August 13, 1864. Houghton Library, Harvard University.

soldiers as it is of the latter's appreciation of it. But THE ANGLO AFRICAN seems a great favorite with not only us soldiers, but also the dear friends in civil life, I judge, considering its many able contributors from all parts of the North. Several officers in this regiment take it. I trust, however, that it has more *buyers* among its host of readers than *borrowers*; otherwise it cannot long exist. But I am forgetting all this while that the paper I receive every week is the bounty of some kind-hearted stranger friend. However I am a poor soldier, serving without pay, because not offered the wages of a freeman. Yes, we want our noble sisters who send us the spicy ANGLO to know how heartily their soldiers-brothers appreciate their kindness. Bless them! How we poor fellows miss their pleasant smiles! Excuse my levity, Mr. Editor, and I will try to write not more earnestly, but on a topic more serious.

To any individual noting with solicitude the progress of our down-trodden race toward elevation in this great crisis, it is a source of much joy to observe the rapid literary development of our young men and women. See how eagerly the opportunity offered in the columns of THE ANGLO is embraced. Look in the soldiers department, what a goodly number of letters are there every week!

No one complains now as formerly that the soldiers do not keep them posted as to their doings. And I opine that the many well-written letters go unpublished for want of space so great is the number sent you. But Mr. Editor, without claiming to possess more judgment than any one person ought to have, or without wishing to be considered a critic, I must say that a few of the boys who write to THE ANGLO make some very grave military mistakes in some of the conclusions to which they come, which conclusion I might as well say, will not stand the test of the commonest kind of sense. I refer to some letters setting forth grievances. For instance, a short time ago, a writer complained that he was obliged to extinguish his lights after nine o'clock. And again that he was not allowed to visit a certain town without a pass. Now, however reasonable these complaints may seem to civilians, they are, nevertheless, to all military men, perfectly laughable, and a soldier wonders that a military man ever made them. Evidently the writer had never seen much active service or he would have discovered the utility of "keeping dark" after "Taps." He will soon learn however that the freedom we enjoyed at home is just the thing that will not make an army.

But I would speak of another error into which some are falling, which I consider a very grave one indeed; one which if persisted in, must certainly produce untold damage to the cause which lieth next to our hearts and for the success of which we all willingly and enthusiastically offer our lives. I refer to the habit which some colored soldiers have of speaking falsely of, vilifying and charging cowardice upon other colored regiments. How foolish, and how it delights our enemies and pains our friends.

We should possess more national pride. At present we cannot afford to have any cowardice exhibited by our colored regiments, (and they do not exhibit any; even our enemies are forced to call us brave), but least of all can we afford to have men of color so foolish and villainous as to be continually asserting that "the 54th fought bravely but the 55th run away." "The 5th Cavalry were as cool as veterans, but the 4th U.S. were much confused." All this is child's talk, unworthy of colored men fighting to establish a noble reputation and the freedom not only of the people of one State, or of one regiment, but the *liberty of all*. Bear in mind that the brave deeds of one colored man or of any one colored regiment, reflects credit on the race and goes in the balance. Let us rejoice therefore, in each others successes. Let "Veritas" and the "Triple Star" (* * *)[28] vie with each other in celebrating the one, the brave deeds of the other regiment and leave it to the Copperheads to do the dirty work of trying to defame.

The usual monotony of camp life here was the other day disturbed by an expedition to James Island. There was also a movement made on Johns Island. Another to Sullivans and the navy was busy. In truth we waked the rebs up all along our front; and had we had more reliable material, to-day my letter would be dated from Charleston, S.C.

Conscript regiments here will not fight, and I only assert what an impartial person will admit to be the truth when I say that had there been as many colored regiments with the expedition as there were colored and white together, Charleston to-day would either be ours or else we would be at her gates instead of

28. Other nom-de-plumes appearing in the *Weekly Anglo-African*.

occupying an old post. The only success achieved was that of the 55th Mass., which charged upon and under a murderous rebel fire of grape and canister captured Fort Wright, mounting two brass field pieces. The cannon have been brought to camp with us and they are in position on Head Q'rs Hill. Of course the boys feel quite proud of their conquest. It cost dearly however, the regiment having lost nine killed, 19 wounded, some of whom have since died. I append their names.

KILLED

Sergt. W. Stedman, Co. I, shot in the head.
Corp. H.T. Powell, " C, from wound in head.
James Davis,　　　" A,　　"　　neck.
L. Peck,　　　" B,　　"　　head.
W.H. Russell,　　" C,　　"　　head.
W.H. Johnson,　　" I,　　"　　head.
Benj. Griffin,　　" K,　　"　　chest.
Sergt. A. Boon,　　" K,　　"　　leg.
I.H.Thompson,　　" C,　　"　　arm and leg.

Total killed.　　9.

WOUNDED

Capt. Frank Goodwin, Co. E. flesh wound in both thighs by canister, severely; Capt. James D. Thurber, Co. F., slight wound in right shoulder, now on duty.
1st Sergt. W.H. Evans Co. A severely—
W.H. Dallas, Co. A, flesh wound in shoulder.
J. Chatman,　　" B,　　"　　right temple.
F. Herb,　　　" E,　　"　　slight.
James Malone," E,　　"　　in cheek.
J.H. Peterson, " F,　　"　　thigh.
Peter Jones,　" F,　　"　　slight.
J. Murphy,　　" G,　　"　　slight.
B. Burrows,　　" H, in left arm (arm amputated).
M. Darnell,　　" I, (finger amputated).
C. Crummer,　　" I, flesh wound in back of neck.
C'l T.J. Brown, " K, arm broken by ball, arm amputated.

R. Chatman, " K, flesh wound in leg, slight.
L. Payne, " K, slight.
S. January, " K, " , now on duty.
F. Richman, " K, severely in left heel.

Total wounded   18.

Sergeant Boon and Private Thompson died after reaching camp. The other seven killed were left unburied upon the field, owing to the fact that the rebels barbarously shelled Dr. [Burt] Wilder and assistants from two forts while they were endeavoring to perform their humane duties and they could do no more than bring off all the wounded.[29] The wounded have been sent to general hospitals at Beaufort, S.C., where good care will be taken of them. Nearly all it is thought will recover.

Twenty-eight killed and wounded, and yet our noble government will still deny us just treatment. Our noble Col. [Alfred S.] Hartwell, recommended and Gov. Andrew commissioned as 2nd Lieut., 1st Serg't. J. F. Shorter; 1st Serg't. W. H. Dupree, and Serg't. Major James M. Trotter; but the U.S. government has refused so far to muster them because *God did not make them White.* No other objection is, or can be offered. *Three cheers for "our country."*

MON.

55th Mass. Vols.,
Folly Island, S.C., July 26, 1864[30]

. . . I have seen considerable service, one way or another, both in the infantry tactics and also in artillery practice, both light and heavy. It was my privilege to be the first non-commissioned officer that reached the enemy's guns in the fight we had on James

29. Following the evacuation of Charleston, members of the 55th returned to the site of the Rivers Causeway fight and found the scattered bones of those who had died there and had been left unburied since. The remains were given a fitting ceremony and burial.
30. *The Liberator,* October 4, 1864. Reprinted in Redkey, *A Grand Army of Black Men.*

Island, on the 1st [2d] of July. I found one of them loaded, and fired it; afterwards, loaded it with another charge which the rebels failed to take away, and fired that also. The two guns were afterwards given in my charge (two twelve-pounders, Napoleon guns, manufactured in Richmond, Va.) by the Colonel of our regiment, who commanded the successful charge.

I selected from our company (F) two gun detachments, and during our stay on James Island used the guns pretty effectively on the Rebs. I also covered the retreat of our forces from James to Cole's Island with them. The guns are now in front of the quarters of our colonel; the General having granted the Colonel the privilege of keeping them, in consideration of the valor of the 55th.

For the services of myself and the men under my charge, I received, through our Colonel, the thanks of the chief of artillery.

Today I can say, without depreciating any other regiment, that none stand higher than the old 55th in the estimation of our Commanding General.

Could you have been on the battle-field on the morning of July 1st[2d], and see them under a shower of shot and shell deploy into line of battle when it seemed as though the day was lost by the giving way of two regiments—(one white, and the other colored, both rushing back discomforted)—I say, could you have seen the old 55th rush in, with the shout of "Remember Fort Pillow!" you would have thought that nothing human could have withstood their impetuosity. We know no defeat. The guns we were bent on having, and there they are, near my tent door. . . .

Sept. 11th:—Two large tents have been erected and floored adjoining each other, making a room some 45 by 25 feet, with suitable desks and benches for its furniture. Evening schools have been established. The valuable accessions to the reading matter of the regiment, recently received from Massachusetts, have given us quite a library. God bless the noble friends at home for their philanthropic efforts in behalf of the soldiers in the field! The appreciation of their effort is attested in the interest manifested by the large numbers in attendance every evening. I find there are not a few in the regiment, who, although never having been slaves, are unable to write their names, and many are unable to read. A year's experience in the army has shown most of them the disadvantage of being dependent upon others to do their writing

128

Chaplain John R. Bowles

John R. Bowles joined the 55th as its chaplain on March 27, 1864.
His reports on the history and moral condition of the 55th are on file at
the National Archives. He resigned in June of 1865 and died in
Xenia, Ohio, on September 3, 1874.

Second Lieutenant William H. Dupree

William H. Dupree joined the 55th Massachusetts on June 5, 1863.
He was promoted to second lieutenant on July 1, 1865.
He was mustered out on August 29, 1865.

Second Lieutenant James Monroe Trotter

James Monroe Trotter was a schoolteacher who began his term as an officer on June 11, 1863 when he was made first sergeant of the 55th Massachusetts. He was promoted to second lieutenant on July 1, 1865. He wrote several letters to Edward Kinsley in gratitude for Kinsley's support. Trotter was mustered out on August 29, 1865, and died at Hyde Park, Massachusetts on February 26, 1892.

Sergeant Charles L. Mitchell

Charles Mitchell was made sergeant of the 55th on June 20, 1864.
He was commissioned second lieutenant on September 20, 1865, but
was never mustered as such due to a disability discharge from
wounds received at Honey Hill, South Carolina.

Sergeant Major Abram W. Shadd

Abram Shadd was commissioned second lieuenant on September
20, 1865, after serving as both sergeant and sergeant major.
He was mustered out on August 29, 1865, and died at Greenville,
Mississippi, on November 15, 1878.

Second Lieutenant John Freeman Shorter

John Shorter was made first sergeant of Company D on June 22, 1863, and second lieutenant on July 1, 1865. He died in Delaware, Ohio in September of 1865.

Sergeant Nicholas Saib

Nicholas Saib was born in Mali, Africa.

Private Sam Sharp

Sam Sharp enlisted at age twenty-two, and was discharged
because of wounds received at Honey Hill. He was never in a
color company nor is there any indication that he was wounded
in an effort to protect the colors. This, in addition to the fact
that Sharp here looks much older than twenty-two, may indicate
that this is a post-war photograph.

The reverse of this tintype reads:

"Joe"
Headquarters
Camp Meigs
Readville, Massachusetts
Oct. 1862

Tintype of an unidentified soldier in the 55th Massachusetts

Tintype of an unidentified soldier in the 55th Massachusetts

Tintype of an unidentified soldier in the 55th Massachusetts

here it is

1

December the 9 1863
my cousin i taoke my pen
band to inform you that i
am well at present and i
these lines may find you enjoy ing
the same blessing you all a pear
to be dead and whether you be
or no i can not tel it you are not
dead you are very car less a
bout either friends or re lation
as for writing you do not give a
dam whether you all write or
not though i might write
every day which i do every
two or three days and some
times every and to get once a
month i can not it looks as
though you might once in a
while every three or four
months and i would get a
leter now and then but the

John Posey letter, December 2, 1863

Colonel Alfred Stedman Hartwell,
Brevet Brigidier General, U.S.V.

Alfred S. Hartwell was made lieutenant colonel of the 55th on May 30, 1863. He assumed command as its colonel on December 11, 1863, after Colonel Hallowell's discharge. He was mustered out on April 30, 1866.

Colonel Norwood Penrose Hallowell

Norwood P. Hallowell was the first commander of the 55th
Massachusetts Volunteers, becoming its colonel on June 24, 1863.
He was honorably discharged on November 2, 1863, due to
wounds he received at Antietam.

Lieutenant Colonel Charles Barnard Fox,
Brevet Colonel, U.S.V.

Charles B. Fox was made major of the 55th on June 1, 1863 and lieutenant colonel on December 1, 1863. He commanded the regiment after Colonel Hartwell was seriously wounded at Hilton Head. He resigned on June 24, 1865, and died in Boston on March 30, 1895.

Lieutenant Colonel William Nutt,
Brevet Colonel, U.S.V.

William Nutt began his service with the 55th as captain of
Company D, John Posey's company, on May 31, 1863. He was
mustered out on August 29th, 1865.

Major Sigourney Wales

Sigourney Wales became major of the 55th on December 1, 1863.
He resigned on November 22, 1864, and died on September 14,
1895, in New York City.

Surgeon William Symmington Brown

William S. Brown was born in Glasgow, Scotland on February 9, 1822. He was promoted to surgeon of the 55th on June 9, 1863. He resigned on July 1, 1865.

Surgeon Burt Green Wilder

After serving the 55th as its assistant surgeon, Wilder was made
surgeon on July 11, 1865. He was mustered out on August 29,
1865, and later published a short history of the regiment.

Captain Frank Goodwin,
Brevet Major, U.S.V.

Frank Goodwin was made captain of the 55th on July 20, 1863, and was mustered out on August 29, 1865, after being severely wounded in the defense of James Island.

Captain William Dwight Crane

William Crane became captain of the 55th Massachusetts on June 19, 1863. He was killed in action on November 30, 1864, at Honey Hill.

Captain John Gordon

John Gordon was made captain of the 55th Massachusetts on June
30, 1863. He resigned on July 26th, 1864.

Captain James Danforth Thurber,
Brevet Major, U.S.V.

James Thurber joined the 55th Massachusetts as second lieutenant on June 15, 1863. He became a captain on December 1, 1863, and was mustered out on August 29, 1865.

Captain Charles Carroll Soule

On June 19th, 1863, Charles Soule was made captain of the 55th.
He was later breveted major, but declined. He was mustered out on
August 29, 1865. Soule wrote an account of the Battle of Honey
Hill for the *Philadelphia Weekly Times.*

First Lieutenant Winthrop Perkins Boynton

Winthrop P. Boynton was made second lieutenant on July 8, 1863, and first lieutenant on November 21, 1863. He was killed in action on November 30, 1864, at Honey Hill, South Carolina.

First Lieutenant Charles L. Roberts

Charles Roberts became first lieutenant of the 55th on July 25,
1865. He was mustered out on August 29, 1865, and died at
Weston, Massachusetts on October 13, 1870.

Second Lieutenant Leonard Case Alden

On May 12, 1863, Leonard C. Alden was made second lieutenant
of the 55th. He died at Hilton Head, South Carolina on October 5,
1863.

First Lieutenant and Adjutant William Penrose Hallowell

On May 20, 1863, William Hallowell was made adjutant of the 55th Massachusetts. He resigned due to disability on February 25, 1864.

First Lieutenant Dennis H. Jones

Dennis Jones was made first lieutenant of the 55th on June 19, 1863.
He was killed while on a scouting party in Yellow Bluff,
Florida on March 23, 1864, when Captain Charles C. Soule's pistol
accidentally discharged.

John Albion Andrew
John Andrew was governor of Massachusetts, 1861 - 1866. He is
pictured here with his military staff.

Edward W. Kinsley

Edward Kinsley was a friend of Massachusetts governor John Andrew. He was an active supporter of Massachusetts' black regiments and maintained a frequent correspondence with the 55th Massachusetts.

and reading of letters; and they are now applying themselves assiduously with spelling book, pen, ink, and paper. Another class are equally, if not more desirous of improving their mental faculties. I allude to those whom the withering, blighting, cursed system of slavery has robbed of the golden moments of youth and the maturer hours of manhood. Many of these are destined to make their marks bright ornaments . . . to their homes.

Sergeant

Burt Wilder, one of the surgeons who served with the 55th, intended late in life to complete his own history of the regiment, To that end he corresponded with both the rank and file, seeking information on the major actions in which the 55th was involved. The fighting on James Island on July 2, 1864, was a subject of especial interest to Wilder.

Springboro, Warren County, Ohio
April 17th, 1906[31]

Hon. Sir [Burt Wilder], M.D., Comrade and friend:

Having received a pamphlet written by you[32] from Comrade D[avid] Lee [of Company C], I will state what I saw or remember [of] the charge on the 2nd of July 1864. We slept on our arms and we soon formed in battle line, and moved forward several hundred yards. We were then under fire. Col. [Charles B.] Fox gave the command change front forward on first company by companies right half wheel. As the last company came into line, Col. F[ox] said, forward double quick. Col. Fox said with an adjective, remember fort pillow.

This fired the men. We all commenced to yell Ft. Pillow. We fixed bayonets and charged without orders I think. One of our leaders said we could not go up in that shape, guide on a line. I immediately reversed my gun so that the men could dress on me. Col. Fox said 55th take that battery. Capt. [William D.] Crane said don't let them get another shot on you. As I stopped and

31. Burt G. Wilder Papers. Cornell University.
32. Burt Wilder authored a short pamphlet, which he published in 1914, containing an address on the 55th Massachusetts that he had given before the Brookville, Massachusetts Historical Society.

reversed my gun, Wm. Russell of My Co. C, did dress on me; but ran from my right to my left probably about six feet in advance of me; at the flash of the cannon he stopped just low enough for the canister to take him in the head, so lost his life. I am telling you in part what I heard and saw.

> Yours in F.O. & G.
> Jordan M. Bobson, late of Co. C 55th Mass[33]

In his letter to 55th Massachusetts infantryman George S. Walker, Dr. Wilder posed eleven questions regarding the July 2 action: 1. Who else was in the color guard? 2. Who was the color sergeant? 3. What company had the colors and who commanded it? 4. You say you led the charge, how did that happen? 5. How did you get the order from Col. Hartwell? 6. You say his order was "By the right flank, file left;" would not "by the right flank" take you to the right? 7. Did you see anything of "Andy Smith" of Co. B, then or later? 8. As we lay in the trench during the day do you remember how the three regiments were located? 9. During the advance across Legare's Place were we in line or column? 10. Did you see the other regiments during the advance? 11. It is uncertain where the two guns were, in the lunette or at a little distance from it on the right; do you remember? The following is Walker's response.

[October 1914][34]

[To Burt G. Wilder]

For your informatioon for reference to the battle of James Island, S.C. at Rivers Causeway, July 2nd, 1864, there appears to be a conflict of dates between you and I; as my recollection is [that] we were to have staged the advance on the night of the 1st of July, and for some cause not explained to us, [the order] was countermanded, and the expedition did not advance until the night of the 2nd of July. We advanced from Morris Island to

---

33. Jordan M. Bobson was twenty years old at the time he joined the 55th. He was a farmer from Wilmington, Ohio.
34. Burt G. Wilder Papers. Cornell University.

Long Island to Tiger Island and across the extreme west end of Cole's Island, where the [Rebel] picket was awakened and raised the alarm by firing one shot and falling back on the reserve, the reserve fired a volley and fell back on the inner post. This was the morning of the 3rd of July 64, and General [Alexander] Schimmelfenning [sic] was in command of the expedition. The 103rd N.Y. was in the advance and deployed skirmishers, and skirmished with the Confederates across Legare's place. This took place between 3 and 4 o'clock in the morning. The 54th N.Y. was next formed [into] line and advanced as the 103rd N.Y. drove the Confederates back. The next was the 1st North Carolina U.S.C.T., which formed line and advanced in regular order. This was Col. J.C. Beecher's Regiment, then came the 55th Mass, Col. A.S. Hartwell's regiment, formed in line. On the firing of the first shot, 1st the Color guard—Sergeant U.S. Flag Wilson Eddy, State Flag Corpl E.A. King, Corpls Jas. Spear, Jas. Cochran, Jacob Payne, William Dobbins and John J. Johnson.[35] I place my name last there not the least, and not wishing to claim any glory to myself; (2) Wilson Eddy was color Sergt. [3] Company H was color company, Capt. W.D. Crane Co[manding]; (4) I was at the right of the color sergeant and when Col. Hartwell gave the command, by the right flank file left, I motioned to Sergeant Eddy and we took our place in line of battle, 5 paces in advance of the line, and, cheering, started for the guns, the regiment following us. *I was the first man on the parapets of the* lunette. You no doubt will remember the 55th was held in reserve to cover the retreat, in case we should have to retreat. Now during the skirmish I could see there was only one alternative; when our turn would come [it] was to rush the works and take them at the point of the bayonet.

(5) I did not get any order to make the charge from Col. Hartwell. We had been the spectators under fire from the beginning, and constantly coming under the concentrated fire of guns as we drew nearer to them, and during our advance I saw by the topography of the ground, that the only way to silence the guns would be to take them (the guns) as they were on the heights above us. The closer we could get to them the less harm they

---

35. Not all these names can be identified from the roster of the 55th printed in its regimental history. Jacob Payne, a 21-year-old barber from Illinois is noted, as is the author of this letter, John J. Johnson.

could do us; and I had intimated to the color sergeant that, when it came our turn. We must take the guns. (6) Now, had we have executed the order as given, it would have exposed our left flank to an enfilading fire of shrapnel from the guns while we were executing the order, and would have thrown us between the lunette and Secessionville, and Fort Lamar, as the guns in the lunette were light artillery and they could train them in any direction, and did during our advance. I could hear the gunners giving [the] command[s] trail right and trail left, and the attack would have been a failure as the other regiments had been repulsed and could not have supported us under existing circumstances. Therefore we were compelled to take the lunette, or go down in defeat and humiliation. This resulted in the capture of the guns and as I was standing on the parapet of the lunette, Captain Crane, the commander of the color company, said to me, get down corporal, they will shoot you.

(7) I did not see anything of Andy Smith of Co. B then or at any time during the engagement to distinglish him from any one else. My recollection are that Gen'l. [John P.] Hatch was to have formed a junction with us from John's Island, he was to have gone up the Stono River, take Fort Pringle to the west of the lunette and advance up John's Island. The result was he did not get into position until the morning of the 4th of July, after we had taken the lunette. The morning of the 4th of July he attacked and took Pringle about 2 A.M. and drove the Confederates well back toward Charleston, and Fort Lamar and Secessionville, but we had struck our blow and fallen back and intrenched ourselves, he having farther to go than we did could not make the connection with us and we had aroused the Confederates onto the dangers that confronted them. The result was that they were on the alert when Hatch came on them, and gave him a stubborn resistance. I always understood we were to have managed a concentrated attack on James Island, and John's Island, had General Hatch been able to have gotten his troops into position at the same time we did; which would have resulted [in the] capture of Forts Pringle, Lamar and Secessionville. This lunette was intended to temporarily check any advance that might be made in that direction, and give Forts Pringle, Lamar and Secessionville warning of the attack, which proved successful as Lamar and Secessionville felt for our position all day after we took the

lunette, and as Hatch did not form the junction with us, it was fortunate for us that the trench was there for us to cover in. The trench here referred to in your diagram, was built by Gen'l [Ambose] Burnside in latter part of 62 when he made the attempt on Charleston. This was the expedition which was partly lost at Cape Hatteras and was strengthened by Gen. [Nathaniel P.] Banks, [David] Hunter and [John G.] Foster, and Hunter went from James Island and took Hilton Head and Beaufort and emancipated the slaves. The lines between the lunette and trench indicate a sallyport the Confederates had cut through which they could retreat, and have the trench as a cover between them and the aggressive forces.

(8) Now as to how the regiment was located in the trench after taking the guns, now as near as I can recall the locations, the 103rd N.Y. or the (strangely to say I cannot see how you only have 3 regiments, there was three lines ahead of us) as I remember it was the first in the east end of the trench. The 54th N.Y. next, 1st North Carolina next, and the 55th Mass. at the extreme left in the trench.

(9) We were in line during the advance across Legare's Place, had we been in column, it would have [been] unnecessary for Col. Hartwell to have given the command by the right file left. All that would have been necessary would be to say right or left oblique as the case might be, but being in line it became necessary to change the formation into column, in order to flank the works.

(10) Yes, I saw all 4 of the regiments as we advanced. Now Comrade, I am giving you the benefit of a reasonable doubt. My recollection of the formation is the [WORD ERASED]. While you have it the 103rd N.Y. and next was the 54th N.Y. and the next was the 1st North Carolina Colored, then you have the 33rd U.S.C.T. and the next was the 55th Mass. which was supposed to be in reserve to cover the retreat. The regimental formation was as above indicated, and the 103rd N.Y. advanced from Tiger Is[lan]d, the picket fired the alarm, and the 103rd N.Y. deployed as skirmishers and skirmished with the Confederates as they fell back across Legare's Place, on the Reserve Post, and all the lines advanced in regular order and took position as their turn came to be engaged. The 103rd came under fire of the guns when they

were about 250 or 300 yards from the fort or lunette; 54th N.Y. took position as the 103rd fell back, the guns were sweeping the lines from right to left, with shrapnel, by trailing the guns from right to left. The next was the 33rd U.S.C.T. They were ordered to fix bayonets and had to fall back without firing a gun.

(11) As to the position of the guns, there is no uncertainty in my mind as to their position. They were up to and projecting over the parapet as they had been depressed as low as they could to sweep the ground over which we had to pass to take them; had they been back any distance from the parapet they could not have depressed them as low as they were, or the charge would have went into the parapets instead of into our line; as I remember as I was standing on the parapet, one of [the] Company K men, named Jarvis,[36] jumped astride one of the guns and said, O God, I've got you, and after Col. Hartwell had commanded to cease firing, Captain Crane came as I was standing on the parapet and said get down from there corporal, they will shoot you.

Now as regards the action at Rivers Causeway, James Island, July 2nd 64, and in reference to the formation of the expedition, and the cardinal points in the diagram and topographical formation of ground over which we had to pass in our advance, they had trees felled to impede our progress. These trees had apparently been felled for some time as they were dry, probably they had been felled when Burnside attacked Charleston from James Island in 62. Now, Dear Doctor Wilder, it seems strange that we differ in the number of regiments. As I remember there were 4 regiments in [the] expedition, the 103rd N.Y. and the 54th N.Y., the 33rd U.S.C.T. and the 55th Mass. as here in before described. Now Doctor, I am giving you the right of a reasonable doubt again; I was as calm during this action as I am now and I am at this writing as I was teasing the corporal next to me until it came our turn to engage the works. I should think it was between 2000 and 3000 yards between us and the guns when they first fired. This was intended to have been a general assault on Charleston, as General Birney moved with an expedition from the North end of Morris Island, on fort Johnson on the north end of John's Island. With the 127th N.Y. and the 52nd Penna. they en-

36. Likely Henry Jarvis, a twenty-year-old farmer from Northhampton County, Virginia.

tered Fort Johnson on the 3rd of July, but were overpowered and captured. This was all from an imperfectly organized concert of operation by reason of General John P. Hatch's inability to form a junction with us in order to draw the forces from Forts Johnson and Lamar. Had this action have been a success, we would have cleared the islands of all Confederates to the Santee River, which would have been the only barrier to prevent us from entering the City of Charleston at that time.

[Geo. S. Walker][37]

---

421 E. 3rd St.
Xenia, Ohio Dec. 2nd, 1914[38]

Dr. Burt G. Wilder. Dear Comrade:
    . . . Of the fight on James Island when Capt. [Frank] Goodwin was wounded I was there during that charge. I was about to lose one of my shoes. I halted to pull or tighten the strings. Capt. Goodwin called to me as though he thought I had been shot. He did not go far until he was wounded. I have no personal knowledge what happened when he was being taken to the rear. . . . Did not see Col. [Alfred S.] Hartwell in the first advance. 103[rd New York] was to our right, perhaps in the advance for some reason they became confused. The 55th took the advance and kept it for there was not any troops in our advance. I did not see Col [Charles B.] Fox. Second line of works was taken by a portion of the 55th or 33rd [U.S.C.T.], Col. Hartwell was on his Horse. Co. E was halted just in the rear of the advance. Some one in the advance said to Co. Hartwell, why don't you have your own wounded cared for, don't you see your one man there. This was said after the works had been taken, It appears to me that we were then under the cover of a gunboat. . . .

William Scott[39]

---

37. Dr. Wilder's annotation to this letter indicates that Walker enlisted and served in the 55th under the name "John J. Johnson."
38. Burt G. Wilder Papers. Cornell University.
39. Eighteen-year-old William Scott, a farmer from Ripley, Ohio, was a corporal during 1864, not being promoted to sergeant until 1865.

135

Co. E, 55th Mass.

421 E. 3rd St.
Xenia, Ohio Dec. 18, 1914[40]

Dear Comrade [Burt Wilder].

I will state in my own way as I recollect the actions of the forces at Rivers Causeway, July the 2nd, 1864. Line was formed, my company was instructed not to fire our guns; we were to charge and holler Fort Pillow. I think the Ny. or 103—I had it my mind that was the 54th N.Y. was on the right of the 55th. I do not think the 33d [U.S.C.T.] was to the left of the 55th. We were in line, I think the Confederates had more than two guns, one or two pieces light artillery. They escaped withdrawal by horses, for some reason the 103 became confused and 55th assumed the lead. I don't recollect of seeing the 33d during the charge or first advance. I think that some officers continued to lead, 33 came up, the commanders of the 33 & 103 were white. When we reached the Causeway there were not any troops in our advance, did not see any dead horses. I know of two shots being fired, one before we reached the lunette, one afterwards. Col [Alfred S.] Hartwell was on his horse. At the 2nd line of works our advance as indicated in your diagram is correct as I recollect.

Respectfully yours,

William Scott
E, 55th Mass.

Grand River, Ky. Feb. 19, 1918[41]

B. G. Wilder
St. Augustine, Fla.

Dear Doctor.

In reply to yours of the 16th inst. I did not see the incident you

40. Burt G. Wilder Papers. Cornell University.
41. *Ibid.*

write of—Capt. [Frank] Goodwin being on stretchers and the stretchers being hit by a shell or some part thereof. But I did hear Col. [Alfred S.] Hartwell criticize the Drum corps for dropping the stretchers on which Capt. Goodwin was being carried when the shell exploded.

I don't see how he (Capt. Goodwin) could have been in a boat. My recollection is that we went back by Cole's Island, crossed on the bridge that was between Cole's Island and James Island. I am very sure that was the route.

I was on Long Island on picket duty under Capt. [Robert James] Hamilton and he (Captain Hamilton) refused to relieve me until [we were] relieved by Col. Hartwell. I was anxious and did go, but did not come back the same route.

I heard some one say that [the] shell came from the direction of Fort Lambert.

With best wishes for your success,
I am your humble comrade,

Andrew J. Smith[42]

———————◆•◆———————

Xenia [Ohio] Mar. 11th, 1918[43]

Mr. B. G. Wilder
86 Cedar St.
St. Augustine, Fla.

Dear Comrade:

I rec'd your letter and was so very happy to hear from you. I was not in the battle at James Island on July 2d, 1864, because of being ill and unfit for service. I did go with my company to where they crossed the Stono river. At evening you and Col. [Charles B.] Fox rode to where the Col. was laying on horse back. And you ordered me to take the horse of you and Col. Fox back to the camp and remain in your tent. *I was in your tent* convalesc-

---

42. Andrew Smith is noted in the roster of the 55th as a "boatman" who was twenty years old at the time of his enlistment.
43. Burt G. Wilder Papers. Cornell University.

ing *when Captain* [Frank] *Goodwin was brought into your tent on a stretcher wounded.* He did not remain in your tent over night. *I fanned the flies off from him while he was there. To my best recollection, my information was that the stretcher was broken on the battlefield by the explosion of a shell.* I don't know of a single one that was in the stretcher corps at that battle. You might correspond with Jordan M. Bobson of Springboro, Warren Co., O. Sergeant of Co. C. You are now about 10 or 12 miles from our camp at Yellow Bluff. I hope you will visit the place. It is up St. John's River from St. Augustine. I am always very glad to hear from you. I am still able to work for my living at the same position that I have held for thirty-three years. I know that Captain Goodwin was wounded. I saw his wounds, but that is about all the information that I can give. I will write and see if I can find any one that knows any thing of the circumstances and will gladly give you all that I can find out.

Hoping that you and wife are well, I am yours truly,

David Lee[44]

531 East Market Street
Xenia, O.

———————— ✦•✦ ————————

The regimental history of the 55th Massachusetts described Edward W. Kinsley as "the constant and enthusiastic friend of the regiment." This letter is further conformation of that.

Folly Island, S.C.
August 1st 64[45]

Dear Sir [Edward W. Kinsley]:

I received your kind letter and was extremely glad to hear from you. I am well and hope this may find you in as good health as it leaves me. I am happy to think that such a small object as my unworthy self has a small share of the thoughts of so good

44. David Lee was twenty-one when he enlisted. He noted his occupation as "farmer."
45. Edward W. Kinsley Papers. Duke University Special Collections.

and kind [a] person as yourself and as you say, I myself think it best for us to hold on for the darkest hour is just before day, and I am not the least afraid that the good and kind people of good old Massachusetts will see or have us suffering for want of anything. I feel doubly assured since I received your letter that all will yet be right.

I think I will be able to see you soon as I am going to get a furlough soon. It has gone in now for approval. Our Colonel is acting general commanding Post at present. I think Gov[ernor] Andrew is a man who I would gladly die for. May God bless him and keep him from harm and we will yet show the world what the Gov[ernor]'s colored volunteers can do and that we are ever indebted to him for giving to us the chance to show the world that the colored man will and can fight. I hope you will please answer and believe me to be your

Humble Servant,

Sergeant Wm. L. Logan[46]

———◆•◆•———

Co. H, 55th Mass. Vols. Infantry
Folly Island, S.C.

One of the few rank and file members of the 55th to emerge with any substantial profile is James M. Trotter. He was born in Mississippi in 1842. His mother was a slave named Letitia and his father was her owner, Richard S. Trotter. When James was twelve his mother took him and his siblings (there were two other children by this "marriage") to Cincinnati where he attended a school for blacks that had been started by an English clergyman named Hiram Gilmore. Trotter's studies continued in a local academy, where his interests were music and art, and he went on to teach for a short time. In 1863, when Trotter learned that the state of Massachusetts was raising black regiments, he made the long journey to Boston to enlist. Once in the Bay State, Trotter came to know several members of that first family of abolitionism, the

46. William L. Logan, twenty-two when he enlisted, was from Boston. He noted his occupation as "waiter."

139

William Lloyd Garrisons. How close that friendship became might be deduced from this letter Trotter wrote to one of Garrison's sons, Francis Jackson Garrison.

Camp of 55th Mass., Vols.
Folly Island, S.C., Aug. 2, 1864[47]

Dear Franky,

Your very entertaining favor came late but was welcome. Your last like your first was full of good sense and happy bits and I regret that I am not equal to the *task* of sending you pay in the same coin; but, relying on the charity that distinguished all Garrisons I nevertheless write hoping that this time it will please you to write, at least, inside of a year. I have a little nephew at home, 12 years, who lately wrote me his first letter and I hope you will pardon me for sending *your* letter to him for certain good reasons, Your brother,[48] I saw a minute ago, looking as well and cheerful as usual. He has so much improved (grown fat) since we were at Readville that you would scarcely know him now, and is not in the least altered in those noble principles of manliness that won the highest regard from all who knew him there.

Some time ago he served in a position in our Regt. peculiar for the arduous labors that belong to it as well as a very great temptation to dishonesty (Q[uarte]r M[aste]r) and when he retired our noble Col. issued an order complimenting Lieut. G. for "serving with industry and fidelity in this most important Dept." So everybody thought. His earnestness every body remarks and a kind and gentle-manly bearing while performing the vexatious and difficult duties belonging to his position have won the love of all the Reg't. You complained that he tells you nothing of himself. I fear you will always have reason to do so, Franky, for he is perfectly self forgetful; and I do not recollect hearing your bro. allude even to himself a half dozen times since our acquaintance.

47. Francis J. Garrison Papers. Schomberg Collection, New York Public Library.
48. George Thompson Garrison, who was commissioned as a second lieutenant on June 22, 1863, and promoted to first lieutenant on December 1. Following the practice of naming all his children for abolitionist heroes, Lieutenant Garrison was named for the British antislave agitator George Thompson.

That "Arrest" affair was *simply nothing*. It was the result not of his fault but of the capriciousness of some military *misrule*. Nearly all of our excellent officers have been "under arrest," even Col. [Alfred S.] Hartwell, the "Noblest Roman of them all." You spoke of him very truly. Frankly, I never met a more perfectly honorable gentleman in my life. The same is true of Col. [Charles B.] Fox. You have heard that 1st Sergts. [John F.] Shorter and [William H.] Dupree & Sergt. Maj. Trotter have been commissioned by Gov. Andrew as 2nd Lieuts. So far, very good; but Gen'l [John G.] Foster will not discharge them as enlisted men and muster them into service as officers claiming that "there is no law *allowing* it, they being colored men." Do you know any law that *prohibits* it? I am assigned to Co. K, and am performing the duties for which I was commissioned. So also is Shorter and Dupree. But this half and half arrangement is very unpleasant to us. I am sorry to have to tell you also that most all the line officers give us the *cold shoulder*. Indeed, when our papers, returned the other day, disapproved those who have all along claimed to be our best friends, the line officers, seemed to feel the most lively satisfaction at the result. O how discouraging! How maddening, almost! A few, however, are *sensible* enough not to deny a poor oppressed people the means of *liberating themselves*.

An officer told me that it was "too soon," that time should be granted white officers to *get rid of their predudices*. So that a white Lieutenant would not refuse to sleep in a tent with a colored one. Of course he *supposed* that an objection of this kind would be made always by the white Lieut., and that an educated decent colored officers would never object to sleeping with the former whatever might be his character. Yes, Franky, there is really more turning up the noise on account of the commissions *in our very midst* than elsewhere; *and no other reason is given except Color*. Several have resigned on account of it, and the disapproval of the muster papers alone prevent others from doing the same thing. This is a model way to promote military discipline and efficiency. They differ with Napoleon. He always secured the perfect good behavior of his soldiers by promoting the deserving. Every man, knew that if he did well that he would be rewarded. But according to the "*Modern* Mode" no such rule is to be adopted because the soldiers are so *blamable as to have their skins dark*. Most awful crime! I wish, if they hate

141

us because we are black, that the colorphobia and "Negro Elevating" class would white wash us. But our noble Cols. are true noblemen and so is Gov. and this matter will probably be agitated.

Old Company "K" is all right, the most orderly and soldierly in the Regiment. This could not be otherwise as its Captain is one of nature's noblemen and almost a perfect soldier. I am sorry to say that Sergeant Boon, Benj. Griffin and Finlay Rickman are dead.[49] They were foremost in the brave charge on "Fort Wright" on James Island, and they died while nobly battling for country and Freedom. Poor Sergt. Boon! Do you recollect him? He was only Corp'l when at Readville. No one's death has made me feel so sad as his. In truth I loved him. At Readville he could neither read nor write. I spoke to him of the importance of learning, telling him that I would gladly help him, and that when he could read I would recommend him for Sergt. Right manfully he took hold, and before he died he had acted orderly Sergt., and could make out all the papers and written three letters home. He went to James Island with no gun and only side arms. His arm was sore and he could not carry his rifle. But his brave spirit would not rest quiet while his comrades were gone forth to battle and therefore he sought and obtained permission of his commander to join the expedition. He was wounded by a large grape [shot] in the leg, which was amputated, causing instant death. He was cheerful and brave to the last. In camp, on the hill-side near to where stands the cannon out of which was hurled the ball that caused his death, he is laid. A while ago I was at the grave. We have placed a board at his head bearing this Inscription:

Sergeant B.
    lived in
        Boston

In Memory of
Sergeant Alonzo Boon
Died of Wounds
July 3d, 1864

49. Benjamin Griffin is noted in the regimental history roster as having been "killed in action, July 2, 1864." Of Finley Rickman it is noted: "Wounded July 2, 1864; died Beaufort, S.C., July 25, 1864, wounds."

As He died to make men holy
Let us die to make men free

The other boys are well and send their best love to Frank Garrison, whom they all remember. Capt. [Charles C.] Soule sends his love also. Franky, I wish you to give my high regards to your noble Father. I cannot of course ever forget *him*, he is too distinguished a friend of my race for that, but I remember particularly the happy speech he made to Co. "K" and the sword presentation. Do you recollect how you begged me not to call on "George" for a speech? Ah! we have seen some service since that time so have those swords.

We are looking for the P[ay] M[aster] up from the "Head" every day now and *hope* that we will be paid *justly*. If we are, Col. [Alfred S.] Hartwell says that Dupree and myself may have a furlough. I would not go if this matter of muster was settled; but as my present *double* position is not pleasant perhaps 'twould be as well for us to go north while the question is pending.

Please tell Mr. Garrison about the refusal of the Government, or Gen'l Foster, to muster as officers colored men duly commissioned, so that it may be referred to by him in the influential "Liberator."

Franky, what "friend is that who wants my unsightly picture." I wonder where's his taste? I send one to *you* and if you think proper you can give him one of the *two* you have. Tell him not to take it near the mirror. In return for the one I herewith send you must be sure and send yours. Any papers or books sent me for the reading room will be distributed there. Excuse all errors and no postage stamp. When we get out down here it is a long time before we get in. Write soon, Good bye.

Jas. M. Trotter

(P.S.) I had the pleasure to recommend for Sergeant Major Sergeant Chas. Mitchell, whom I suppose you are well acquainted with. He is a true gentleman, and is giving good satisfaction. He sends his regards to yourself and all the family. P.S. Will you be kind enough to ask Mr. Garrison how it is about the *Allotment arrangement* that was made at Readville. Whether the amount

143

allotted will be taken from the wages as we understood it would be.

Trotter[50]

More return fire, this time directed at a critic of the Massachusetts men who identified himself only as "Wild Jack."

55th Mass. Regt.
Folly Island, S.C., August 19, 1864[51]

. . . I notice an article in the columns of your truly important paper which has a tendency to occasion bickering and contention among the soldiers now in the service of the United States. We, as soldiers, writing for the inspection of the public eye, should be very careful not to assert anything that does not meet the hearty concurrence of our comrades engaged in the same cause. . . .

Perhaps "Wild Jack" was not impressed with thoughts like the above, or he would not have written so scathingly of the 54th and 55th Massachusetts Volunteers. He should remember that our contending manfully for our rights as volunteers is his gain.

The reason why we refused to receive the pay offered us was on account of its not being according to our enlistment. Consequently we refused to take it. After which, we were assured that Congress, when in session, would settle the matter of pay.

We agreed to await the action of Congress, willingly and uncomplainingly doing our duty as soldiers and men. After the session of Congress was over, we found ourselves no better off than we were before, that body having done nothing for us. "Wild Jack" must have been ignorant of this, or he would have spoken differently.

I desire the public to remember that we were not allured into the service of the Government by money, as some have thought. We were enlisted as a part of the quota of Massachusetts. We

50. This letter is printed in Jack Abramonwitz, "A Civil War Letter: James M. Trotter to Francis J. Garrison," *Midwest Journal*, IV (1952), 113-22. More about James M. Trotter can be found in the biography of his son by Stephen R. Fox, *The Guardian of Boston: William Monroe Trotter* (New York: Atheneum), 1970.
51. *Christian Recorder*, September 3, 1864. Reprinted in Redkey, *Grand Army of Black Men*.

were promised the same clothing, rations, pay and treatment that other soldiers from the Old Bay State received. The Governor of Massachusetts assured us that he did not think any thing would occur to occasion faction among the soldiers composing the 54th and 55th regiments.

We have had a holy and sacred object in view, not for the sake of having the name of soldier, but for the sole purpose of striking the fatal blow to slavery, that the oppressed may be set free. . . .

Bellefonte

Another letter written to that great friend of the 55th Massachusetts, Edward W. Kinsley.

Folly Island, S.C.
Aug't 25th [1864][52]

Dear Sir [Edward W. Kinsley].

I received your kind and welcome letter and was glad to hear from you. I am well at present and hope this may find you well as it leaves me. We have not as yet received payment and there is as yet no sign of our being paid up. The men all stand to the settling of their full pay from the day of their enlistment and say that they will not take any thing but the full pay from the government while they are in the field. They say it would not be right for the state to pay them what the government owes them unless she chooses to draw us home and pay us the whole amount, as we feel it an insult to principle and the good old state to receive the pay from her and continue in the field. I am very much obliged to you for the Herald which you sent me as it is something I do not often receive. Our company [Company H] is now on detached service. We are in the large fort at Stono Landing and are drilling on the large guns. The men like it very well and they drill surprisingly well for so short a space of time. They are almost the

52. Edward W. Kinsley Papers. Duke University Special Collections.

same as old veterans, so perfect are they in the drill and discipline of the service. The clarinet which you sent to the band arrived and it makes a great improvement on the music and the boys were very glad to receive it from you. Hoping that you will please answer as soon as received, I will style myself your very obedient servant,

Sergeant,

William L. Logan

In the national dialogue about slavery before the war, one of the more popular solutions to the problem was to remove it completely—return all negroes in the United States to Africa. Among those who at first subscribed to this solution was Abraham Lincoln. It was a response that neatly ignored the fact that by 1860 the majority of blacks in this country were truly African Americans—individuals who were born in the United States.

Even the onset of fighting and the issuing of the Emancipation Proclamation did not entirely remove the "back to Africa" argument from the dialogue of the times, as this letter from the 55th shows.

Morris Island, S.C., May 24, 1864[53]

. . . I am not willing to fight for anything less than the white man fights for. If the white man cannot support his family on seven dollars per month, I cannot support mine on the same amount.

And I am not willing to fight for this Government for money alone. Give me my rights, the rights that this Government owes me, the same rights that the white man has. I would be willing to fight three years for this Government without one cent of the mighty dollar. Then I would have something to fight for. Now I am fighting for the rights of white men. White men have never given me the rights that they are bound to respect. God

53. *Christian Recorder*, June 11, 1864. Reprinted in Redkey, *A Grand Army of Black Men.*

has not made one man better than another; therefore, one man's rights are no better than another's. They assert that because a large proportion of our race is in bondage we have a right to help free them. I want to know if it was not the white man that put them in bondage? How can they hold us responsible for their evils? And how can they expect that we should do more to blot it out than they are willing to do themselves? If every slave in the United States were emancipated at once, they would not be free yet. If the white man is not willing to respect my rights, I am not willing to respect his wrongs. Our rights have always been limited in the United States. It is true that in some places a colored man, if he can prove himself to be half-white, can vote. Vote for whom? The white man. What good do such rights ever do us—to be compelled always to be voting for the white man and never to be voted for?

Now, the white man declares that this is not our country, and that we have no right to it. They say that Africa is our country. I claim this is my native country—the country that gave me birth. I wish to know one thing, and this is this: Who is the most entitled to his rights in a country—a native of the country or the foreigner? This question can be very easily answered. Now there are foreigners who have flooded our shores. They bring nothing with them but antagonistic feelings to rule and order, and they are without the rudiments of education, and yet they can train their children to be law-abiding citizens. In their own country mis-rule reigns. Generally very poor, they have no leisure for the cultivation of their hearts' best feelings; for in their case, poverty degrades human nature. In this country their social influence is much greater than in their own. Here every avenue to distinction is open to them. The foreigner, when he enters this country, enters into life in an age full of a progressive spirit in the elective franchise. Such persons are the first to take up an offensive position against the Government, instead of marching under the banner of the Prince of Peace. Such people have ruled this country too long already.

The ignorant Irish can come to this country and have free access to all the rights. After they have gained their rights, they cannot appreciate them. They then want to bully the Government. They soon get tired of living under the laws of the country and commence to mutiny, riot, ransack cities, murder colored children, and burn down orphan asylums, as was done in New York. Is the power to be given to such men to direct and govern the affairs of the Union, on which the weal or woe of the nation depends? This is productive of moral degradation and becomes one of the fruitful sources of evil in our land, from which we shall suffer most severely unless some plan is specially adopted to check its onward course. How can this nation ever expect to prosper? I wonder that God does not bring on them present deluge and disaster. I do not wonder at the conduct and disaster that transpired at Fort Pillow. I wonder that we have not had more New York riots and Fort Pillow massacres.

Liberty is what I am struggling for; and what pulse does not beat high at the very mention of the name? Each of us, with fidelity, has already discharged the duties devolving on us as men and as soldier. The very fact of such a union on grounds so commonly and deeply interesting to all, undoubtedly cannot always fail, by the blessing of God, to exert a hallowed influence over society, well fitted to break up alike the extremes of aristocratic and social feeling, which too often predominate in society, and to beget unity, love, brotherly kindness, and charity. . . .

J.H.B.P.[54]

Comments about the fight on July 2 could still rankle as this note, penned two months later, attests.

Folly Island, S.C., September 2, 1864[55]

Mr. Editor:

I was looking over your paper, dated August 18th, 1864. I saw an account of the expedition which took place on the 2d of July. I also saw the burlesque which some kind writer sent you con-

54. Probably written by Corporal John H. B. Payne, a thirty-year-old teacher from Bellefontaine, Ohio.
55. *Christian Recorder*, September 24, 1864. Edwin Redkey Collection.

cerning the bravery of the second sergeant of Co. G. Mr. Editor, I do pronounce it a burlesque for the writer went so far as to say that the Lieutenant Colonel gave the order to retreat, and I screamed out, "Colonel, we will take this fort to-day!" I can only speak for myself, and I can say that I heard no such order; but whether others did nor not, it is more than I can say. But I can say that Lieutenant Colonel [Charles B.] Fox is as brave a man as any regiment can afford, and not only he, but all the officers connected with this regiment.

Why should that writer distinguish me from all the rest? Am I braver than any other man? Or else is my life not as sweet to me as any other man's is to him? Or is my face made of iron, that a shell bursting against it would take no effect? I claim that I did my duty as a soldier, and no more. Why did he not say that the Ohio, Pennsylvania, Massachusetts, or the New York "boys" fought well? Or why did he not say that the 55th Massachusetts regiment fought well, and the men behave bravely? If he had said that, it would have given me all the praise I wanted; for it would have made me feel happy to think that I was a member of such a regiment as the 55th.

As I said above I did my duty as a sergeant; and if the writer had done his duty as a soldier, I claim that there would have been one more rebel sent to his long home, whereas he is now waiting for a chance to shoot the writer.

Yours truly,

Wm. M. Viney[56]

———————— •◆• ————————

The issue that had dominated the thinking of the men of the 55th Massachusetts was resolved in October, 1864. This letter explains it all.

56. At the time of his enlistment, twenty-two-year-old William M. Viney, of Boston, listed his occupation as "broommaker."

Camp 55th Mass. Vol. Infantry,
Folly Island, S.C., October 14, 1864[57]

Mr. Editor:

Doubtless you will have heard before this reaches you, that the
54th and 55th Mass. Regiments have been paid. The paymaster
"filed his appearance" with us on Friday, September 30th, commencing operations with Co. B at present doing provost duty.
There was some little delay before he got fairly to work with the
other companies, but in the course of a week from the time it
began the paying of the 55th was among the accomplished facts.
It came at last after being kept out of it nearly a year and a half,
so you can imagine how we all felt. We felt over-joyed, and at
the same time thankful to God for the successful termination of
our suit.

Now don't be surprised at what followed. We resolved to have
a celebration, it was thought by the wise ones that an event of
so much importance to us, and ours, deserved it. A meeting was
therefore called at which a committee was appointed to prepare
for the occasion a programme and resolutions expressive of the
sentiments of the regiment. The committee, with a promptness
as commendable as it is rare in such bodies, submitted in a short
time, everything "cut and dried" to the next meeting which was
large and enthusiastic. Their report was unanimously accepted.

THE CELEBRATION

Monday, the 10th was the day selected for the celebration. It
came, and precisely at 3 o'clock the assembly was sounded, each
company issued forth from its street in charge of a non-commissioned officer, and being formed in line by acting Sergt.-Maj.
[Charles L.] Mitchell, Marshall of the day, and Sergt. Geo. Bazil,
Assistant Marshall, the procession headed by the band marched
by the right flank in two wings with a space between, which was
occupied by the speakers and officers of the day. After marching
a short distance beyond camp the procession turned and proceeded directly to the place of meeting, in front of the Colo-

57. *Christian Recorder*, November 12, 1864. *Weekly Anglo-African*, November
12, 1864. Houghton Library, Harvard University.

nel's quarters. We were saved the trouble of erecting a platform, as there was a piece of rising ground just the right thing and in the right place. On top of this, seats were arranged for officers of the regiment, officers of the meeting and the band. Now, Mr. Editor, please take in hand a list of the officers and the programme, and you will understand better what follows:

President—1st Sergt. P.R. Laws, Co. I.

Vice-President—Sergt. [Martin F.] Becker, non commissioned staff; 1st Sergt. J. Jackson, Co. B; 1st Sergt. P. Fleming, Co. K; 1st Sergt. J. Gardner, Co. E; Sergt. [Elmer B.] Miller, Co. H; 1st Sergt. J. Ruffin, Co. F; 1st Sergt. I. Welch, Co. C; 1st Sergt. G. Worthington, Co. G; Sergt. G. Bobson, Co. C; Sergt. A.R. Lewis, Co. D.

Secretaries—1st Sergt. J.F. Shorter, Co. D; Sergt. W.H. Sanders, Co. A; Ex-Sergt. N. Said, Co. I; Marshall of the day, Acting Sergt.-Maj. Mitchell; Assistant-Marshall, Sergt. Geo. Bazil, Co. B.

Speakers—Sergt. H. Johnson, Co. I;[58] Sergt. R. White, non-commissioned staff; Sergt. G.P. Iverson, Co. B; 1st Sergt. I. Welch, Co. C; Sergt. G. Shadd, Co. B.

Committee on Resolutions—Sergt G.P. Iverson, Co. B; Sergt. R. White, non-commissioned staff; 1st Sergt. P. Laws, Co. I; 1st Sergt. J.F. Shorter, Co. D; Sergt. H. Johnson, Co. F; Sergt. Becker, non-commissioned staff; 1st Sergt. J. Ruffin, Co. F; 1st Sergt. I. Welch, Co. C; Sergt. Miller, Co. H.

PROGRAMME

Prayer by the Chaplain.
Opening Address by the President.
Singing by the assembly.
Music by the band.
Speech by Sergt. H. Johnson, Co. F.
Music by the band.
Speech by Sergt. I. Welch, Co. C.
Music by the band.
Speech by Segt. White, non-commissioned staff.
Reading resolutions by Sec'y Shorter.
Music by the band.
Speech by Segt. G.P. Iverson, Co. B.
Song "*Vive L'America.*"

58. There is no Sergeant H. Johnson in Company I. This is likely a reference to Sergeant H. Johnson of Company F, who appears elsewhere in this letter.

151

A few comments about the above and we are done. It was a most impressive scene. A regiment of brave men celebrating, in the midst of war, one of the triumphs of peace without arms, in the presence of their officers a band of veteran warriors doing honor by solemn ceremonies to the recognition by government of their citizenship and equality.

President Law's opening address was appropriate and eloquent. He stated the object of the celebration was to be the triumph of freedom and equality over despotism and prejudice. The Sergeant not only spoke well, but presided throughout the day with great dignity. Sergt. H. Johnson of Co. F. was very brief, but his speech was *Multum in Parvo*. His language was correct, arrangements good, and manner earnest. He has in him the true elements of the orator and deserved the cheering he got at the close of his speech.

Sergt. Welch spoke with touching earnestness, sprinkling his speech with some very fine historical allusions.

Sergt. White gave us one of those solid and manly speeches that Western men know so well how to make. It was easy to see that he meant all he said, and that he meant a great deal.

Sergt. Iverson was introduced by the President as orator of the day. I wish I could give you his speech. We all felt proud of him as he stood there describing in the most beautiful language our triumphs, its legal bearing, the Slave Power, the past sufferings of our race, and the bright future which awaits it as "the reward of its wisdom, patriotism and valor." It was plain to see his legal culture in his style of speaking, although limited in time he nevertheless managed by skillful reasoning and lucid expression to make perfectly clear every point he took up. He was enthusiastically cheered. Our splendid reigmental band played a number of popular airs. There could be nothing finer than their performance. Mr. John Moore of Philadelphia, its accomplished leader deserves all the praise for the manner in which he devotes himself to its improvement. We all love our band, "music had charms" of a very superior kind in a place like this, and in a business like this. It seems to link us with home, recalling to the mind its pleasant associations, thereby going far towards ennobling and refining the character of the soldier.

The management of the procession and the entire arrangements of the day, reflected the highest credit upon the abilities of Sergt.

Mitchel and Sergt. Bazil, showing them worthy of the high opinion in which they are held by their comrades.

Finally, Mr. Editor, I must tell you about the supper in the evening. The gentlemen of the committee and officers of the day sat down to an elegant supper. The usual exercises took place: speeches, toasts, songs, and cheers. Gentlemen sang that night who never were known to sing before. The supper was got up in Mr. Lee's best style, and I think it deserved the justice which it received, in other words both the supper and the eating were admirable. The whole affair went off with *eclat*.

J.F.S. [John F. Shorter]

The following resolutions were adopted at the celebration:

Whereas, the just claims of the 55th Regiment Massachusetts Volunteers on the pay question having been admitted, on the basis of equality; and whereas, we, the non-commissioned officers and privates of the regiment, anxious to take advantage of this and every opportunity of giving expression to our loyalty to cause and country, especially when we behold that country in the midst of its perils rising to the dignity of giving freedom and knowledge to an unfortunate race, and bestowing upon it the rights of citizenship; therefore,

Resolved, That we stand now, as ever, ready to do our duty, wherever our country requires it, in the work of crushing this wicked rebellion, and preserving the National unity.

Resolved, That we are determined to make it our first duty as soldiers—by promptitude, obedience, and soldierly bearing—to prove ourselves worthy of the responsible position assigned us by Providence in this, the grandest struggle of the world's history, between Freedom and Slavery; our first duty, as men, by every means possible, to contradict the slanders of our enemies, and prove to be true our fitness for liberty and citizenship, in the new order of things now arising in this, our native land.

Resolved, That while it deeply grieved us to find many who should have understood and appreciated our motives in connection with the pay question, failing to give us support and sympathy, sometimes even going so far as to condemn, thereby unconsciously giving aid and comfort to the enemy; nevertheless, we have no hard feelings against such, being convinced that, ere long, if not already, they will see the error of their way, and discern the wisdom of our acts, as surely as that they are to enjoy the benefits of our successes.

Resolved, that even as the founders of our Republic resisted the British tax on tea, on the ground of principle, so did we claim equal pay with other volunteers because we believed our military and civil equality its issue, independent of the fact that such pay was actually promised, and not because we regulated our patriotism and love of race by any given sum of money.

Resolved, That we do most sincerely thank those of our friends at home who have stood by us throughout our trials and deprivations, and whose sympathy and practical kindness went far toward softening the rigor of our condition; especially are our thanks due to Wm. L. Garrison, Wendell Phillips, Gov. Andrews, Senators Sumner and Wilson—those heroic champions of liberty —for their untiring and successful efforts in our behalf.

G.P. Iverson
Chairman of Committee on Resolutions.

John F. Shorter, 1st Sergt. Co. D.
Wm. H. Sanders, 2d Sergt. Co. A. } Sec's.

———————◆•◆•◆———————

Something of what the receipt of pay meant in real terms to the soldiers can be found in this letter home written right after the money arrived.

Folly Island, 55th
Regt Mass. Vols. /October the 15th 1864[59]

Dear Mother

I am ever happy to drop you a few lines to let you know that I am well. I hope these few lines will find [you enjoying] the same. Mother, I will send you some money, which is to the amount of $125 dollars, which was as much as I could send at the present un-

---

59. Lyne S. Brown Pension File. National Archives.

der the circumstances. Mother, I want you to use this as you please. I received $167.70. Now you know how much I kept for my self. I should of sent more but from all probability we won't be paid off very soon again, so, mother, I did the best I could.

Mother, when you get this write [me] without delay, for I shall be eager to [hear] from home concerning this money. They paid us off to day from the date of enlistment—all the back pay.

No more at present.

But I still remain, your son,

L[yne] S. Brown[60]

The pay issue may have been resolved, but, as this letter to Edward W. Kinsley makes clear, the battle for equality was far from over.

Head Quarters 55th Regt. Mass. Infantry
Folly Island, S.C. Nov. 21, 1864[61]

Mr. Edward Kinsley,

Dear Friend:

Much time has elapsed since I last saw you or had the honor to receive a letter written in your interesting and very genial style, and feeling that you never forget the soldiers of our Country and especially the 55th Mass. Vols. I write to let you know how we do. While I was north on furlough the regiment, after serving 16 months without it, received their pay. You cannot imagine what a day of rejoicing this event occasioned. I had the misfortune to be absent at the time, but returned not too late to see very delightful signs of the festal scenes that were. You may be a little surprised when I tell you that the 55th Regt. seemed an entire new set of men from those I left, so down-hearted and soul-crushed on account of the deep injustice so long meted out to them by the Government. Yes, every thing wore a very different

60. Lyne S. Brown was a twenty-two-year-old mason from Delaware County, Ohio. He was mortally wounded at Honey Hill and died in the hospital at Beaufort, South Carolina.
61. Edward W. Kinsley Papers. Duke University Special Collections.

aspect. You have heard that the 54th sent money to wives and friends to the amount of $64,000 and the 55th $65,000 by Adams Express. A large amount was also sent through letters &c.

The great day of victory was marked by a celebration. The men were paraded in companies; commanded by their 1st Sergts. A procession was formed which was marched for some distance from Camp headed by our excellent brass band, Prof. Moore [directing], and then back to the stand where was to be speeches by the sergeants, music, vocal & instrumental. The remarks made by all the gentlemen who spoke were eloquent, pointed, and full of the enthusiasm the great event created. You will not believe, Mr. Kinsley, that the mere attainment of dollars and cents occasioned this rejoicing. No, it was because a great principle of equal rights as men and soldiers had been decided in their favor —that all this glorious excitement was made. I wish you could visit the Regt now for I know you would go back favorably impressed with it. Treating men who thirst and hunger after freedom like dogs and then treating them as soldiers and men make great changes in their morale you would tell our friends. But, Mr. Kinsley, candor compels me to make one confession here, which, however great a discord it may make with the above, I cannot supress. Does any one wonder that there are men in the 55th, who are just like all other men, be they of what color they may; and who strive by military acquirements, by soldierly conduct, and by all honorable means to so faithfully serve their country as to have those services recognized clearly and substantially. Call it ambition or not, it is certainly true, and they cannot help it if they would. *Who can?* Should you, then, talk with a goodly number of our sergeants, you would find much *hidden* discontent, and I say hidden because they too dearly love to serve the cause to utter their discontent among the men and thereby make them also gloomy. Still they wait with patience for a better day. But an event has lately transpired which has opened wide all of our eyes (*enlisted men* I mean) and we wonder what the *next* mail will bring forth. Last mail brought an order from Adj't Gen'l [of Massachusetts, William] Shouler's Office announcing the *Commissioning Private Chas. L. Roberts 2nd Lieut. instead of* [William] *Dupree commissioned but not mustered.* You recollect Dupree, he was with me when I was north, and is the most soldierly and accomplished military colored man in the regiment, and is also acknowledged to be superior to many of our officers. *Mr. Kinsley, in the name of justice, what does this mean?* Is he whom we thought and still think the noblest, finest and most influential friend we have—is *Gov. Andrew going to forsake us*[?] If not, what does all this mean? Is the Gov., who is celebrated for taking no back hand steps, would he crush Dupree, aye & all of us, because the Government at Washington and the present commander of this regt, Lt. Col. [Charles B.] Fox, and his officers *(all save the noble absent one)* think that he was too soon? Is he who said to us, "boys take your muskets and wear your swords," going to discard us? I can't believe it to be so. None of us can. It must be that some deep trick is formed to defeat the magnanimous plans of Col. [Alfred S.] Hartwell and I wish he knew what has taken place before his return.

Lt. Col. Fox, comd'g regt the last two months, sent for me to come to his tent last night, and when there told me that a person had been commissioned instead of Sergt. Dupree and that *he did not know how it had been brought about.* He wanted to make the announcement himself to myself and [John F.] Shorter, thinking, he said, that if we should learn it from other sources, and as it has happened during his administration of affairs, we would think it was done by his recommendation. Mr. Kinsley, how else could it have been done? *Col. Fox dissented with Col. Hartwell when he recommended colored men for commissions.*

I hope, Dear Friend, that my revealing all this, to us at least, painful and burning wrong, will not displease you. We look upon you as a *true friend,* one who makes no *bad professions,* but is such a friend as would see us treated like men when we prove ourselves worthy, and would not give us the cold shoulder when a simple act of justice is done us such as the giving of a commission. Will you please investigate this matter, above referred to and let me know what we may next expect? Please believe that I will act with prudence about any information you may give me. Dupree & Shorter joined me and so do all the men in sending their love and thanks for all your efforts on our behalf. Hoping soon to have a letter from you, I remain, truly yours,

[James M.] Trotter

157

Part Four

"It was like rushing into the very mouth of death"

November - December 1864

Honey Hill

On November 23, 1864, the officers of the 55th Massachusetts received orders to have the regiment ready to move at a moment's notice. Four days later, all the companies (save two detached for duty on Folly and Long Islands) went on board the steamers Mary Boardman *and* Frazer, *and were transported to Hilton Head. There everyone shifted onto the* Mary Boardman *and, on morning of November 29, they were landed at a point along the Broad River known as Boyd's Neck. On the next day the 55th joined an expeditionary force that was to march west to cut the Charleston & Savannah Railroad near Grahamville, but at Honey Hill, the Federals came upon a well-entrenched enemy holding a strong line. Attacks were launched against this position, all of which failed. When night fell, the weary Union troops withdrew back to the river. Black units, especially the 55th, suffered heavily in this engagement.*

Headquarters, 55th Mass. Vols.
Mainland, S.C., December 5, 1864[1]

Mr. Editor:

We left our camp on Folly Island Nov. 27th, embarking on board the *Mary Boardman* for Hilton Head, to join an expedition

1. *Weekly Anglo-African,* December 24, 1864. Houghton Library, Harvard University.

159

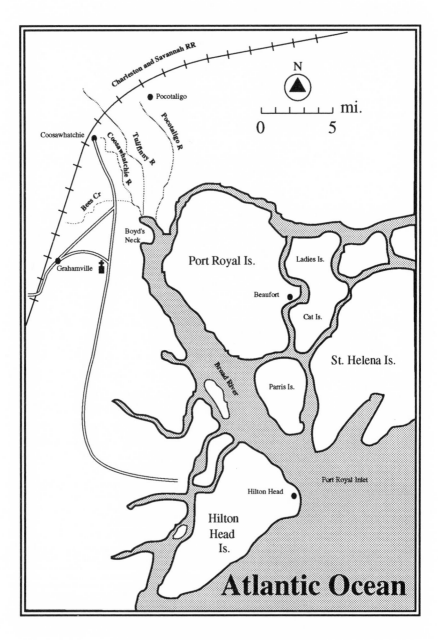

Port Royal Inlet and Broad River

160

inland, for the purpose of cooperating with Sherman's forces, which were reported near.

Arriving at Hilton Head, we lay at anchor for a while, and on Monday, after coaling at a landing up the river, we returned and joined the expedition, and on Tuesday landed at Boyd's Neck, on the Broad River.

At daylight the next morning, we were on our way to the railroad with the remainder of the expedition, which consisted of about six thousand troops, artillery, cavalry, and infantry.

We met the enemy after marching about five miles and skirmishing and fighting immediately commenced. We drove them for some three or four miles, when, coming to a battery or earthwork, situated on a hill and surrounded by woods and swamps, it was attacked and charged on several times, without capture. Night threw her mantle of darkness around the hotly contested field of strife and slaughter, and our forces withdrew a few miles and fortified, where we now remain, but expect soon to move forward again. We are now cannonading.

The following are the casualties:

Killed—Capt. W.D. Crane, Lieut. [W.] P. Boyington.
Company A—W. Punell, H. Morgan, E. Porter.
Company B—J. Smothers, A.L. King, W. Jones, C. Brown, J. Haren, G.W. Bush, I. Boyer, E. Lewis.[2]
Company C—A. Haggins, O. Duncan.[3]
Company D—Sergt. A.R. Lewis, Corp. G. Taylor, E. Allen, C. Stafford, S. Ward, W.H. Griffin, J. Posey.
Company F—E. Major, W. Gibbs, H. Viner.
Company I—[John] W. Brown.
Company K—Sergt. R.H. King, color bearer.

Missing—A. Butler, W. Charleston.

Wounded: Col. A.S. Hartwell, Lieut. [E.R.] Hill, Capt. M. Woodward, Capt. C.C. Soule, Lieut. J.C. Hall, Lieut. E.H. Jewet, Sergt-Major J.M. Trotter.

2. The roster for the 55th shows no indication that G.W. Bush of that Company was injured in this engagement.
3. Orin Duncan was not killed but captured.

161

Company A—Sergt. W.H. Saunders, Sergt. D. Spears, Sergt. D. Moss, Corp J. Patterson, A. Clayborne, James Manly, W. Lewis, James Gowens, P. Spencer.

Company B—Sergt. G. Bazil, Corp. A[lbert] Adams, Corp. Eli Hall, Corp D. Oglesby, Corp. [W.H.] Dobbs, W. Bowdry, J. Chism, W. Christy, S. Cox, R.H. Curtis, W. Fox, W. Howard, J. Kees, W.H. Moore, P. Mitchel, Thos. Overton, B. Richie, J. Smith, E. Thomas, T. Ventris, F. Whetzel, A. Wiggin.[4]

Company C—Corp. G. Barret, Corp. D. Adams, D. Barret, W. Bolin, A. Jenkins, S. Hill, Wm. C. Roberts, B. Scott, T. Cannon, E.J. Stewart, P. Gibbs, James Bowlin, John Crocket, Lewis Roberts, J. Roberts, J.P. Hightower, D. Harrison.[5]

Company D—Sergt. J.F. Shorter, Sergt. P. Fountain, Corp. P. Crowder, Corp. B. Henry, Corp. M. McFarlin, Corp. Thornton Parker, L.S. Brown, W. Crainshaw, E. Deericson [Dericks], W. Glaspy, W.J. Peel, D. Thorpy, J. Riley, R. Burk, C. Dixon, T.H. Fitzgerald, F. Hall, Trotman Sarmons, Ben Lee.[6]

Company E—J. Black, W.H. Miledam, J. Scott, M. Thompson, Thos. J. Wells, G. Washington, E.G. Flood.[7]

Company F—Sergt. Chas. L. Mitchell, Corp. J. Raddox, Corp. O. Dungan, N. Champ, B.F.B Ditcher, S. Davis, J. Gillard, A. Northup, D.A. Paine, W. Wicker, S. Webster, J. Shipp, J.H. Hurley, Edward Lee.[8]

Company I—Sergt Matthews, Corp. R.M. Morrison, J. Goens, J.K. Graham, G. Roberts, I. Kayne.[9]

4. According to the regimental roster, Eli Hall was not injured in the engagement, nor was Jacob Chism though James Chatman was. R.H. Curtis was uninjured, and B. Richie is noted as having been killed.
5. There is no indication in the regimental roster that D. Barret was injured in this fight. There is no W. Bolin on the list, although a W. Baldwin is noted as having been taken prisoner at Honey Hill. Lewis Roberts is not listed as having been wounded, nor is J. Roberts or D. Harrison.
6. There is no indication in the roster that Thornton Parker was injured in this fight, the notation for W.J. Peel and Trotman Sarmons indicates they were killed, and there are no listings for anyone named D. Thorpy or Ben Lee.
7. There is no indication in the regimental roster that Private George Washington was injured at Honey Hill.
8. The reference to J. Raddox is probably Jasper Haddox. There is no O. Dungan on the 55th Roster, and B.F.B. Ditcher is shown as having deserted in 1863. There is no indication that Samuel Davis was wounded, A. Northup is shown as having been killed, and J.H. Hurley is not shown as having been wounded.
9. There is no Matthews on the roster of Company I and the only Morrison listed was not injured in this fight. G. Roberts is shown as having been killed, and J. Goens and I. Kayne are probably J. Jones and I. Cain.

Company K—Sergt. P. Flemming, Sergt. O. Turner, Corp. R. Jackson, Corp. G. McPherson, A.A. Williams, C. Redman, E. Cross, S. January, I. Wheeler, H. Jarvis, J. Lewis, J.W. Stevenson.[10]

Yours for Union and Libery,

J.R. Bowles
Chaplain, 55th Mass. Vols.

In the Field
Boyd's Landing, S.C.
Dec. 18, 1864[11]

My Dear Friend,
E.W. Kinsley, Esq.—

Your kind and very satisfactory reply is received. I thank you for the kindness done me in laying before the Gov. mine of the 24th ult. I have shown yours to several and they are greatly encouraged and will heed the sensible and friendly advice given both by the good Gov. and our constant friend, yourself. I do not fear that the Gov. will withdraw his teeth without bringing the object. I only wrote for information which I could not get here. I am content to await future developments.

You speak of the Col. I thank God that in the awful charge of the 30th ult. he was not killed. His favorite Rebel steed was shot [from] under him, but the Col., though wounded in two places and nearly crushed by his horse falling on him was bravely rescued by the men and borne safely off the field.[12]

---

10. The regimental roster indicates that E. Cross and I. Wheeler were not injured.
11. Edward W. Kinsley Papers. Duke University Special Collections.
12. Lieutenant Thomas F. Ellsworth later received the Medal of Honor for his role in saving Hartwell.

The Battle of Honey Hill, November 30, 1864

Colcock
(1,400)

Broad River

Gordon's

Boyd's Neck

Hatch
(5,500)

Stoddard's Marine Battalion

NY 144

USCT 33

OH 25

MA 55 (Colored) [5 cos.]

USCT 35

SC 3 Cav.

State Line Brigade

GA 1 Militia

NY 127

NY 56

NY 157

MA 55 (Colored) [3 cos.]

USCT 102

O'Kane's
Naval Battn.

Bolan Church

① MA 54 (Colored) [2 cos.]
② MA 54 (Colored) [4 cos.]

Augusta Local Defense

Athens Local Defense

GA 47

mi.
0   1   2

164

But he is with you now and you will have from his own lips the story of unavailing bloodshed. I wish he knew how much all think of him and wish for his speedy revovery and return to the command. He has won a name for himself which will make him and all his friends feel proud. The men and line officers desire to see the *American bird* superseded by the *star*, but do so hate to lose him from the command of the 55th. But fortune certainly favors the brave and we must abide this inexorable and just law.

But for the fact that you have long since learned all the particulars of the Battle of "Honey Hill" from the Col., I would go into details. Our loss is about 30 killed, including the dead at Hospital, and 108 wounded. We went in with 502 muskets. Thus you see our loss is very heavy. The 54th and likewise *6 or 7 of our regts were not engaged.*

We fought in a forest dense and marshy and it was almost impossible on this account to maneuver more than half our troops. Some think that the generalship displayed was very poor on our side. We fought from 11 o'clock A.M. until dark, when under its cover we silently withdrew to this point, bringing nearly all our wounded and were not followed by the enemy.

The battle was a drawn one. Our total loss is 802 killed and wounded. The enemy's could not have been, under the circumstances, much smaller, although they try to make it so. They had advantage, not in numbers, but in such natural positions as more than make up for such deficiencies.

The battery in which the 55th charged was situated on a hill on the only road through the wilderness. Between ourselves and this battery, on either side of the road, was an impassable marsh. In passing up this road to the battery, of course, the men could only go by the flank—4 men in a breast. Every shot, therefore, from their guns would mow down nearly a hundred of our brave fellows. It was like rushing into the very mouth of death going up this road facing 7 pieces of death dealing cannon. Col. Hartwell and all of us knew this. But when commanded to charge 'twas not his to refuse, and so waving his hat while his eye looked upon his men, he smiled and cried, "Forward!" The order was promptly obeyed and in we rushed cheering and yelling. But ah! 'twas useless. The cannon on the hill opened. Shot, shell, grape and canister was hurled down the road as thick as hail and soon the Col. was wounded. Poor Capt. [William D.] Crane & Lt. [Winthrop P.] Boynton killed, Color Sergt. [Robert] King killed, and 2/3 of all that started in that desperate charge were either killed or wounded. Only part of our men were in the charge. Major [William] Nutt had the other part trying to make a flank movement. All that were left in the wood were returned. The Col. will tell you that 5000 men could not have taken that Battery, much less, our little band of 300. I was slightly wounded in two places. I am now on duty. We hold this point, while the other Regiments are 10 miles further up the river and within 2 miles of the Charleston and Savannah R[ail] R[oad]. Sherman we learn is at Savannah and we are under marching orders to join him. I will write you any news that will be interesting. Please write soon.

I remain very truly your obedient servant,

[James M.] Trotter

[P.S. William H.] Dupree is at Folly comd'g Fort Delafield. I will send your letter to him.

Boyd's Neck, S.C., January 7, 1865[13]

Mr. Editor:

In your issue of Dec. 24th, 1864, giving an account of the casualties in the 55th Mass. Vols. at the Honey Hill fight, November [30], I noticed several errors, which I wish to correct for the benefit of the friends of the unfortunate heroes.

Co. I—John W. Brown, not W. Brown (killed); James Jones,

13. *Weekly Anglo-African,* February 4, 1865. Houghton Library, Harvard University.

not Goens; John N. Graham, not Gregham; Isaac Cain, not Kayne; Corp. Richard Morrison, not R.M. Morrison.

Corp. Morrison died from his wound, Dec. 7th. Private Brown was a young man who had recently made his escape from that hell of slavery, Kentucky, and at the time he was killed, he had secured about his person the round sum of three hundred and twenty-five dollars, which, no doubt, the rebels considered "contraband," and therefore "confiscated" it. The other three are doing well as the nature of their wounds admits.

P.R. Laws,[14]
1st Sergt. Co. I, 55th Mass. Vols.

———————————•◆•———————————

Jan. 14/86[15]

Mt. Pleasant, Jefferson County, Ohio

Governor Andrew

Dear Sir.

I have the honor to inform you that I was a member of the 55th Massachusetts Colored Regiment, Company F, Private, and that I was wounded in the right hand at the fight at Honey Hill, South Carolina. And was sent from the field to the hospital at Beaufort, S.C. I remained there one month and then I was transferred to the General Hospital at David's Island, New York Harbor. I stayed there about seven weeks, and got a furlough to come

14. Peter R. Laws was a thirty-six-year-old bootmaker from Boston.
15. Nelson Champ Pension File. National Archives.

home. And when my furlough was out, I was not able to go back to the Hospital and I got my furlough extended, and after that I received an order to go to the Chief Mustering Officer at Columbus, Ohio, and there I mustered out, and [I expected that] my descriptive list would be forwarded immediately. I went and was mustered out and my descriptive list has not been received as yet and I have not received any pay. I have been sick ever since I came home and stand greatly in need of my money. I put my papers in the hands of Lewis, Givens & Hutchinson, Military Claim Agents, Columbus, Ohio, and they informed me that I would have to write to my Captain, Captain James D. Thurber, Co. F, 55th Mass., and he would send my descriptive list. But as I do not know his address I thought that I would write to you, as I am sure you can give me the required info and oblige,

Yours Respectfully,

Nelson Champ[16]

---

421 E 3rd St
Xenia, Ohio
Nov. 21, 1914[17]

Dr. Burt G. Wilder.

Dear Comrade. I saw your letter to the National Tribune touching on some of the happenings of the battle of Honey Hill. I am of the opinion that the Rebels had a trap set for us and we were marched right into it. When we attacked them or their advance, they kept firing and falling back until they got us where they wanted us. Then we were unable to gain any more ground that we could hold. Colonel [Alfred S.] Hartwell was wounded,

16. Nelson Champ was nineteen when he joined the regiment. He listed his occupation as "farmer."
17. Burt G. Wilder Papers. Cornell University.

Capt[ain William] Crane was killed, Lieutenant [W.P.] Boynton, I think, was killed, also our color bearer Rob. King was killed. Major [William] Nutt's horse was shot from under him right close to me. When night came on and we could no longer see we had orders to gather up the wounded and take them to the rear to a little Church in the woods. I helped carry a man shot in the knee. He belonged to the 25th Ohio. I have several things I would like to say pertaining to the service of the 55th. If you are informed as to where I could obtain a history of the service of the 55th I would be glad to know. The National Tribune published from time to time the narratives of the army of the coast or Southern Department. I don't recollect of seeing the 55th mentioned. Let me hear from you.

Fraternally yours,

William Scott[18]
Sergt. Capt. Frank Goodwin's
Co. E, 55th Mass Vol. In.

———————◆•◆•◆———————

Springboro, Warren County, Ohio

May 14th, 1917[19]

[To Burt Wilder]

In regard as to who saved the flag of the 55th Mass. Regiment Vol. at the Battle of Honey Hill, November the 30th, 1864, I am quite sure that the honor belongs to Andrew J. Smith of Co. B 55th Reg. Mass. Vols. My reason for knowing the above to be a fact, in the charge by column by company, my Company, C 55th Mass., was the Color Company in that Battle, in the charge that

18. William Scott, a farmer from Ripley, Ohio, was eighteen when he joined the regiment. He became a sergeant in 1865.
19. Burt G. Wilder Papers. Cornell University.

169

Col. [Alfred S.] Hartwell's horse was killed. My Company was in front, I was to the left of Sergt. [Robert] King when he was killed. He was the Color Sergt. I obliqued a little to the left of the color guard and I was a few feet from Sergt. King when he was killed and Corp. Andrew J. Smith of Co. B 55th Mass. picked the flag up. This was our last charge in that Battle.

This is as near as I now remember at this late day, and I here sign my name and affix my official seal this 14th day of May, A.D. 1917.

P.O. as above.

Jordan M. Bobson,[20] late Sergt.
in Co. C 55th Mass. Regt.

Notary Public in and for Warren County, Ohio

———————◆•◆———————

In the years following the war, survivors of the 55th took part in several reunions and exchanged occasional letters regarding their participation in the war. The spiritual closeness between the 54th and 55th Massachusetts can be inferred from the fact that M.M. Lewey chose to write to Luis F. Emilio, an officer and historian of the 54th.

The Florida Age
M.M. Lewey, Publisher
P.O. Box 125

Pensacola, Fla., January 11, 1896[21]

Lt. L.F. Emilio

Very dear Sir and Comrade:

. . . I volunteered in the 55th Mass. Infantry in May, '63, and [was] discharged in April, '65, from the camp, general hospital,

20. Jordan M. Bobson was a twenty-four-year-old farmer from Wilmington, Ohio.
21. Massachusetts 55th Volunteers Association of Officers Records. Massachusetts Historical Society.

David's Island, N.Y. on account of gun shot wounds through [my] right elbow d[itt]o shoulder and left leg. My full name is Mathew McFarlan Lewey. When I enlisted I was going to school in N.Y. city, living with my grand father there (Rev. Wm. McFarlan) and whose name I bore at the time, which accounts for the omission of (Lewey) when in the service. Some years ago the pension department corrected my name. I draw a pension in this very lengthy name: Mathew McFarian Lewey alias Mathew McFarlan.[22]

I was personally in all the engagements of the regiments up to the battle of Honey Hill and in the second charge of the regiment led by Col A.S. Hartwell was disabled. As a member (Corpl) of the color guard and in the second charge of this memorable engagement, Sergeant [Robert] King of the guard, was touching elbows with me on my right when he fell. It appears to me just now, and I am quite sure it is correct, that Col. Hartwell, Capt. [William D.] Crane—a most excellent soldier and a gentleman, Lt. [Winthrop P.] Boynton, Sergeant King fell simultaneously —before the flag could be recovered from King's lifeless form over which I laid for one or two seconds, three bullets struck me in places of my person already described.

Had it not been for a member of my company ("D") whose name I cannot recall at this moment, I would have been left on the field. This brave and thoughtful comrade took me up bodily and landed me in an old church where the surgeons were busily at work with the wounded.

Six men of 26th N.Y. Col'd Troops were detailed for my special ambulance. These men placed me in a blanket and carried my doubled up form to the landing. From that day I never again saw the regiment. . . .

I remain very truly yours,

M.M. Lewey

———————◄━●◆●━►————————

22. The published regimental roster of the 55th lists a "Matthew McFarlin" as a member of Company D, with the notation: "Corporal Dec. 2, '63; wounded Nov. 30, '64; discharged June, 1865, wounds."

171

Capt. L.F. Emilio
New York City

Dear Sir:

. . . I was a member in the 55th in the engagement at Honey Hill, S.C., was shot through the right elbow carrying away a part of the joint, through the left leg and right shoulder. That battle ended my services. I was color bearer, Corporal. In the charge of Honey Hill I saw Sergeant [Robert] King fall immediately by my side, and within ten and fifteen feet of me. Capt. William D. Crane and Lieut. [Winthrop P.] Boynton fell dead. . . .

Very truly,

M. McFarlan (Lewey)
Late Co. "D" Corp 55th Mass. Vols.

———————————— •●• ————————————

The indefatigable Dr. Burt Wilder also sought information after the war from members of the 55th regarding their participation in the battle of Honey Hill.

Xenia, O. April 26 – 1918[24]
from David Spears, late Sergeant, of
Company A, 55th Mass Vol Inft to

Dr. B.G. Wilder, Regimental Dr.

Dear Sir

Your communication of a few days ago has been duly noted. I thank you much for the history of the 54th and 55th Regts in part, some of my notes got lost soon after I got married, but my

---

23. Massachusetts 55th Volunteers Association of Officers Records. Massachusetts Historical Society.
24. Burt G. Wilder Papers. Cornell University.

mind is fresh as to some incidents, not accurate as to dates. Can't remember the case of Captain [Frank] Goodwin on James Island, but I can remember going over there in the night, and waited till next morning and then the charge was made on that battery, and took it, and the 2 guns & the gunners too, and then loaded and shot down that road at the fleeing enemy. I was in the color guard at that time. Our orderly sergeant, William H. Evans,[25] was wounded in the thigh and he was promoted Lieutenant after he got well. He belonged to my Company. My mind was on the 3d of July, but your record reads that it was on the 2nd. I know we stayed over there a few days and the enemy hit us hot with shells from their forts and we were not long in digging a trench to hide in either—ha-ha. The next we had was that long march from Jacksonville, Fla. to Baldwin Station, if I have the right name of the place, at any rate, we covered the retreat of General Seymour back to Jacksonville, Fla. I can't tell how many miles we marched that day, but got tired—ha-ha. Next we went to Palatka, Fla., down the Saint Johns River. I have no dates of this but can remember the trip all right and the next trip was to Honey Hill. These two dates I can remember. November 29th and 30th and on our way the 29th, the mail boat overtook us and give us our mail. Can you remember that? That was before we got to our landing place and that night we landed. The name of the landing place I can't remember, but we struck camp till morning and took up our march on the 30th for Honey Hill, and on our way we came to a large plantation, a wilderness of weeds, and the enemy had set fire to it and the enemy sent a slave out as a spy. Can you remember that? and he was instructed to call hogs as a sign that the Yankees was coming. Can you remember that, and when he was told to come to us he started to run, but the boys made him come in—ha-ha, General [Alfred S.] Hartwell and his staff took charge of him. I don't know what he told them, next we came to an old building. My mind is that we turned to our right there. This building we used for a hospital that day, and our men went to work fighting fire for a few hours. We had come a ways from this building and came to a halt, and there was where we took on refreshments and before we left there Hart-

25. Twenty-three-year-old William H. Evans was a farmer from Wayne County, Indiana. There is no record that he was ever commissioned a lieutenant.

well gave us our instructions (don't dodge men, step high, shoot low and keep your powder dry).

After we had received instructions we stood there for a little while, and I could hear the musketry and cannons roar, and hear some one hollering, O my left, oh my arm. Things had begun to get serious then and Captain Geo. M. Woodward said, there is a mighty rattling among [the] dry bones down there now. Then came the orders for us to march down. The first dead I saw was Captain [William D.] Crane, and a horse dead close to his side. I had to step right, among the wounded was General Hartwell; he wounded in his right hand & the next I saw was Thomas Ventris of my company[26] and he was wounded in the hand. I saw Hartwell when he raised his [arm] up with his handkerchief, then took his sword in his hand and rode to the front, and when I saw him again he was in that old Building, his head on his coat or some one's knapsack. He knew me as soon as I came in and he said to me, Sergeant Spears, they got you too did they?, and I said yes, I was wounded before the first gun was recaptured. What I have stated is what I can remember and was an eye witness, to as to the mail boat overtaking us and delivering our mail, my letter was from my brother, Henry in Ohio, and in it I read that David Reede an old friend was buried in August. I have a memorandum of the letter to this day. Your records give the name of one of these engagaments, [River] Causeway, and I never would have known it by that name. Yes, my Brother Henry who wrote me that letter that I received from that mail boat on the 29th of November, 64, he was buried the 18th day of February last. I am the last of the family.

I shall be pleased if my letter will help you in anyway that will convey to your mind any incident that will help you along with your history. Thanking you for your past favors, hoping success and all your people as even yours,

respectfully,

Sergeant David Spears,[27] Co. A 55th

26. Actually, Thomas Ventris was a member of Company B.
27. David Spears was nineteen when he signed up with the 55th. The Shelby County, Ohio man listed his occupation as "farmer."

Mass Vol Inft
P.O. Box 183, Xenia, Ohio

P.S. David Lee and his wife join me in kindest regards to you. He still tries to hold his job but he is failing.

Part Five

"Our best officers do not manifest any 'Colorphobia'"

January - September 1865

Georgia -- South Carolina Massachusetts

Following the battle at Honey Hill, the 55th performed garrison duty around Savannah.

> 55the Regt. Mass. Vols
> January 22nd, 1865[1]
>
> Fort Jackson, Savannah, Ga.

Dear Wife

I take these few moments to write you a few lines to let you know how my health is, which is very good at present, and hope when you receive this you will be enjoying the same blessing. I have got the box at last; the pies was all spoilt and as hard as a stone, the cake was a little mouldy, but we ate it; the can of peaches was good and it was a Godsend to me when I got it we had [just had] a long march and it was night and I was cold and hungry and you know it must be a Godsend. The baloney was good but I am sorry to say that John Little[2] was not with me to get some. We left him sick on Folly Island. The medicine came in good time and I am very much obliged to you for them. Dear Amanda, do send me some more as soon as you can and be sure to send me a can of good whiskey, the same as Mrs. Woods sent,

1. John H. Jenkins Pension File. National Archives.
2. When twenty-nine-year-old John Little enlisted in the 55th, the Boston native listed his occupation as "cook." He is noted in the regimental roster as a member of the band.

177

so I can give some to John Little. What did you sent that white coat to me for? You have never told me what it was that I had when I left you in New York. I cannot think what it was. Dear Amanda. I did not know what a soldier's life was when I was at home. We have been 2 months in the field with but one suit of clothes on our backs and part of the time nothing to eat. Yesterday I had nothing to eat, last night they gave us 4 hard crackers, and this morning 6 to last all day with a small piece of fat pork but it cannot be helped, and we thank God that it is not even worse than it is; for some of Gen. Sherman's men went 3 days without anything to eat and fighting all of the time. We whipped the Rebs and travel so fast that we cannot get rations, but I think the 55th has done all the fighting she will have to do before our time. I think we will stay here and do garrison duty the rest of our time, for Gen. Sherman says he will not fight with our colored troops and I am sure that your Uncle John will not cry, for I have had my share of fighting, so he can take his white men and fight as much as he likes as long as he lets John alone. When he came to Savannah he did not have to fight, for he had so many men the Rebels gave up and some run over the river into S.C., and Sherman after them, but when he gets to Charleston he will find that his big Army will have to fight and then he will find out what Gen. [John G.] Foster's black troops have been doing. The city is pretty decent place, but nothing to brag of. It [is] like all of the holes in the South. I see no beauty in them. The Fort that we are in has been a good one, it is made of brick but the Rebs destroyed it. They burnt the houses inside it and blew up the magazine, and spiked all of the guns. Dear Amanda, do send me some tobacco and paper envelopes and post stamps in a small box as soon as you receive this letter. Give my love to mother and Sister Maria, Mary Ann, Mrs. Dawson and children and all of my friends. I must close by biding you good day and may God ever bless you is the prayer of your and affectionate husband,

John H. Jenkins[3]

P.S. Direct your letters to Fort Jackson, Savannah, Ga.

---

3. John H. Jenkins was a thirty-eight-year-old porter from Boston, Massachusetts.

Head Qrs 55th Mass. Vols
"Fort Barton," 4 miles from
Savannah, Ga., Jan'y 29th, 1865[4]

Mr. E.W. Kinsley
   Boston, Mass.—

Dear Friend:

I have read your kind favor of the 9th, inst. I was happy to hear from you again. Indeed I know of no greater pleasure than that I experience while perusing your pointed, straightforward and very friendly letters. Since my last we have again moved as you will see by the heading "Fort Barton"—named after a prominent slave holding Rebel—is very large, covering 5 acres, and almost impregnible—except to flanking Sherman and [his] troops. It is surrounded by a ditch *30 ft. deep and 15 wide.* The Rebels had only 15 guns mounted—must have been short—which they dismounted and spiked before *retiring.* They are generally old-fashioned Columbiads of small caliber. Some of them were filled to the muzzle with slugs &c. They tried, in a hurry, to render them useless to us, but it seems they were too much hurried by "Old Billy" to do the work well. Barton was built 2 years ago as a defence for the City. Sherman, the sly fellow, visited the City at the other side and "Barton" did no good. Three companies of the 55th garrison Fort Jackson, a regular brick U.S. fort built, like "Pulaski," before this war, and two companies were left at Folly [Island]. You will see that we are in 3 parts. [William H.] Dupree is on Folly, [John F.] Shorter is at Beaufort, S.C., recovering from severe wounds got at Honey Hill. I hope we may not lose him to the service. I hope you have seen and talked with brave, noble Sergt. Charles Mitchell of Boston. He was badly hurt, had part of his foot torn off while bravely doing his duty at "Honey Hill."

We have just heard that Col. [Alfred S.] Hartwell is at Savannah and Col. [Charles B.] Fox has gone down to bring him *home.* The non-commissioned staff were at supper when we heard of him, and we made the old tent ring with cheers. Everybody is

4. Edward W. Kinsley Papers. Duke University Special Collections.

jubilant because of his arrival. I tell you, sir, that we believe in Col. A.S. Hartwell! He is so *true* and such a perfect soldier. Ours is the only colored Regt. so near Savannah and, of course, [we] create much sensation among the Georgians. They have great fear of colored troops and are trembling because of our proximity and the expectation of our coming to town to them was [as] Belshazzar reads the handwriting on the wall. The men are in no condition to go to Savannah at present. The campaign has caused nearly all to wear flesh colored clothing. However, we are expecting soon to draw clothing. The silver horns and drums will soon arrive from Folly (I wish they were here tonight so that we might give the Col. a musical welcome) and we shall then be in better trim.

Some traitors tried to burn Savannah last night. They set fire to the Arsenal in which was considerable powder and over one hundred shells. The explosion was most terrific, reminding us here of [a] rapid and continuous cannonade on the battlefield. It is a miracle that only two or 3 persons, as far as I can learn at present, were killed.

The flames communicated to adjoining buildings and a great many structures were burned. Genl [Cuvier] Grover has up to this time made 50 arrests, and has now the most scrutinzing rules in force. Please excuse all mistakes. All send their highest regard to Mr. Kinsley. I hope to hear from you soon and will be pleased to write in reply.

I remain with highest regard, sir, your obedient servant,

Jas. M. Trotter

From Savannah, the 55th was returned to South Carolina where it took part in the occupation of Charleston. Then came the inevitable garrison duty at various posts throughout the state. It was a time of victory in both the military and social spheres.

Head Quarters 55th Mass. Vol's
Orangeburg, S.C.
Folly Island, S.C. May 27, 1865[5]

5. *Ibid.*

Mr. E. Kinsley
    Boston, Mass.—

Dear Friend:

I write to sincerely thank you for the files of Posts you are kind enough to send every mail. I distribute them among the various Sergeants in the Regt and from there they are circulated through the Regt, affording pleasant & instructive entertainment for many. An order from the Sec'y of War, for the mustering into this Regt as 2nd Lieuts. Serg Maj J.M. Trotter [and] 1st Sergt. W.H. Dupree, came to Col. [Charles B.] Fox yesterday. Our discharge papers are now being made out, preparatory to our being mustered as 2nd Lieuts at once.

Some of our Officers have not yet got rid of their prejudices and consequently threaten to resign in case we are mustered into this Regt. I do not believe that Gen. [Alfred S.] Hartwell will allow this thing to change him from his course. Our *best* officers do not manifest any "Colorphobia," and only a very few of the others, I think, will resign on account of these promotions. I suppose all will come out right. You have heard of the promotions in the 54th?

Mr. Kinsley, you will please excuse this short letter. I am very busy at present making out our monthly reports. I shall not forget to write you an account of the Freedmen before long. I know you are deeply interested in the welfare of these poor people.

With sincere wishes for the health and happiness of yourself and family, I remain very gratefully yours,

Jas. M. Trotter[6]

———————— ◆•◆ ————————

Office of the Commission on Labor
Orangeburg, S.C. July 1, 1865[7]

Edward W. Kinsley, Esq.
37 Franklin Street
Boston, Mass.

6. Trotter was himself mustered in as a Second Lieutenant on July 1, 1865.
7. Edward W. Kinsley Papers. Duke University Special Collections.

Dear Friend:

I embrace with much pleasure a few moments of leisure to address you a few lines. I wrote you some time ago. The Regiment is at present at Orangeburg, S.C., has recently been paid the 2d time since its enlistment, and all are in good health and spirits. Genl [Alfred S.] Hartwell is quite well, and is as highly respected by his troops and the citizens generally as an honorable, just, and skillful officer can be. He has lately returned from a visit to his command at Columbia. A short time ago he arrested [George Alfred] Trenholm (formerly Rebel Sec'y War[8]) at Columbia and sent him to Charleston. You have since heard of him from Washington. The Genl, although admired by the citizens within his command as a high toned gentleman (one of the true chivalry) is at the same time firm and strict, allowing no disloyalty either in word or deed. I am at present a member of the Commission on Labor appointed by Genl Hartwell to see that the planters make contracts with the freedmen, giving them an equivalent for their labor. The duties are quite arduous but I am very glad to be here, as I have ample opportunity to be of service to the freedmen.

When our Regt arrived here, nearly 2 months ago, we found the old system of slavery in full operation as it had always been. Matters assumed a different shape, however, in a little while. Now no one is allowed to have people working on their farms without having made a fair written contract signed by both parties, signature being witnessed, and approved by the President of this Commission. The former slaveholders wince under this new order of things. It seems to hurt them sorely—having to treat as intelligent free men and women, and draw up a written agreement to compensate for labor done those whom they have tyrannized over with impunity, treating them as so many cattle, but they have to do it. A few do it with seeming cheerfulness. Some are too sharp to exhibit their chagrin. These contracts bind the freedmen to remain on the plantation until the present crop is harvested, this to mean its cultivation and thereby prevent starvation. Of course the colored people are all very happy, and they are working faithfully. I have several times been out on the plan-

8. Actually, Trenholm served as Confederate Secretary of the Treasury.

tations. I went 22 miles, without any guard save a good Colt revolver, which I had no occasion to call on. The Chivalry all treated me with respect and were very skillful in concealing whatever bitterness they may have felt when seeing a "nigger" with shoulder straps riding along the road to Columbia visiting their plantations in order to see that they were treating properly the colored people. We have had but a few cases of maltreatment of the freedmen by their former owners. Gen. Hartwell has a Military Commission for all such.

Mr. Kinsley, the people of South Carolina who have been in this wicked Rebellion are now perfectly cowed down. They began the Rebellion and talked more of eternal fighting than those of the other states, but I do not think any other state are so completely satisfied that they are whipped, and so willing to stay whipped as this. They seem to expect that, as they were first to rebel that Gov't will show them no mercy. Several Union meetings have been held in the interior, and the people are very anxious for a return of civil government under the new order of things. Royce is the choice of the people in the northern part of the state, while those in the southern part want [William] Aiken for Provisional Governor. Uncle Sam does not seem anxious to give them either at present. Troops are to be scattered all through the state. Provost Judges are to be selected from among the officers. This looks like Military Government for some time. Arrangements are also to be made for the education of the children of the poor. Soldiers to be teachers. We have given up hoping to get home soon. If you can tell me whether or not there is any prospect of the 54th & 55th being mustered out soon, I will very much thank you. More may be known at Boston than we can learn here. [William H.] Dupree and myself were mustered in on the 22nd & 28th of June respectively. I was assigned to Co. G and Dupree to Co. I. Co. I is commanded by 1st Lieut. [George T.] Garrison. The Commanding Officer of Co. G requested that I be assigned to his company. I mention this in order to acquaint you of his sentiments. There is much feeling in the Regiment among the officers against these promotions of colored men in respect with white officers; but all the best officers are in favor of it.

Some of the officers are trying to get Gen'l Hartwell to advise

183

us to resign. He has not done so yet, nor do I think he intends to. Some talk of resigning on account of these promotions. I cannot say that they will do so. Several of our best officers want to go home, but say they will not go just now, lest it might be thought they were dissatisfied with the situation. I do not know how it will all turn out, but Dupree and I will try to do our duty as officers, let prejudice be as great as it may.

Major William Nutt, at present commanding the Regt, is all right. He says we must not think of resigning and that he will stay with his Regt if all resign. He is very popular with the Regt and with everybody whose regard is worth anything. He has distinguished himself in battle several times. The papers came as usual. I renew my thanks for your kindness. All send their best regard to you. Dupree will write soon. I would be pleased to have a letter from you when convenient.

> With sincerely wishes for the health and
> happiness of yourself and family,
> I remain with deep regard,
>
> James M. Trotter

Even before the 55th mustered out of U.S. Service, its members were looking ahead to the struggle for equality that faced African Americans following the Civil War.

55th Mass. Vols.
Fort Motte, S.C., August 1, 1865[9]

. . . I have a matter of much importance to write to you and all true Christians at home. My subject is the freedmen of this part of South Carolina. They inform me that a great many who desire to assemble themselves in a body for social worship are deprived because they have no elder to minister to them. They have a few exhorters, who labor for them, but the greater portion of the [religious] professors appear to be on the barren mountains, desiring a pastor and finding none.

9. *Christian Recorder*, August 12, 1865. Edwin Redkey Collection.

They want colored ministers to establish a church and preach the gospel to them. They informed me that it has been a long time since they heard the truth of the gospel, preached to them. Bro. Fralem came to camp, and requested me to try and pay them one visit in the settlements. They were in a very lonely situation, and desired some one to come and expound the great mysteries of salvation, and the wonderful works of God.

After a few days had expired, I consulted with the brother, and told him I would go for the comfort of the children of God.

The commanding officer of the post gave me permission to go and assemble at the Bethel Station Church, near Fort Motte Station. I was accompanied by three other soldiers of my company. On reaching the Church, we found a large number of other spectators. They were seated in good order. There was a number of white persons present. They did not think that colored men could expound the true gospel of Christ.

Never, there, were colored men admitted to the pulpit to preach before. On July 11th, at 1 o'clock, I took my place in the pulpit, and ministered to my beloved brethren and sisters. They all seemed to be fed from the Holy Spirit of God, and greatly rejoiced in the deep mysteries of Christ. I was truly happy to find them in such good spirits, and I contended for the faith once delivered to the saints. It was very interesting to myself, and I think it would have been much more so to my beloved brethren and friends at home, to see how

> God moves in a mysterious way,
> His wonders to perform

Because it is the power of God unto salvation to every one that believeth in Him. May the great God be with you all. "Come over and help us."

B.J. Butler,[10]
Co. I, 55th Massachusetts

---

10. Benjamin J. Butler was a nineteen-year-old farmer from Vincennes at the time he enlisted in the 55th.

Many years later, after a new century had arrived, survivors of the 55th Massachusetts kept alive the flame of memory of their service and sacrifice.

421 E. 3rd St.
Xenia, Ohio 10/12/1917[11]

Dr. B[urt] G. Wilder:

Dear Dr. and Comrade

I received the printed matter you sent, was glad to get it. In speaking of the 54th and 55th Mass Regts there was not any discount in their patriotism. When their native states did not accord them the privilege of enlisting that they might take part in the suppression of the rebellion, they left their homes and all that was dear to them, and traveled hundreds of miles that they might enlist. Then they were refused, paid only the pay of laborers, they were held without pay for over a year. With all that they were patriotic and true to the stars & stripes.

Sincerely yours,

William Scott

One of the longest living survivors of the 55th Massachusetts was Andrew Smith. Smith was all of twenty when he enlisted; he listed his home as Clinton, Illinois, and his profession as "boatman." Smith was the only black member of the 55th to have his life story published during his lifetime in a "white" newspaper, Washington's National Tribune, *which looked after veteran's affairs. Smith could not read or write, and so dictated this recollection of his life.*

11. Burt G. Wilder Papers. Cornell University.

Adventures of a Colored Boy in War

by Andrew Smith, 55th Mass. Grand Rivers, Ky.[12]

My owner had been in the Confederate army since September, 1861. He came home on the 4th or 5th day of January, 1862. I was in the field gathering corn with his two sons, William and Harrison. We looked down the road and thought that we recognized him, and when we drove the wagon to the barn, sure enough, it was he.

We all shook hands with him. There was another colored boy by the name of Alfred Bissell who was at the house. He had overheard a conversation between my owner and another man. Our owners had come to take us to the Confederate army. This occurred about 10 o'clock in the day.

Later my owner sent his two boys away and we suspected that he had sent them to get help to take us away. We left the wagon with the team hitched and climbed over the fence into the woods. We know that Smithlands Landing was about 25 miles away and we struck out for that point, where we expected to find the Union Army.

GET TO UNION LINES

Alf and I walked until about 2 o'clock the following morning before we reached the picket line of the Union Army.

We both had left home in our shirtsleeves. It was a bright, sunshiny morning when we left home, but about nightfall it began to rain a slow drizzle. With the constant rain there came a sudden change in temperature and our clothes, having become soaking wet by the rain, began to freeze upon us.

All night we walked around the picket line half frozen. Near daybreak we approached the picket line and were taken in by the guards and warmed and fed. This outpost was held by a company of the 41st Ill. in charge of a Capt. Bacon. This company had been sent out to block the Cumberland and protect the Ohio.

The company was afterward sent back to Paducah, Ky., to join the rest of the regiment. This was about the last of January.

Other troops continued to come to Paducah to join the command. These troops were in Gen. [Andrew J.] Smith's division

12. *National Tribune,* March 21, 1929.

and we stayed there about two weeks. Gen. [Ulysses S.] Grant then made up an expedition to go up the Tennessee River to Fort Henry.

We landed in Tennessee below Fort Hyman, which was on the Tennessee. The rest of them landed on the other side of the river. They were intended to cut off the enemy from Fort Henry and keep them from retreating to Fort Donelson.

There were four gunboats, two ironclad and two wooden, in this expedition. The two ironclad boats were sent to attack Fort Henry. The intention was, I suppose, to have the ironclad boats attack the fort, bombard it, and excite them so the land forces could capture them.

The boats, however, attacked before the land forces arrived and captured all the men in the garrison. The rest retreated to Fort Donelson.

We stayed there about three weeks, then crossed the river and joined the rest of the command. We then marched to Fort Donelson. The two ironclad boats had been sent up the Cumberland to repeat the attack on Fort Donelson. But the Confederates had been at Fort Henry and had learned a thing or two, so the boats were not successful.

ACTION AT PITTSBURG LANDING

The attacks were made on Thursday, Friday, and Saturday mornings from the 12th of February. Gen. Smith's division charged the fort on Friday evening. Seven regiments were selected for the charge and warned of their duty.

On Saturday at daybreak he led them in a charge on 15,000 men. The enemy planned for them to retreat up the Cumberland River and go out at Dover, on the Tennessee, but the other men cut them off and they surrendered on Sunday morning, Feb. 16.

I shook hands with the captain of my master's company about 11 o'clock Sunday morning. Quite a number of the men had been reared around my home town of Eddyville, Ky. We lay around in camp about a week or so, then marched down the Tennessee River and took boats to Savannah, Tenn., just below Pittsburg Landing.

We got off there and cleaned up our boats, then went up to Pittsburg Landing and camped.

Early in April a Confederate army camp up from Corinth, Miss., under Gen. Albert Sidney Johnston. It was spoken of among us soldiers as an army of 150,000 men—an army, to my inexperienced eyes, which seemed so grand that it could hardly be beaten.

On Sunday morning early they were in our camps. It was said that they shot some of our men in their bunks before they could get out. The troop that I was with was about a half mile from the firing line. We heard the guns firing but did not know what it was.

About sundown some messengers came to us and gave the news of the attack. Lieut. Col. Tuper, of the 41st Mass. (colored),[13] ordered an attack. I was then only about 18 years old and not a regular soldier. I had gone out on the field just to look at the soldiers.

Col. Tupper ordered the company to lie down behind a breastworks made of fence rails. Lieut. Col. Warner[14] asked me to take his horse to the rear, and as I was doing so I was knocked down by a minie ball. This was my first wound, though nothing serious.

After that Maj. Warner saw that the fight was raging, and he told me to go to the rear, but begged me to stay and watch the soldiers fight a little longer.

After he saw that he was in danger of being killed he told me where he lived and asked me to promise to take his trunk to Clinton, Ill., to his family, and assured me that I would be well taken care of.

After much persuasion I took his horse and started to the rear. I was in full view of the whole southern army. When I had gone about 50 yards from him he called to me, "Hurry: don't stop, but go like hell!"

I started again, but was struck by another ball over the left ear. The ball plowed its way under the skin and was taken out in the center of my forehead. I went back to the hospital and the doctor took the ball out and screwed a piece of sponge in my forehead.

The battle went on until night. Someone told me that Maj.

13. This is undoubtedly an error, probably made by the newspaper typesetter, Lieutenant Colonel Ansel Tupper served in the 41st Illinois at the battle of Shiloh.
14. As the text later correctly states, this reference is to Major John Warner of the 41st.

Warner was wounded, and I was ordered to meet him Tuesday after the battle and give him his horse. He obtained a leave of absence and took me to Clinton.

I stayed there until 1863 with the Warner family. Lieut. Col. Warner resigned and came home with the promotion to full colonel.

I heard him reading about the 54th Mass. being formed. He learned that I was eager to join, so he wrote for transportation money for me and I then went to Chicago and joined some more recruits and went to Massachusetts. When I arrived at Boston the 54th Mass. had been formed, leaving five men to start the 55th Mass.

With the five men three companies were formed. There were two men in Co. A, two in Co. B, and one in Co. C. In about two weeks all three of these companies were filled. We were all officered by able men who were well experienced.

The noncommissioned officers were picked from the regiments. We drilled there about three months and then were sent to Port Royal, S.C. We stayed there and, under Gen. [Quincy] Gillmore, helped in the siege at Fort Wagner. We took it from the enemy.

We were stationed at Folly Island, five miles from Charleston and four miles from Fort Sumter.

We had no occasion to fight with our small arms, being with the cannoneers until we moved to James Island.

The first time the regiment was ever in battle by themselves was there in the Battle of the Causeway. We were led by Capt. Charles E. Grant. We captured the intrenchments and two pieces of artillery.

In July, 1864, it seemed that the war was getting near the end. The enemy moved about in squads. We had been in South Carolina, Florida, and Georgia. I do not know the purpose. It seemed to have been to run them down. We were supposed to tear down the railroads between Savannah, Ga., and Charleston, S.C., so the Confederate troops could not reinforce the armies in front of Sherman.

My regiment intended to take Honey Hill, S.C., but we found the enemy too strong. We made three charges and lost one-third of the men engaged, and were driven out. I had been placed in the color guard. My position was on the left of the sergeant, who was Robert King. He said to me: "Will you go with me? I am going to carry the flag into the fort or die."

We had nearly reached the muzzles of the guns when he was killed. I caught him with one hand and the flag with the other when he staggered back. Lieut. [Thomas F.] Ellsworth, who was commander, screamed at me when he saw the sergeant fall, "For God's sake, Smith, save the flag!"

This action was under Gen. Gillmore and Gen. Foster.[15] I brought the National flag from the field of Honey Hill. Beside me was Comrade [John H.] Patterson, who carried the State flag. When his arm was broken by a bullet I carried both flags. Later, I was promoted to color sergeant.

I got my final discharge at Mt. Pleasant, S.C., in August, 1865. Shortly afterwards we sailed to Gallop Island, near Boston, from whence we returned to Clinton in September or October. I stayed there until May, 1866, when I went to Kentucky to visit my mother and three sisters. Col. Warner and his daughter came to the train and told me to come back to Clinton whenever I was ready, as I had a lifetime home there.

I went down to Cairo and took a boat to Moses Ferry, a mile below Birmingham, about 8 or 10 miles from where I was born. Later I went to Eddyville and saw all my former playmates, who were ex-Confederate soldiers. I then saw my former owner, who came to me and gave me good advice. He told me that he was as poor as I.

15. Actually, the commanders were Generals Foster and Hatch.

Appendix One

Annals of the War
CHAPTERS OF UNWRITTEN HISTORY

Battle of Honey Hill
A Federal Account of the Fight on Broad River, S. C., in 1864.

FAILURE OF THE UNION EXPEDITION
Gallantry of the Troops,
Who Fought Well Under Blind Leadership.[1]

BY CHARLES C. SOULE
Formerly Captain in the Fifty-fifth Mass. Vols.

The battle fought at Honey Hill, S. C., November 30, 1864 is not even mentioned in most histories of the war. It was a disastrous episode in a comparatively unimportant expedition on the coast, occurring at a time when public attention was absorbed in the great movements of the armies under Thomas, Sherman and Grant. It deserves, however, some sort of record in our military annals, on account of the stubborn gallantry of most of the troops engaged, and because a successful issue would have given the Charleston and Savannah Railroad into our hands and compelled the immediate evacuation of Savannah or the ultimate capture of its garrison. So important did the action appear to the enemy that the Legislature of Georgia passed a resolution March 9, 1865, thanking General Smith and his command "for their unselfish patriotism in leaving their State and meeting the enemy in the memorable and well-fought battle-field at Honey Hill, in South Carolina." To the Fifty-fifth Massachusetts this engagement gave the opportunity which the Fifty-fourth Massachusetts had at Fort Wagner, of proving that a black regiment, well disciplined and well officered, could behave as gallantly under fire as the best troops in the service.

Sherman's army had started from Atlanta on its "March to the Sea" November 15, 1864. On the 30th it had crossed the Ogee-

1. *The Philadelphia Weekly Times,* May 10, 1884.

193

chee river and was halted near Louisville, Ga., two-thirds of the way across the State, the cavalry under Kilpatrick raiding towards Augusta and Waynesboro. It was evident by this time that Sherman was aiming, not for Macon and the Gulf, but for the Atlantic coast, and the Confederate troops which had fallen back on Macon were hurried around the flank of our army towards Savannah, where all available troops from North and South Carolina were also ordered to report to Lieutenant General Hardee.

PURPOSES OF THE EXPEDITION.

In order to co-operate with the movements of Sherman's forces and for the double purpose of offering to them a safe foothold on the coast and of cutting the only avenue by which reinforcements could reach Savannah, General John G. Foster, commanding the Department of the South, organized an expedition to proceed up Broad river, land at Boyd's Neck, march to Grahamsville [*sic*] and take possession of the Charleston and Savannah Railroad at that point. For this attempt there seemed to be every chance of success. Nearly all the Confederate troops in the district had been sent into the interior to oppose General Sherman's advance. The only force on duty at Grahamsville was part of a squadron of the Third South Carolina Cavalry.

THE SITUATION.

The distance from the Broad river to the railroad at this point was only seven miles. The gunboats could cover the landing of our troops and offer a secure base of operations. Hilton Head and Broad river had been in our possession for two years—a sufficient time, it would seem, for the officers of the navy to familiarize themselves with the channels and shoals of a coast already thoroughly mapped out by the Coast Survey. Two regiments of negro troops, recruited from islands and shores around Hilton Head, ought naturally to have furnished guides familiar with every plantation road, every by-path and every landmark. While they were slaves they were used to going fifteen or twenty miles from their homes, day and night, for courting, frolicking or religious meetings. There would appear to be no reason—with ample water transportation at hand—why a force could not be collected, ferried quickly and surely up Broad river and pushed forward promptly to the railroad.

The results would be (to quote from Jones' "Siege of Savannah") to sever the communication between Savannah and Charleston, to completely isolate the former city, and to enable Sherman at pleasure and without hazard to cross the Savannah river at almost any point below Augusta and establish communications with Port Royal, then the principal Federal depot on the South Atlantic coast.

THE EXPEDITIONARY FORCE.

More Than Five Thousand Men Under the Command of General Hatch.

In order to accomplish these results General Foster assembled at Hilton Head, November 28, all the troops which could be spared from the fortifications along the coast, from Charleston harbor to Florida. So many regiments had been sent to Virginia that the force thus collected numbered only 5,500 men of all arms. As General Foster was incapacitated by an old wound received in Mexico from active service in the field the command of the expedition devolved on Brigadier General John P. Hatch. The expeditionary force was divided into two brigades: The First, composed of the Fifty-sixth New York, Lieutenant Colonel Tyler; One Hundred and Twenty-seventh New York, Colonel Gurney; One Hundred and Forty-fourth New York, Colonel Lewis; One Hundred and Fifty-seventh New York, Lieutenant Colonel Carmichael; Twenty-fifth Ohio, Lieutenant Colonel Houghton; Thirty-second United States, colored troops, Colonel Beecher, being commanded by Brigadier General E. E. Potter, the Second, comprising eight companies of the Fifty-fourth Massachusetts, colored, Lieutenant Colonel Hooper; eight companies of the Fifty-fifth Massachusetts, colored, Lieutenant Colonel Fox; Twenty-sixth United States, colored troops, Colonel Silliman; One Hundred and Second United States, colored troops, Colonel Chipman, being under command of Colonel A. S. Hartwell, of the Fifty-fifth Massachusetts. The artillery included one section (three-inch Parrots) of Company A, Captain Harmer; Third Rhode Island Artillery (which did not go into the action); two sections (four guns)—light twelve-pound Napoleons of Captain Mercerean's Battery (B), of the Third New York Artillery, and two sections (four guns) light twelve-pound Napoleons of Battery F of the same regiment, commanded by Lieutenant Titus, the whole under command of Lieutenant Colonel Ames of the Third Rhode Island Artillery. Two squadrons of the First Massachusetts Cavalry accompanied the expedition.

DAHLGREN'S NAVAL BRIGADE.

Rear Admiral Dahlgren, having been asked to assist in the land operations, gathered from his fleet and from blockading vessels two navy field batteries of four howitzers each, organized expressly for the occasion and supported by four half companies of sailor skirmishers and four depleted companies of marines. This "Naval Brigade," as it is designated in General Hatch's report, was commanded by Commander George H. Preble, and did not exceed 500 men, all told. General Hatch's orders from General Foster were to land at Boyd's Neck, push inland and destroy the railroad near Grahamville, to destroy the bridge to the southward, then march with his whole force and attack the work guarding the Coosawhatchie bridge.

To carry and convey the expedition a fleet of gunboats and transports had been collected. Admiral Dahlgren, from his flagship the Philadelphia, commanded a flotilla composed of the Pawnee, Pontiac, Mingoe, Wissahickon, Sonoma, Winona and the tugs Daffodil and Petite. These vessels, with the transports, were arranged in single file with orders that each steamer should show no lights except in the stern, and should follow the light of the steamer ahead. Singularly enough there was only one pilot with the fleet and none of the naval officers had ever ascended Broad river before. The captains of the transports were equally ignorant of the channel, were many of them nervous and incompetent, and at least one of them was so overcome by liquor that the army officers had to navigate his boat as best they could.

UP BROAD RIVER.

How the Fleet, Starting in a Fog, Reached
Boyd's Landing Late in the Morning.

At half-past 2 o'clock on the morning of the 29th the signal for sailing was given, a red and white light, whose brilliant rays shot across the harbor. A few moments later and it could not have been seen from the vessels, for while they were weighing anchor a heavy fog settled over the harbor, rendering any concerted movement impossible. After two hours of anxious waiting the fog became somewhat lighter. "Feeling about" in his flagship, as he expresses it, Admiral Dahlgren collected his vessels and commenced slowly to grope up the channel with the light-draft tugs in advance. After getting over the shoals at the mouth of Broad river (where the Wissahickon grounded and could not be got off in time to take part in the landing), the pilot was sent ahead in the Pontiac and the squadron moved slowly up the river in a fog still so thick that the shore was only visible when the vessels were close upon it, and most of the time the gunboats ahead and astern were indistinctly visible. The two tugs continued to feel their way on either side of the flagship. The transports followed, but all of them lost their way in the fog. Some grounded on the shoals and could not be floated off until noon of the 30th; others went astray up the Chechesser river (among them the Canonicus, carrying the engineers and the material for building landings); others again came to anchor and waited for clearer weather and another tide.

AT BOYD'S LANDING.

While the transports were thus scattered and delayed the navy vessels kept well together and came to anchor in the creek off Boyd's Landing at about 8 o'clock on the morning of the 29th. As the Pontiac in advance approached the landing, a loud whoop was heard through the fog, and a moment later a fresh fire beside a hut on shore showed that the rebel pickets had been surprised and had barely time to escape. "Not a sign of our troops was anywhere visible," says Admiral Dahlgren in his report, "and I began to fear that some mistake had been made, when a transport appeared flying General Hatch's flag." This was about 11 o'clock in the morning. In half an hour the sailors, marines and howitzers were landed and advanced about a mile in skirmishing order. The other transports began to arrive and to land troops, who shouted enthusiastically as the fog lifted and showed a picturesque plantation with large pines and oaks, draped with luxuriant Southern moss. The narrow creek was blocked with vessels. The engineers had not arrived with materials to make proper landings.

197

LANDING THE TROOPS.

The debarkation was necessarily slow. Troops were taken ashore in small boats to scramble up the muddy banks of the marsh. Horses were thrown overboard and swam ashore. A dilapidated plantation wharf was utilized as far as possible by the vessels which could reach it. Instead of getting ashore early in the morning, as had been planned, the troops were thus landing all day and through the evening. General Foster, whose boat had been misled in the fog, arrived at 2 P.M., but returned to Hilton Head at 4 P.M. General Potter arrived with part of his brigade about noon, and Colonel Hartwell, with four companies of the Fifty-fourth Massachusetts, shortly after. The artillery did not leave Hilton Head until 8 in the morning and were landed about dark.

MOVEMENTS OF THE NAVAL BRIGADE.

The Naval Brigade were ordered forward in the afternoon to occupy the fork where the Coosawhatchie road diverged from the road to Grahamville. They had no guide and their map perplexed them by showing roads where there were none and by magnifying byways and cart paths into roads. Instead of stopping at the cross roads they pushed on to the right, away from Grahamville and toward Ree's Creek and Coosawatchie. They met, engaged and drove the Confederate pickets. The Thirty-second United States, one of the first regiments ashore, was sent on to support the Naval Brigade.

ON THE WRONG ROAD.

About 4 P.M. the cavalry and a large portion of the First Brigade having landed, General Hatch determined to push forward without waiting for the artillery and the remainder of the infantry and attempt to seize the railroad. General Potter, in advance, turned to the right after the Naval Brigade and came up with them just as they were halting for supper. Here it was discovered that they were on the wrong road and the column retraced its steps to the first cross road, where the Naval Brigade, thoroughly worn out with the labor of dragging their eight howitzers by hand over the sandy roads, were left for the night, while Generals Hatch and Potter, with the other troops, took the road to the left, on which the advance should have been made at the outset. But

198

bad luck persistently followed the enterprise, for on reaching Bolan's Church, where the Grahamville road turns to the right, and, encountering there the enemy's pickets, the guide persisted in following the direct road toward Tenvey's Landing and Savannah. After proceeding on this road four miles without opposition, the guide and the generals became convinced that they had gone astray and countermarched to the church, which they reached at 2 A.M., so weary with the night march of fifteen miles that the troops gladly went into bivouac.

A PICTURESQUE SCENE.

Meanwhile Colonel Hartwell had been left in charge at the landing, assigning regiments as they landed to position for the night and making arrangements for a move early the next morning. Boyd's Landing and the plantation settlement near it will be remembered by those who camped there as one of the characteristic scenes of the war. The roomy piazzas of the dwelling house, the dingy picturesqueness of the outbuildings, the background of moss-hung live oaks, the gunboats and transports in the creek, the constant landing of artillery and stores at the wharf, all strongly illuminated by the glow of the camp-fires, formed a picture to fasten upon the memory of the men, who sank to sleep between the ridges of the old cotton fields that night.

MOVEMENTS OF THE ENEMY.

Georgia Militia Under General Smith
Cross the Savannah to Protect the City.

Meanwhile the Confederates had not been idle. The companies of cavalry which were picketing the coast were called together at Grahamville. Colonel Colcock, commander of the military district, was summoned in hot haste from the Savannah river, where he was superintending the erection of works to protect the crossings. General Hardee, at Savannah, was promptly advised of the landing of Hatch's expedition. He was in great-straits for troops to meet this attack, but by singular good fortune reinforcements arrived just in the nick of time. On the withdrawal of the Federal forces which had been threatening Macon (November 25), General Gustavus W. Smith, who commanded the Georgia troops concentrated there, was ordered to move south by railroad to Albany, Ga., thence to march across the country to Thomasville and there to take cars for Savannah. This detour of one hundred and fifty miles south and then two hundred miles northeast was made with great promptness and celerity. The march of fifty-five miles from Albany to Thomasville was made in fifty-four hours. At Thomasville, where five trains had been expected, "the energetic General Toombs" had only been able "to frighten the railway officials" into furnishing two trains. In these the First Brigade was started after dark, November 29, and reached the outskirts of Savannah at 2 o'clock on the morning of the 30th.

GENERAL SMITH URGED FORWARD.

At Savannah General Smith received peremptory orders from General Hardee to proceed at once to Grahamville and repel Hatch's advance. "The officer in command at Pocotaligo," says General Dick Taylor, meaning probably Grahamville or Coosawhatchie, "had reported that he must abandon his post the following morning unless reinforced." "It was absolutely necessary (to quote from Jones' 'Siege of Savannah') that this communication (the Charleston and Savannah Railroad) should be preserved. Upon it depended the further occupation of Savannah. Over this road must the garrison retreat in the event that it become expedient to evacuate the city. By this route also were reinforcements expected. General Hardee had no troops which he could detail for this important service, except two regular cavalry regiments from Charleston, and it was feared that they would arrive too late. Not a moment must be lost and it was urged upon General Smith that if he would move at once and hold the enemy in check until 2 P.M., several thousand troops en route from North and South Carolina for the reinforcement of the garrison of Savannah would arrive and insure the effectual repulse of the Federals."

INTO SOUTH CAROLINA.

Although the statute organizing the State forces (of which General Smith's command was composed) "confined their services and operations to the limits of Georgia; although strictly speaking there rested upon these troops no legal obligation to move beyond the confines of their own State, whose territory they were instructed to defend, although General Smith has a qualified authority from Governor Brown to withdraw the Georgia troops under his command from the Confederate service in case they were ordered beyond the limits of the State, and although the commander and command were almost broken down by fatigue and want of rest, realizing that the battle for the salvation of the metropolis of Georgia was on the instant to be fought on South Carolina soil; and after a full conference, with the Lieutenant General becoming perfectly satisfied that it was right and proper the movement should be made, General Smith issued the requisite order." The trains were switched across to the Charleston and Savannah Railroad and carried the sleeping Georgians across to South Carolina soil; thus, as General Toombs expressed it, "making them unconscious patriots."

READY FOR THE FIGHT.

General Smith, with his leading brigade, reached Grahamville at 8 A.M. on the 30th, the day of the battle. While Smith remained at the railroad until 10 o'clock, when his second train arrived and also the Forty-seventh Georgia, from Charleston, Colonel Colcock, who had been anxiously awaiting with a mere handful of troops the arrival of reinforcements, at once led forward the First Brigade toward Bolan's Church. As the Federal advance had occupied before his arrival the position which he had selected for defense, he countermarched the brigade and posted them at works constructed two years before at Honey Hill equidistant (two miles and a half) from Grahamville and Bolan's Church. In order to delay Hatch's advance until the Confederate troops could be placed in position, Colonel Colcock pushed forward one twelve-pounder Napoleon of Kanapaux's Battery, under command of Lieutenant Zealy, together with Company K, Captain Peeples, of the Third South Carolina Cavalry. While they held in check the whole Federal column General Smith hastened forward the rest of his brigade and made his dispositions for the defense of Honey Hill.

THE BATTLE-FIELD AT HONEY HILL.

The situation was an excellent one to repel an attack in front, though weak on the flanks. A substantial open earthwork, pierced for four guns, extended two hundred feet on each side of the road, on the crest of an abrupt slope of about twenty feet. The ground immediately in front of the entrenchments was comparatively open, but at the distance of about one hundred and fifty yards a shallow and sluggish stream, expanding into a swamp, with a heavy growth of trees and dense underbrush, ran along the whole Confederate front. General Hatch says of this swamp that "it was not impassable, but presented a serious obstacle to our advance." The only practicable approach was by the narrow road, which made so sharp a turn as it passed through the swamp that the earthwork was invisible to a force approaching by the road until they were close upon it.

THE CONFEDERATE FORCE.

The force under the command of General Smith was as follows: Infantry—The First Brigade of Georgia Militia, Colonel Willis; State Line Brigade of Georgia, Colonel Wilson; Seventeenth Georgia (Confederate Regiment), Lieutenant Colonel Edwards; Thirty-second Georgia (Confederate Regiment), Lieutenant Colonel Bacon; Athens Battalion, Major Cook; Augusta Battalion, Major Jackson. Cavalry—Companies B, E and C and the "Rebel Troop" of the Third South Carolina Cavalry under Major Jenkins. Artillery—A section of the Beaufort Artillery, Captain Stuart; a section of De Pass Light Battery; a section of the Lafayette Artillery; one gun from Kanapaux's Light Battery; seven pieces. General Smith says that he brought five pieces of artillery into action and that his infantry force, "which was all engaged," numbered 1,400 "effective muskets." This seems rather a low estimate, for on December 5, 906 rations were issued to the First Brigade and 469 to the State Line Brigade, 1,375 to the two organizations, and no mention is made in this schedule of the Forty-seventh Georgia, which General Smith says arrived from Charleston at 10 in the morning. But counting in officers, artillery and cavalry, the Confederate force, before the arrival of reinforcements in the late afternoon, could not have amounted to 2,000 men.

General Hatch's expeditionary force was about 5,500. Deducting two regiments not arrived and one regiment and detachments from others left at the landing as guards, he brought into action on the morning of the 30th about 4,000 men, certainly more than two to one, though the Confederates had the advantage of position and of knowledge of the country. Captain Dessaussure, who served on General Smith's staff for the day, was thoroughly familiar with the ground, as were also Colonel Colcock and Major Jenkins.

<hr/>

THE EVE OF BATTLE.

The Position of the Confederate Force—The Forward Movement of the Federals.

The Confederate forces were arranged in a convex semi-circle, the right resting along a fence above the swamp, the centre, with the artillery, occupying the earthwork and the left retired toward the Coosawhatchie road, through "an open pine barren." The earthwork seems to have been defective in construction. One account says that it was too high for use by infantry, another that the artillery could not use the embrasures and had to take position in front of the entrenchments. An inspection of the works, as they still stand, contradicts both these statements and the small loss of the Confederate troops shows that they found satisfactory protection.

Although General Smith was on the field during the action the immediate command of the main line was given to Colonel Colcock, in deference to his position as military commander of the district in which the battle was fought. Colonel Gonzales; of General Hardee's staff, had charge of the artillery and Major Jenkins of the cavalry.

At about 3 o'clock in the morning of the 30th, an attack was made on the Federal pickets beyond the church, but it was repulsed without loss. Desultory picket firing was kept up until morning.

ADVANCE OF THE FEDERALS.

The troops at the landing were astir early. Colonel Hartwell sent forward before daybreak the Fifty-sixth New York, Thirty-fifth United States, colored troops, and part of the Thirty-second United States, colored troops, to join the First Brigade. Leaving the Thirty-fourth United States, colored troops, at the Neck he marched at daylight with eight companies of the Fifty-fourth Massachusetts, eight companies of the Fifty-fifth and two batteries of artillery (eight guns), under Lieutenant Colonel Ames. The Twenty-sixth and One Hundred and Second United States, colored troops, comprising the rest of the Second Brigade, had not yet arrived. It was a lovely morning, sunny and mild, as these troops marched between the hedges of the plantation roads and along the abandoned cotton fields. They left at the landing a secure base of operations. The double-enders of the fleet, with the Pontiac, lay in line, stern to stern, close up to the bank of the creek, presenting a broadside of nineteen heavy cannon and sixteen howitzers.

WORK OF THE NAVAL BRIGADE.

At the Coosawhatchie cross roads the Naval Brigade, which had camped there for the night, fell into the line of march and four companies of the Fifty-fourth Massachusetts, under Captain Pope, were left to replace them. Shortly after the column had gone on a force of Confederate cavalry came down the Coosawhatchie road and attacked Pope's detachment. Two rifled howitzers of the Naval Brigade, which had been sent back from the church to his support, arrived just in time, and coming up noiselessly (being drawn by hand) behind the hedge-rows opened on the enemy with such effect that they retired in haste. These companies of the Fifty-fourth were relieved at half-past eleven by the Thirty-fourth United States, colored troops, and marched to the battle-field arriving between twelve and one. In the afternoon Major Anderson, of Foster's staff, with two companies of the Thirty-fourth and part of the heavy detachment, advanced some distance up the Coosawhatchie road, until fired on at close quarters by the Ree's Creek Battery, when he retired to the cross roads. The enemy made no other demonstration in this part of the field.

TIME LOST BY POTTER'S BRIGADE.

At Bolan's Church (which was about three miles from the landing) Potter's Brigade was under orders to march before daylight. If these orders had been executed and a bold push had been made there was no reason why our advance—even after the loss of twenty-four hours, which had been wasted in missing the way —might not have reached Grahamville without substantial opposition before General Smith's leading brigade arrived by railroad. But for some reason—perhaps because the men were worn out with their night march, perhaps because General Hatch was waiting for the artillery and the Second Brigade—the start was not actually made until nearly nine o'clock, when the One Hundred and Twenty-seventh New York was sent forward to skirmish. The cavalry had previously reported that the enemy had appeared up the road with artillery and infantry (these were the guns of Kanapaux's Battery and the company of cavalry, now dismounted and serving as skirmishers, which Colonel Colcock had pushed forward to delay our advance).

<hr />

OPENING OF THE BATTLE.

The First Skirmish Begun Near Bolan's Church—The Enemy in Force.

At 9:15 A.M. the first skirmish was opened half a mile from the church by a solid shot from Kanapaux's gun, which struck with fatal effect in one of the leading regiments advancing by flank in the narrow road. On our right was a large open field; on our left, for a quarter of a mile from the church, woods with that dense jungle of vines and undergrowth which covered most of the battle-field of Honey Hill. Beyond this was a cotton field and then a wooded swamp, crossing the road and impeding our progress on each flank. The Confederate cannon was placed on a rising ground some distance beyond, commanding the narrow causeway which was the only avenue of approach and the dismounted cavalry were posted as skirmishers on the further side of the swamp.

UNNECESSARY MANEUVRES.

A vigorous charge of our skirmish line would have brushed away the meagre force—only one company—which they disputed our passage, but much time seems to have been lost in maneuvering. The Twenty-fifth Ohio, One Hundred and Forty-fourth and One Hundred and Fifty-seventh New York were advanced and

205

deployed in line to support the skirmish line of the One Hundred and Twenty-seventh New York. A section of Battery B, Third New York Artillery, under Lieutenant Wildt, advanced to the edge of the swamp and opened on the enemy, firing seventy-five rounds at six hundred yards. The cavalry went around the right of the swamp to take the enemy in flank and our excellent force of infantry appears to have been held in check until the artillery and cavalry could produce an effect. Finally an advance was ordered and the Confederates fell back.

THROUGH THICK WOODS.

Beyond the swamp, up to the entrenchments at Honey Hill, extended on the left heavy woods, with tangled undergrowth. On the right was a large field, in which the Confederates, retiring, had set fire to the tall grass, sedge and broom corn. A strong wind blew this fire down upon our skirmishers and threw them into temporary disorder, by which the enemy gained further time. Beyond this field were heavy woods so thick that our skirmishers were withdrawn and the leading brigade marched in column on the road. At the end of this straight stretch of road the Confederates made a short stand with their piece of artillery. The advance section of Battery B was again brought into action and fired twenty rounds at eight hundred yards. The Confederates having sufficiently delayed our advance soon retreated, but one of their last shots struck in the groin Lieutenant Wildt, commanding the section, and so nearly carried away his leg that the surgeon who accompanied the advance amputated it with his pocket knife on the field. Our loss in these skirmishes did not exceed twenty men killed and wounded. Among the latter were Lieutenant Colonel Geary, of the Thirty-second United States, colored troops, and Captain Penet, of the One Hundred and Forty-fourth New York.

THE ENEMY FOUND IN FORCE.

These operations consumed nearly the whole morning. Meanwhile General Smith had brought up from Grahamville his whole force and placed them in position along the line already described. The preparations were hardly completed when the advanced gun, having made its last stand at the bend of the road, came back into the entrenchments. Our advance, having withdrawn its skirmishers on account of the density of the thickets on each flank, was marching in column on the road with a few flankers straggling through a vine undergrowth when, on turning an abrupt bend, it came "unexpectedly" (as General Hatch states in his report) upon the enemy in position. Although the works were said to have been built two years before their existence was until now unknown and unsuspected by our commanders.

AS IT APPEARED TO THE ENEMY.

Jones, in the "Siege of Savannah," gives the following account of the commencement of the action: "Upon its appearance about one hundred and twenty yards in front of the works, in a curve of the road, the infantry and artillery opened a murderous fire on the head of the Federal column, before which it melted away. They were advancing in apparent ignorance of the line of field works, and of the serious opposition they were to encounter. Staggered by this fire the enemy recoiled and some time elapsed before they deployed in line of battle. The low ground was wooded to an extent sufficient to conceal the movements of the enemy, but not to protect them from the heavy fire of infantry and artillery which crushed through their ranks."

THE UNION LINE OF BATTLE.

The Lack of a Strong Hand Felt by Most of the Regiments on the Field.

What regiment constituted the advance at this time the accounts do not state, and indeed it is somewhat difficult to ascertain the movements or position of each regiment during the rest of the action. The left of Potter's Brigade was at once thrown into line to the left of the road, facing the enemy, along the edge of the swamp. The One Hundred and Twenty-seventh was next the road, then the One Hundred and Fifty-seventh New York and the Fifty-sixth New York, which held our extreme left. The attempt of the right of the brigade to deploy was apparently hindered by the thick undergrowth, and the regimental commander's ignorance of the situation both of our forces and of the

207

enemy. The Thirty-second United States, colored troops, seem to have formed in line and to have met an advanced force of the Confederates posted along an old dam, at right angles with the main road, which formed our line of defense later in the afternoon. The Thirty-second wavered and the Twenty-fifth Ohio, which was advancing behind them by the right of companies through the thicket, came into line and charging through the Thirty-second and a portion of the One Hundred and Forty-fourth New York, drove the enemy from their position, inflicting little loss, however, as they were afraid to fire here for fear that some of our own troops were in front of them.

ATTEMPTS TO TURN SMITH'S LEFT.

A line was formed on the road which branched off from the main road, parallel with the dam; the Thirty-second United States on the right, the Twenty-fifth Ohio next and part of the One Hundred and Forty-fourth on the left towards the Grahamville road. There was no firing in front and no enemy visible. After sending forward a party to reconnoitre, Colonel Houghton, of the Twenty-fifth Ohio, led his regiment forward into the woods, changed front partially towards the left and advanced to the edge of the swamp, where he says "a strong force of the Confederates was met and a severe-fight took place." The Savannah *Republican*, in an account of the action, says of this episode: "Our (Confederate) left was very much exposed and an attempt was once or twice made by the enemy to turn it by advancing through the swamp and up the hill, but they were driven back without a prolonged struggle."

LITTLE DONE ON THE FEDERAL RIGHT.

The One Hundred and Forty-fourth New York does not seem to have advanced at the same time. They were lying down in line shortly after this time, considerably in rear of the Twenty-fifth Ohio, and no further mention is made of them in the report and accounts of the fight until the retreat in the evening. The Thirty-second United States, colored troops, are said by Colonel Hampton to have come up "somewhat tardily" on his right. The further action of the right wing will be shown later on. It may be said here, however, that no general officers or aids appeared and no orders were received by the right wing while they were in this advanced position. General Hatch says that he "ordered the right to press forward, swing around to the left and flank the enemy, but the dense undergrowth and deep swamp prevented;" but he is mistaken. The undergrowth and swamp were entirely passable, as reconnoissances showed. What was lacking was orders and a commander.

BATTERY B.

Meanwhile the section of Battery B, already twice engaged (commanded, after Lieutenant Wildt received his wound, by Lieutenant Crocker), was moved to the intersection of the main and branch roads, the only place where artillery could be put. It was a very unfavorable position for the use of artillery. The forest was so thick that the enemy was invisible and the guns could only be sighted at the puffs of smoke which arose over the intervening branches. Shortly afterwards Captain Mercereau brought up the other section of Battery B and the four guns were rapidly worked, although only one section could be placed even in sight of the smoke of the enemy's guns, the left section being masked by woods so dense that there was great difficulty in bringing the two sections into battery. "They were in a very dangerous position," says the author of "Cayuga in the War," "being under an unremitting fire of cannon and sharp-shooters. Obscured by smoke and shrubbery, however, their exact position was as difficult to make out as that of the rebel battery on the hill. Here seven men of the two sections were wounded. Lieutenant Crocker's eye was shot out, but he drapped a handkerchief around his head and fought his guns for an hour after the hurt. Captain Mercereau said of him in his report: 'I never saw any one display more cool judgment and bravery than he during the whole engagement.'"

THE BATTLE WELL ON.

Progress of the Second Brigade from Bolan's Church to the Enemy's Works.

The Thirty-fifth United States, coming up in rear of the First Brigade, was ordered to charge up the road. Forming in line obliquely, with their right resting across the road and their left overlapping in front of the One Hundred and Twenty-seventh New York, they opened fire and attempted to advance; but the fire they encountered was so hot that they fell back to the rear of the artillery, where they lay down in line and remained during the rest of the afternoon. In the advance Colonel Beecher was twice wounded, but refused to go to the rear. It was now somewhat past noon.

The whole of the First Brigade, except the Naval Brigade (held in reserve on the main road), had already become engaged. It was probably of this time in the action that General Smith writes in his report as follows: "In an hour the enemy had so extended and developed their attack that it became absolutely necessary for me to place in my front line my last troops, the Forty-seventh Georgia. From time to time alterations had to be made in our lines by changing the positions of regiments and companies, extending intervals, etc., to prevent being flanked." The gallant Thirty-second Georgia," says "Jones' Siege of Savannah," "acting as a moveable reserve, always appeared at the most opportune time." The noise of the battle at this time was terrific—the artillery crashing away in the centre, while volley after volley of musketry ran down both lines and were reverberated from the surrounding forests.

ADVANCE OF THE SECOND BRIGADE.

At the time the first skirmish occurred the Second Brigade was halted near Bolan's Church. As the First Brigade advanced the Second followed marching by the flank in the road and leaving at the church, as a guard, two companies of the Fifty-fourth Massachusetts. With this slender brigade, of which only eight companies of the Fifty-fifth Massachusetts and two companies of the Fifty-fourth Massachusetts were now left, Colonel Hartwell deployed in line in the first cotton-field on the left of the road, then passed the swamp by the flank and crossed the second field (in which the grass was still burning fiercely) in column by company. Halting on the edge of the woods at the further end of the field the brigade rested for half an hour. There was nothing in sight except a battery of artillery in the road at the left. The sound of skirmishing had ceased and the fields and woods wore a Sabbath quiet, when suddenly and violently firing by volley began at the front and the artillery opened again.

ORDERS FROM POTTER AND HATCH.

The brigade was put in motion and was struggling in column by company through the dense woods, when orders came to Colonel Hartwell to double-quick to the front. Moving by flank to the road, which was so narrow and so thronged with cannon and caissons that the brigade had to thread its way along the roadside and was strung out almost in single file, the brigade passed General Potter, who ordered Colonel Hartwell to support the One Hundred and Twenty-seventh New York—and afterwards General Hatch, who directed him to support the Thirty-fifth United States, but not to go into action, if possible to avoid it, without further orders, which would be sent to him by an aid.

MOVEMENTS OF THE SECOND BRIGADE.

When the head of the column reached the cross roads Lieutenant Crocker's section of artillery was firing rapidly in the road, and the Thirty-fifth United States was in line obliquely across the road beyond, firing at will, and wavering excitedly forward and back. The fire at this point was very hot. It was within close range of the enemy's guns, and as the trees near the road were somewhat thinned out it was more exposed than other points in the line to their infantry fire. Colonel Hartwell directed the leading companies to file to the right down the cross road, from which the Twenty-fifth Ohio had just advanced, further to the right. His intention was to form the brigade in line to support the Thirty-fifth United States. Before the Fifty-fifth Massachusetts could be closed up and formed the Thirty-fifth had fallen to the rear, and there was nothing to support. Colonel Gurney of the One Hundred and Twenty-seventh New York, informed Colonel Hartwell that the left was hard pressed (which appears, by the way, to have been a mistake). The two companies of the Fifty-fourth Massachusetts were sent to the left and front of the One Hundred and Twenty-seventh. By the time the Fifty-fifth Massachusetts was in line, under a hot fire, it became a grave question what should be done.

ATTEMPTS TO CHARGE.

Colonel Gurney, in his report, says that "Lieutenant Colonel Woodford had reported to General Potter that he would charge the front of the work if a simultaneous charge could be made on the road to his right. The Fifty-fifth Massachusetts immediately came up and charged. Colonel Gourand, of Hatch's staff, brought the order for the charge." Colonel Hartwell gave the order to advance in line of battle, but the difficulties of the ground, the swamp and thickets, which had already broken the ranks of the Thirty-second United States, colored troops, and the Thirty-fifth United States, colored troops, allowed the regiment to go forward only two or three rods. The three right companies in this advance got astray in the woods. Forming the other five companies, as well as possible, in column by company on the road, Colonel Hartwell again led them to the front, until the enemy's guns met them at the turn of the road with such a fire of canister that they again fell back.

FORWARD UNDER HOT FIRE.

How Colonel Hartwell Led His Men Where Shot and Shell Flew Fast.

With the assistance of Colonel Gourand their gallant commander rallied his men, formed them again in column and led them in a third attempt to charge. This time they fairly turned the corner in the road and crossed the brook, where a rude bridge had been torn up by the Confederates and its planks staked down as an abattis. The shallow stream here spread up and down the road thirty or forty feet, and as the little band of less than three hundred men, stumbled through sand and water, the five guns of the fort were trained on them with spherical case and canister at one hundred and twenty yards range, and all the infantry of the centre and flanks poured in a destructive fire, across the comparatively open ground in front of the works, upon the narrow gorge in the woods through which the road emerged.

DEADLY WORK OF SHELL.

Colonel Hartwell had been wounded in the hand in the first

212

advance. As he turned the corner his horse was killed and fell on him in the road. Captain Crane, acting as aide, while shouting, "Come on boys, they are only Georgia militia!" was killed, with his horse, by a charge of canister. Lieutenant Hill, of Hartwell's staff, was knocked from his horse by the explosion of a shell. Lieutenant Boynton, commanding the leading company, was shot in the leg, fell in the water, gained his feet and pressed forward, only to be killed by a canister as he reached the bridge. Color Sergeant King was killed by the explosion of a shell. Sergeant Mitchell and Sergeant Shorter (the latter had been commissioned, but not yet mustered in as a lieutenant) were severely and Sergeant Major Trotter was slightly wounded.

THE GROUND STREWN WITH DEAD.

In an account of a visit to the field next day, the Savannah *Republican* thus describes the carnage at this point: "We found the road literally strewn with their dead. Some eight or ten bodies were floating in the water, where the road crosses, and in a ditch at the roadside, just beyond, we saw six negroes piled up one on top of the other. The artillery was served with great accuracy, and we doubt if any battle-field of the war presents such havoc among the trees and shrubbery." "The road," says Colonel Hartwell in his report, "seemed to be swept of everything." No troops in the world could have stood such a fire under such circumstances.

RESCUE OF COLONEL HARTWELL.

The repulse was instant and final. The five companies had lost over a hundred men killed and wounded in less than five minutes. The survivors fell back, but rallied in the rear of the artillery. Colonel Hartwell would have been left to fall into the hands of the enemy but for the bravery of Lieutenant Ellsworth, who turned back, under that terrific fire, and while one of the men, who was killed the next moment, partly lifted the horse and thus released him, the Lieutenant dragged Colonel Hartwell across the ditch into the woods and then to the rear. In thus going from the field Hartwell was hit three times by spent balls, but Ellsworth escaped unharmed. When the Fifty-fifth were repulsed the Confederates flocked out of their works with loud yells of triumph

213

and trooped down toward the brook, but were quickly driven back by the fire of the regiments on our left.

OTHER COMMANDS IN THE FIGHT.

What General Sherman Thought That General Hatch Should Have Done.

While the Fifty-fifth was thus engaged Lieutenant Colonel Woodford led the One Hundred and Twenty-seventh New York on the left of the road, in line across the swamp, nearly at right angles with the advance of the Fifty-fifth. They advanced to within a hundred yards of the Confederate works and remained ten minutes there in a boggy marsh, with water ten or fifteen inches deep, when they were withdrawn to the front and flank of the artillery, and there lay down and remained during the rest of the afternoon. There is no record of any movements by the Fifty-sixth and One Hundred and Fifty-seventh New York on our left flank, but, as their loss was light, it is probable that they simply held their ground during the afternoon, without attempting to advance and without receiving any attacks from the enemy.

A QUESTION ASKED BY SHERMAN.

Lieutenant Colonel Hooper, with the two companies of the Fifty-fourth Massachusetts which had come to the front with Colonel Hartwell, lay all the afternoon to the left and front of the One Hundred and Twenty-seventh New York, his men lying down and reserving their fire. It was his belief from what he saw in his advanced position that the Confederate right could be easily flanked and he sent a written message to that effect to General Hatch, which, however, had no effect. He writes that General Sherman, riding over the field afterwards with General Hatch, said in his blunt way: "Hatch, why in .... didn't you flank them on their right?"

CAPTAIN POPE'S COMPANIES.

Captain Pope, who had come up from the cross roads with his four companies of the Fifty-fourth, hearing no further firing at the front, had halted at the church for dinner, when (just after noon) the sudden burst of firing occurred which indicated that

214

our advance had struck the Confederate works. He double-quicked his command at once to the front and on passing General Hatch was joined by Colonel Bennett, of Hatch's staff, who led the way to the cross roads, where he ordered Captain Pope to charge. This was after the repulse of the Thirty-fifth and Fifty-fifth and was an insane order. Captain Pope's men had been separated in coming up by the artillery which still filled the narrow road, and when he received the order to charge he had only one officer and eight men with him. Taking the only view of the situation possible for a sensible man, he led his men back of the artillery and formed them, as they came up, into line. These companies, with the two others which had been first left at the church and had advanced to the front before Pope came up, formed to the right of the Thirty-fifth, behind the guns, and there lay until dusk.

THE GREAT DISPROPORTION IN LOSSES.

The Confederate Loss Trifling and That of the Union Troops Heavy.[2]

BY CHARLES C. SOULE

Formerly Captain in the Fifty-fifth Mass. Vols.

The three right companies of the Fifty-fifth Massachusetts, advancing with the regiment in line from the branch road, did not hear the order to form column by company and continued on through the woods and swamp, continually diverging from the rest of the regiment, which had turned to the left of the main road. No enemy was in sight, but the air was full of bullets and of the noise of firing to the right and left. Without orders the men opened fire, and, as their formation was much broken by the underbrush, the fire of those in the rear was so dangerous to their comrades in front that Colonel Fox ordered the bugler to cease firing. The right company passed over the One Hundred and Forty-fourth New York, which was lying down in line of battle, and

2. *Philadelphia Weekly Times*, May 17, 1884.

on reaching the stream, at a considerable distance from the main road, the Twenty-fifth Ohio was found standing in line and firing excitedly at an unseen enemy—unseen, but not unfelt, however, as a storm of bullets from our left swept away the tops of the grasses and shrubs. Here the companies of the Fifty-fifth lay down without firing. It was an anxious and perplexing time, for they had entirely lost their bearings and in the thick of woods could not tell if the firing on their left came from friend or foe.

THE FIFTY-FIFTH DURING THE AFTERNOON.

A reconnoissance of the front developed no enemy, but there was no general officer nor aide present to give orders for an advance, and after remaining by the stream for nearly an hour the whole line—now including the battalion of marines and the Thirty-second United States, colored troops, to the right of the Twenty-fifth Ohio—fell back to the branch road and took position behind the old dam, where the Confederates had made a stand earlier in the day. Here they lay all the rest of the afternoon. Occasionally the enemy would creep down through the woods and open fire, to which our forces would vigorously respond. But our ammunition was so nearly exhausted and the supples which were sent up from the rear were so scant that our men were directed to reserve their fire except when thus attacked. The left of this flank, near the corner where the artillery was posted, was much exposed, being in the line of fire down the road from the Confederate works. Here the Fifty-fourth and Fifty-fifth Massachusetts lay, losing many men and officers during the afternoon.

HOW THE ARTILLERY FARED.

By 2 P.M. Battery B of the Third New York Artillery, having been in action since 9 o'clock, was completely exhausted. One of the guns had recoiled into the ditch and the gunners had not energy enough to extricate it. The other three guns were overheated and the ammunition was nearly exhausted. Only one of the guns was firing at intervals. Battery F was therefore ordered to replace Battery B. Coming up over the rough corduroy road at a reckless pace, the infantry and stragglers springing aside to right and left to let it pass, it went into battery at the cross road. Just as they arrived a shell from the enemy exploded the two ammunition chests of a limber of Battery B, severely scorching

216

Lieutenant Breck. Lieutenant Titus had the guns of this battery taken to the rear by their prolonges, the soldiers lending a hand at the ropes. Two of Titus' pieces were then run up and opened fire, receiving a furious reply. The first gun discharged drew such a fire that nearly every man serving it was wounded. At 4 P.M. this section, its ammunition being exhausted, was withdrawn and its place taken by two howitzers of the Naval Brigade under Lieutenant Commander Matthews.

BRINGING OFF GUNS OF BATTERY B.

The One Hundred and Second United States, colored troops, being landed at 11 A.M., hurrried at once to the front, arriving at 1 P.M. As General Hatch had been informed by deserters that the enemy were being reinforced from the railroad the One Hundred and Second was held in reserve—two of its companies as well as two companies of the One Hundred Twenty-seventh New York being formed across the road to check straggling. At about four o'clock, two companies of the One Hundred and Second were engaged in a gallant attempt to draw off the guns of Battery B from their exposed position. As the first company detailed for this work approached the guns they were met by such a fire that Captain Lindsay was killed and Lieutenant Alvord severely wounded. Sergeant Madry, who was left in command, had not been informed of the object of the movement, and filing his men into the woods faced them toward the enemy. "Lieutenant Bennet, with a detail of thirty men, then brought off the guns in the coolest and most gallant manner," (Hatch's report).

SAILORS ON THEIR KNEES.

The Naval Brigade had little chance to distinguish itself, being held in reserve on the main road. The marines, under Lieutenant Stoddard, were sent through the woods to the right flank, where they formed on the right of the Twenty-fifth Ohio. They also, as well as the Fifty-fifth Massachusetts, send forward a reconnoitering party, without finding any enemy in their front, but were obliged to fall back to the cross road with the rest of the line at 3:30 P.M. and lay there until they were withdrawn at dusk. When the guns of Lieutenant Titus' Battery were withdrawn at 4 P.M., two of the navy howitzers were sent forward to take their place and were worked with great dexterity by the sailors, who lay down in the road under and around the guns while loading them, retreated to the ditch at the roadside when they fired, and after the volley of cannon and musketry which each discharge drew from the enemy sprang again to their guns, thus escaping in a great measure the losses to which the artillerymen of the Third New York had been subjected in the same position. An eye-witness says that it was laughable, even under that heavy fire, to see the zeal with which the sailors served their guns and especially to see the tracks they made with their knees in the sand as they crowded about the howitzers.

CONDITION OF THE ENEMY.

On the Confederate side, although they had been very fortunate during the day, General Smith confesses that he awaited with some anxiety in the early afternoon the arrival of expected reinforcements. At 4½ P.M. Brigadier General Robertson came up with artillery, cavalry and infantry. At midnight Brigadier General Chestnut appeared with 350 South Carolina reserves and at daylight, or soon after, of December 1 General Baker brought up his brigade of nearly 2,000 men and Lieutenant General Hardee arrived at Grahamville. Had the Confederates advanced late in the afternoon or evening of the 30th they would have taken our forces at great disadvantage. But most of their men were worn out by continuous marching and riding upon the cars and General Smith deemed it unwise to attempt any interference with the withdrawal of our troops.

The charge of the Fifty-fifth was really the culmination of our attack, and when the right swing fell back to the cross roads at 3:30 it became evident that our enterprise had been foiled and that the best thing to do was to get back to the gunboats. General Potter's arrangements for retreat were excellent. One section of Titus' Battery, supported by two regiments of infantry, took post half a mile back. Two regiments of infantry were then withdrawn from the flanks of the front line and posted a mile further to the rear. At dusk the retreat commenced. The Naval Brigade was ordered to occupy the cross roads. The One Hundred and Twenty-seventh New York and One Hundred and Second United States, with one section of the Naval Battery, remained at the front, keeping up a slow artillery fire until 7:30 P.M. Meanwhile the wounded were all taken to the rear. The ambulances, which

218

had just come up at dark from the landing, were entirely insufficient for this purpose, so that the Fifty-fourth and Fifty-fifth Massachusetts were broken up into squads to carry the wounded back on stretchers extemporized from muskets and blankets.

IN GOOD ORDER.

At 7:30 P.M., the main body being well on the march, the One Hundred and Twenty-seventh New York and the One Hundred and Second United States with the navy howitzers, were withdrawn and covered by the Fifty-sixth and One Hundred and Forty-fourth New York, which in turn were covered by the Twenty-fifth Ohio and One Hundred and Fifty-seventh New York. The movement was thus effected without confusion, alarm, pursuit or loss. Not a wounded man was left on the field except those who fell directly under the fire of the enemy's works and no stores or equipments fell into the enemy's hands except the blankets and knapsacks which had been thrown aside by our men in their advance through the tangled woods.

The last glimpse our forces had of the scene of the battle was at Bolan's Church, on the way to the rendezvous at Boyd's Landing. On our advance in the morning the little white church, nestled among the moss-hung oaks, presented a beautiful and characteristic Southern picture. As we returned in the evening it wore a very different aspect. Huge fires of rails and brushwood threw a lurid light over the church and the forest behind it. The pews which had been torn out to transform it into a hospital and the stores which had been piled here as a depot were strewn around in wild disorder. Beside the church the surgeons had established their operating tables, and the unconcealed traces of amputations were shocking to behold.

THE LOSSES ON BOTH SIDES.

Our loss was reported as being:

Killed 88
Wounded 623
   (140 so slightly as not to be in hospital)
Missing 43
   (Of whom 13 wounded and 5 unwounded are known
   to have fallen into the enemy's hands.)   ——
Total 754

The Confederate loss was reported at 4 killed and 40 wounded. This disparity is due to the fact that the Confederate forces fought on the defensive, behind breastworks and concealed from us in an unknown position in the woods, while we advanced across their front, over ground which they knew thoroughly. The number of the "slightly wounded" is due to the thick woods, which deflected and partially checked the force of the enemy's fire and increased proportionately the casualties from "spent balls."

THE LOSS BY REGIMENTS.

The loss by regiments was as follows:

	Killed	W'nd'd	Missing	Total
1st Brigade—25th Ohio	20	118	....	138
56th N.Y.	6	14	....	20
127th N.Y.	5	41	....	46
144th N.Y.	17	50	....	67
157th N.Y.	....	30	....	30
32d U.S.C.T.	8	56	....	64
35th U.S.C.T.	7	107	....	114
2d Brigade—54th Mass.	2	37	4	43
55th Mass.	29	108	....	137
102d U.S.C.T.	3	20	....	23
Artillery	2	12	....	14
Cavalry	....	1	....	1
Naval Brigade	1	11	....	12
(At cross roads?) 34th U.S. C.T.	....	5	....	5
Total*	100	610	4	714

GALLANTRY OF THE UNION TROOPS.

To criticize any operation of the war is an ungracious task, but this paper will not be complete without some comment on the conduct of the expedition. To the behavior of the troops engaged only praise can be accorded. Even the few regiments which ap-

* The discrepancy in the totals is due to the fact that this detailed statement is from the New York *Herald* account of the fight, not probably as accurate as General Foster's report, from which the first figures are taken.. Phisterer's Statistical Record puts the Union loss as: Killed 66; wounded 645; total, 711.

pear to have shown momentary disorder remained in line on the field and underfire until ordered to retreat. "The list of killed and wounded," says Hatch in his report, "none of whom fell in retreat, attests good conduct. The affair was a repulse, owing entirely to the strong position held by the enemy and our want of ammunition." "I can not close this report," writes General Potter, "without making honorable mention of the good conduct and steadiness displayed by the officers and men under the most trying circumstances. Exposed to a heavy fire from a concealed enemy, who was strongly entrenched, and laboring under every disadvantage of ground, they maintained their position with the greatest tenacity and endurance. Nothing but the formidable character of the obstacles they encountered prevented them from achieving success." The Savannah *Republican* concedes that the troops in the centre of our line "fought with a desperate earnestness."

DEFECTIVE GENERALSHIP.

But the generalship displayed in the fight was not equal to the soldierly qualities of the troops engaged. There appears to have been a lack of foresight in the preparations. It is strange that only one pilot could be provided for an expedition upon a navigable river, of which our forces had been in full possession for two years. A few reconnoitering expeditions up the river might have familiarized the navy with the soundings and averted the dangers and delays of a fog. And it is more than strange that no better guides could be found in the South Carolina negro regiments, or among the freedmen who had flocked from the mainland to Hilton Head, than those which misled our advance for a whole day and gave the enemy the time they so much needed to assemble their forces. Again, a little reconnoitering up various roads by the first troops landed on the morning of November 29 would have corrected the errors of guides and maps.

BAD MANAGEMENT BY THE FEDERALS.

During the action there seems to have been very bad management—the delay in starting on the morning of the 30th; the irresolution which allowed one piece of artillery and one company of cavalry to hold in check a whole brigade for three hours; the inaction which left a line of battle without orders and made no systematic attempt at reconnoitering and turning the enemy's

221

flanks, which rested without support or defense in open pine woods; the bad judgment which ordered single regiments to charge successively by a narrow road upon a strongly fortified position, defended by artillery and infantry—these faults cannot be overlooked nor passed by without serious censure. General Potter showed on other occasions such excellent judgment and good generalship that the blame must rest upon his superior officer General Hatch, who was present at the front and directed operations during the day. To quote General Jacob D. Cox's criticism of the Honey Hill fight (from his "March to the Sea"): "It was a fresh instance of the manner in which irresolute leadership in war wastes the lives of men by alternating between an ill-timed caution and an equally ill-timed rashness."

GOOD MANAGEMENT OF THE ENEMY.

It is only fair to say that the Confederate management seems to have been excellent from first to last. The energy which brought a force from Western Georgia to the coast of South Carolina so opportunely that it got into position only ten minutes before the action opened; the audacity and adroitness which checked the advance of a brigade for several hours with one gun and a few dismounted cavalry and the soldierly ability with which artillery and infantry were so handled as to inflict a loss of 750 men while losing only 50 all deserves the highest praise. On their side it was all good generalship and good luck; on ours it was the reverse.

Boston, Mass. (37 Court street).

Appendix Two

John R. Bowles became Chaplain of the 55th Massachusetts on March 27, 1864. The black clergyman had been born in Lynchburg, Virginia, in 1826. His duties required that he submit to the War Department periodic reports on the history and moral condition of the regiment, five of which are on file in the National Archives. In addition, Bowles wrote several letters to the Anglo-African.

Folly Island, S.C., June 21, 1864[1]

Mr. Editor:

Permit me through the columns of THE ANGLO to relate, for the satisfaction of your numerous readers, the incidents connected with the execution of Wallace Baker, private of Co. I, 55th Regiment Massachusetts Volunteers.

Early on the morning of the 18th inst., while yet in bed, I heard a gentle rapping at my tent door. Unusually early for visitors or business I thought. On opening the door our Adjutant presented me a paper—a summons from the Provost-Marshal of the post, which I read with mingled feelings of sorrow and regret. It summoned me to appear at his quarters forthwith to administer whatever of spiritual aid and comfort I could, to Private Wallace Baker of Co. I, 55th Mass. Vols., who was about to suffer the extreme penalty of the law. I dressed myself and hastened to the place of his confinement.

The sergeant of the guard having received instructions to admit me, I gained access to him without delay or hesitation.

Baker was sitting on the side of his bunk in his shirt sleeves with quiet indifference.

His quiet indifference led me to think, surely the man is not yet apprised of his approaching execution. So I asked him if he knew what was determined in his case. He said, "Yes. They came in here this morning about 3 o'clock, and told me they were going to take me out at 10 and shoot me. That's a hell of a way to

1. *Weekly Anglo-African,* July 9, 1864. Houghton Library, Harvard University.

do a man—take him out and shoot him without giving him a chance! They have given me no chance. I have done nothing to be shot for. Well, let them shoot—." Here I stopped him, and with various arguments and exhortations tried to fix his mind upon the solemn fact that he would soon stand in the presence of his God, and that he must try and be prepared for it by repentance, prayer, and trust in God, so as to meet him in peace. He sullenly replied, "They have given me no chance." I tried to prevail on him to pray, but his heart was full of wrath and bitterness at the injustice he supposed they were doing him, and his mouth full of cursing. I could make no impression on his mind in favor of religion or a preparation for death.

Finally he consented that I might pray for him. I urged him to pray for himself. We knelt down together, I prayed that God might soften his heart—help him forgive all again whom he entertained a bitterness—but it was to but little purpose. I do not think he prayed or even seemed moved. After a little more talk I left him, hoping when alone he might reflect.

After breakfast I returned to the place of his confinement and found him in about the same state of mind. During the two interviews with him I learned from him that he had no learning whatever—no religious training—raised in Kentucky—had a mother there—his father was dead. He requested that one of his comrades, G.R., should write to her and let her know what had become of him; and to collect his money and send it to her.

I rode in the ambulance with him to the place of execution. Tried several times to call his mind to the subject of prayer, but to no avail.

He showed no sign of a fear of death. When not angry and speaking ugly things, he was eagerly looking at the procession, and seemed to relieve his mind by queer remarks to some of his acquaintances.

Once the procession stopped, and seeing an acquaintance (white) among the guard, he took out his tobacco and gave it to me, saying, "Give this to that man I shall want no more of it."

To one of our hospital attendants who met us, he said, "Good-bye, Doctor, I shant want any more of your medicine." to another he said, "Good-bye, sir, here I go with my wooden jacket with me." On arriving in sight of the ground of execution, and

224

seeing all the troops on the island assembled, he said, "They make a heap of ado to kill one man. If it was Jeff. Davis they could do no more." Such was his manner to the last. Once when the ambulance halted for some time, he said, "I wish they would make haste and do what they are going to do." Said he, "I came out here to fight the rebels and I would not mind being killed in battle, but I don't want to be murdered by my own side." I stayed with him till the bandage was tied over his eyes, his hands tied behind him, and as I walked off the last word that fell on my ear was an oath. He said he had "done nothing worthy of death, and they might shoot and be d--d! God would make it all right."

He fell pierced with five balls. Two in the head, one in his breast, one in his abdomen, and one in the arm, and died without a struggle. His crime was striking an officer.

John R. Bowles, Chaplain

———————◆•◆◆———————

Camp of the 55th Mass. Vol. I.
Folly Island, S.C., June 30, 1864[2]

To the Adjutant General of the United States Army:

Sir,

According to the orders of the War Department requiring Chaplains to forward to you a report each month of their labors and the moral condition of the regiments with which they are connected, therefore, I beg leave to submit the following report:

I received my appointment last Feb. and joined the Regiment —the 27 of March—which was then in Florida. The principle position being at Palatka. While in Fla. we held divine service each Sabbath, besides two or three times of evenings, through the weeks. From Florida we were ordered here. On this island our meetings have not been quite so regular or frequent for want of a place to assemble in. I have also distributed religious papers, books, tracts & testaments obtained of the "Christian Commission" for distribution among the men.

2. Chaplain Reports to Brig. Gen. Lorenzo Thomas. National Archives.

Perhaps the men will compare favorably in a moral sense with other Regiments. Profanity is very prevalent, so is card playing for amusement, very common. The Sabbath is somewhat respected, and most of the men like to go to meeting. The Regiment has been out over a year and never have received any pay, and it causes a very great deal of suffering among the men's families and dissatisfaction among the men in consequence.

We have several times appeared to be on the brink of mutiny for want of pay, but I have labored incessantly to prevent so dreadful a calamity. And I believe so far God has blessed my labor.

Sir: I have the honor to be your obedient servant,

John R. Bowles, Chaplain, 55th Mass Vol. I.

———————— ‹•›‹• ————————

Head Quarters 55th Regt. Mass. Vol. Inf.
Folly Island, S.C., Aug. 1st, 1864[3]

Maj. Gen. L. Thomas,

Sir:

I have the honor as chaplain to submit to you the following monthly Report for July, 1864.

Divine Service for the month of July has unavoidably been neglected in part, for the following reasons: Our Regiment, in company with others, joined in an expedition on James Island, commencing July 2d, lasting 9 days, including two full Sabbaths of the month, and it was not possible to hold services; and until yesterday, the 31st, my health prevented me from conducting service. (I am now so far recovered as to feel no injury from my last Sunday labors.) In connection with my public labors, I distribute books, papers, tracts among the men. I can obtain them from the agents of the Christian Commission. The moral character of the regiment is tolerably good, yet far from what I desire it to be. And yet in the short space of one month I can see no

3. *Ibid.*

real perceptible change either for the better or worse.

In the engagement on James Island our regiment took two brass field pieces from the enemy, and in so doing, we lost in killed 9, wounded 48, three of whom have since died of their wounds. Our men are in good health, this notwithstanding they have been in the field 14 months without pay, yet they respond to every call to duty.

We are expecting to receive pay soon, however, and then I think the regiment will be in still better condition.

I am sir, with much respect,
Your obedient servt.
John R. Bowles
Chaplain, 55th Mass. V.I.

<hr />

Head Quarters 55th Mass. Vol. Inf.
Folly Island, S.C. Sept. 1st, 1864[4]

Gen. L. Thomas, sir:

I have the honor as chaplain of the 55th Mass. Vols. to present to you according to formal orders from the War Department the following report of my labors for the month of August 1864.

I have in the discharge of my duties been permitted through a kind and wise providence to hold public service each Sabbath during the month; and, as a result, our meetings are better attended than heretofore. Men and officers under favorable circumstances love to attend Divine services.

I have been very well supplied with religious papers, books & tracts from the Christian Commission Society, which I have faithfully distributed among the men. And, as there are some who cannot read and write, we have opened an evening school in the chapel for the benefit of those who may work to improve in their education.

The charge of the mail is also assigned to me by our commanding officers.

The condition of the Regiment morally is, I think, improving. And the health of the Regiment is better than it was at the time

4. *Ibid.*

of my last report.

Only [NUMBER OBSCURED BY INK BLOT][5] have died in camp during the past month. (I believe some have died of wounds in the battle of the previous month who were sent to [the] general hospital [in] Beaufort.)

Under the impression that they are soon to be paid off for the first time during the fifteen months hard service, our men are in good heart and fine spirits, and attend to the performance of duty cheerfully.

> I am, sir, your obedient servant,
> John R. Bowles
> Chaplain, 55th Mass Vols.
> Folly Island, S.Car.

———————— ◆◦◆ ————————

> Head Quarters 55th Mass. Vols.
> Folly Island, S.C. Oct. 1st 1864[6]

General:

I have the honor of transmitting to you through the regular military channels as required by General Order 158, War Department, for the month of September 1864 the following report: I have been permitted to pursue though the past months my regular duties as Chaplain of the 55th Regiment without interruption from any source, [duties] which included, holding religious service each Sabbath at 4 o'clock P.M., visiting sick in hospitals, attending funerals of the deceased, and distributing books, tracts and papers among the soldiers. Besides these regular duties I have charge of the mail, also of an evening school (assisted by others) for the benefit of those who desire to learn to read and write &c.

During the last month there has been a slight increase over the previous month of the attendance both of enlisted men and officers at divine worship. The moral condition of the Regiment

5. A search of the regimental roster shows only one member of the regiment to have died during the month of August, 1864: Moses Lee, a farmer from Palmyra, Missouri, the victim of typhoid fever.
6. *Ibid.*

is undoubtedly improving. Cursing, which was almost universal, is now heard less frequent[ly]. Card playing, and other amusements, are decreasing as the men find better and more useful ways of spending their leisure moments. Cases of gross immorality are not very frequent, owing to the strict enforcement of good discipline, and the absence of temptation. The health of the regiment is better than during the same month of last year.

Our men are in fine spirits and jubilant over the news of the recent victories of the Union Army over the rebels, and also the prospect of soon receiving their pay so long withheld. (One company has received pay in full from date of enlistment up to last muster.)

All of which I respectfully submit,

J.R. Bowles, Chaplain, 55th Mass. Vols.

----- •●• -----

Head Quarters 55th Mass. Vols.
Boyd's Point, S.C. [December 1, 1864][7]

General:

I have the honor of transmitting to you through the regular channel, a monthly report for the month of November, as required of me by General Order from the War Department No. 158.

The moral condition of the regiment, so far as I am able to judge, is not much different from what is set forth in my last report. The men are in good spirits and cheerful, even under the hardships incident to soldier life, in the active field of service, and nobly determined to battle for Liberty & Union, to the bitter end.

We were encamped on Folly Island up to the 27th ult., doing garrison and picket duty in front of Charleston. On the 27th eight companies of the Regiment left for Hilton Head to join an expedition up Broad River commanded by Brigadier General J. Hatch.

We landed on the evening of the 29th at Boyd's Point and camped for the night. At daylight of the 30th we took up our line

7. *Ibid.*

of march inland; meeting with slight opposition until we marched about five miles, when the enemy made a stand and a severe conflict ensued.

The Union forces were successful and drove the enemy to their earthworks, which were several times charged on by our forces without carrying them. Night closed the deadly strife. Our forces then withdrew to a suitable place and threw up entrenchments for better protection. The 55th lost in the engagement two officers killed and six wounded. Enlisted men twenty-seven killed and about one hundred and seventeen wounded.

The regiment is at present under command of Maj. William Nutt; Col. A.S. Hartwell, being wounded in the engagement of the 30th ult, Lieut. Col. C.B. Fox acting post commander of Boyd's Point. Company H is doing garrison duty at Fort Delafield, Folly Island; Co. G doing garrison duty on Long Island.

All of which I respectfully submit,

Your obedient servant
      John R. Bowles
      Chaplain 55th Mass. Vols.

Chillicothe, Ohio, August 16, 1865[8]

Dear Anglo:

There are some reformers, and persons of much intelligence, who are prone to be despondent, and always look upon the dark side of the picture of human liberty; but for my part, when I look back and review the past over which we have been travelling for a few years, I find it a source of pleasure to recount the brilliant victories we have gained, although there is much yet to hope and labor for.

Oh! how many loyal hearts in sable skins sank in sorrow and quaked with fear when the dark storm cloud of secession and rebellion was sweeping over the land, and the strong arm of

8. *Weekly Anglo-African*, September 5, 1865. Houghton Library, Harvard University.

government seemed impotent to resist its fury, or in the least, to check its sway; yet through the blessing of God and the aid of the colored men, this mighty rebellion is crushed—the storm is calmed, and the troubled and turbid waters of state begin to assume again a quiet appearance. As the throes of an earthquake elevate the valleys, and the eruption of a volcano raised the submarine islands to the surface, so this mighty upturning and upheaving of the nation has brought to light the latent capabilities of the colored men, and raised them to the level of other men in the nation. As the slaveholder has displayed his treason and hatred of liberty, the colored man has shown his loyalty and love of liberty. As the former has lavishly displayed his barbarism in acts of untold cruelty, the latter has exhibited all the gentler feelings of humanity in deeds of love and kindness: so that some white men begin to think that a loyal black man is almost as good as a white traitor in armed rebellion against the Government, and that the colored man who has periled his life for the nation and comes off with the loss of an arm, a leg, or an eye is nearly as clever as he who stayed at home berating the government, and blathering treason without shame on the streets; or, in other words, that a decent negro is nearly as good as a drunken Irishman.

I am very glad to know that, after long waiting and faithful service, with commissions of promotion in their hands, that J.M. Trotter, W.H. Dupree, and [J.H.] Shorter of the 55th Mass Regt, have at last been permitted to wear straps on their shoulders and cords down the seam of their pants—three as worthy men as ever carried a gun. Of Jas. M. Trotter, after a close examination by Gen. [John G.] Foster and staff on branches of education, bravery, and military tactics, said the General, "I find no fault in the man," yet failed to muster him as Lieutenant; but by special order of the War Department, he is now mustered. The ball does move.

J.R. Bowles
late Chaplain, 55th Massachusetts

Appendix Three

The issues facing military units in the period immediately following the end of hostilities included the question of black officers. How difficult that issue was, even for someone who was as personally committed to having it happen as was Alfred S. Hartwell, can be seen in this letter written during the first months of Reconstruction.

Head Quarters, 1st Prov'l Brig.
  Orangeburg, S.C.
      July 1, 1865[1]

Governor [Andrew].

I have the honor to recommend that 1st Lieutenant Robertson James be promoted to be Capt. vice [Thomas F.] Ellsworth discharged, June 19, 1865.

I would also state that there is a vacancy of the 2nd Asst. Surgeon and that in a few days I think there will be a vacancy of the surgeon, as Dr. Brown has gone to Charleston expecting to muster out.

Captains [William H.] Torrey and [Josiah C.] Hall have tendered their resignations & the vacancies arising therefrom I hope some suitable men will be ready to come at once.

I hear with much repute that Lt. Col. [Charles B.] Fox is about to resign. Your Excellency is aware of the great service rendered by Col. Fox, who has faithfully and unceasingly labored through good report and through evil report for the good of the Reg't and the service. His loss is irredeemable. I propose to await the resignation of officers who have declaimed against this action of Gov't and then if I find their influence not for the best and that the policy of having colored officers is not to be adopted by Gov't I shall recommend them to resign for their own good and the good of the Regt. I find that the best men are not willing to serve as officers under them, and that many of those who urge their promotion do so from low motives of self advancement and to gain popularity. In this transition from war to peace, & in this, the

1. Alfred S. Hartwell Papers. Massachusetts State Library.

heart of Secessia, I find that strict discipline is required for officers & men, to prevent gross outrages upon the people, white and black.

I desire personally to leave the Regt and after resting a while either to obtain a position again in the Army or to go to work at the law books de novo; but I propose if my health allows to wait until the 55th is thoroughly fitted out with officers to whose care I can entrust its interests.

With great respect,

    Your obt servant,
        A.S. Hartwell
    Col. 55th Mass & Brevt. Brig. Gen.

To his Excellency,
    John A. Andrew
        Gov, Commonwealth of Mass.

Appendix Four

July the 11 1863 dear cusin
it with the greats of pleasur i do take my pen in hand to inform that
i am wel at present and i hope when these few linees come to hand
may find you the same we had a hard rain here last night and this
morning we are not going as was reported we were to go too
weeks a go but because of great dis turbance in boston and we
are a going to stay tel by the resisting draft there a white regiment here and they went in once or twice there July 17 and they
have killed 18 or tweny of them they are al irish and have col ad
executions and all so in new york

give Jo sheen one of the coppers let me tel you i am going to
send some money home in a few days and what so evr i write to
do with i wish you will careful do and respectably do i ex pect it
will be in next week by ex press at vin Cin nes 1 of the soldiers
an irish luitenant to day at twelve o'c'ck knocked him down they
put him in guard house take good care the old woman no more at
John Posey Joseph [PAGE TEAR]
rest until i tel you the time i started home you might suppose that
i acted quite presumptious and so do i but for give me but i was
very heavy so heavy that i was like passed home no more at present answer as soon as can john posey to joseph w embry

---

November the 18'63
the my cousin it is with greats of pleasure that i take my pen in
hand to inform you that i am wel at present and seriously hope
these few may find enjoying the same blessing i have ben deeply
interesting in the welfare of my dear kindreds at home and to my
surprise and sorow rather thinking that you all in taring up so
instantly with out terble good luck has created great loses if write
you should write any thing you expect to take place or that you
are a going to do if should not take place or is not done you
should write amediately if the case be certified the next day you
should as soon as the nature of cas would admit so if it were surprise our minds would not be so long flusterated with it i can tel
you that can not write to often for i have wrote several leters and
were sadly disapointed in hopes of geting answers give you to

know that a leter from home is quite con soling to soldiers that cannot get the news of the day as for uncle James i have not received the scratch of a pen though i honored him with two and aunt Sarah wrote three but i never got one of them so i was in formed by luese embry i got one of mary and elen embry i like to get one from home and like get it before i be fore get to boston i had not wrote a leter she did not know precisely where i was the captain said this this morning that Charles newton is now in vaginia was the first of my knowing where he was since he wrote to me from north carolina i herd he was going there but it was dis puted though i suppose it so and i ex pect he is faring bet-er than we are thier several others with him that have got well and they nothing to do but have fun they drill us tel we can not rest some times several of the be hive got sick and had to leave the ranks and some fianted and fel but the old horse never ben faised i was sick which i thought was a bout ras le me down to the foot of the hill i am a bout write now though i have not drilled for 6 weeks take good care of the girls their have been no real move-ments here since wrote last only they have ben great of fortifying and mounting guns morters they that some of them will throw a ball 400 pound in weight the show no great sign of fight 6 colard regiments here the 55 54 first and second South Carolina & 3 Pennsylvania second north carolina is here i have nothing to drik worth speaking of the quarter master gives us a litle when we come from work at night though we have moved camp and now we can [LETTER ENDS HERE]

---

did write and tel me them da gone negroes was maried be fore this time you could have sent a word to as wel as miss thomas did to her brother god bles her dear soul for thinking so much of him i am jest a geting out of umer a bout it for you knowed i wanted to know when that happened if not be fore i supose i must not consider

Mr george Parker

a company keeper of mine any longer but rather consider him my cusin and i ex pect she made her bed as she would by waiting if she young now she is taken out of the family keep that warf rat out the redemer sake nor let Elen keep company if you are doing wel send me some money i lent and spent al that i had and the pay master has not come to pay us of yet but they say he wil be a round in about three months if he comes i will my bil wil be over one hundred dolars and i am a going send it home to vin cenese by ex press and i want you to get it pay strict atention to the office and not let it get lost for if i loos that i had as wel be dead but if posible send me five dolars and i wil the repay by half the amount which is 50 cents interest

we wil now state and inquire of something els we are all doing wel we have a good time and good captain and nothing is our dis tres and as for caring any thing we do not as pesky rebles for we had jest as soon get a many them as not they are stil a bumbarding yet and it not cold here yet we have only had one day or two that a little cold but so much what we could in a camp with out any fire and not be cold the worst times we have is a going on picket and on camp guard the short stay of us here appears to be a very long one but as we have staid so i had rather stay until spring than to go north or east on the acount of the cold wether though we may leave and go north and have to bear it we wanted to go this but we do not want to go now though it is several hundred miles nearer home there is where i ex pect to get my furlow and then you all had been look wild es pesaly if should come

to hear how a bout uncle Elias case and whether he was much woser or not and if you all have not sold it is no use to sel un til you got what your property is worth when you wrote to me and said you was a going a way and i got a leter from lusies embry she stated that they were a going to leave the next wednesday the being wrote on the 1 of September and I never got until the 1 of august in which time i supposed you were gone and i wrote to sims embry and sent a small note in his leter i told if were there to give it to you i am sory that there was every such a mistake you wil get the run of this leter by the number at the top i did not think i would write so much but i suppose maring going on at home and me in south carolina makes a great diference i shall something to write for no more at present

give my love to al the inquiring friends

JOHN POSEY
CO. D 55TH MASS. REGT.
South Corlinia

marse is land near
   Charleston
  JOHN POSEY
CO. D 55TH MASS. REGT.

---

here it is

December the 2 1863

my cusin i take my pen hand to inform you that i am well at present and i these lines may find you enjoying the same blesing you all apear to be dead and whether you be or no i can not tel if you are not dead you are very curless a bout either friends or relation as for writing you do not give a dam whether you all write or not though i might write ever day which i do every two or three days and some times every and to get once a month i can not it looks as though you might once in a while every three or four months and i would get a leter now and then but the you all write it is all or most never i want you to write for i want or will not be home before or under six or seven months i do not want come before the last of august and perhaps by that we will closer home and if not i do not know when i wil be home if hear any more such reports as i have i do not expect i wil come atall one more move like this here to fore taks place and i start and get in ten miles of home and i hear of it i take a little tack and tack right back and catch the old gray goos by the hind then it wil be flip flop old mother hucle backmamy dog baint if i aint gone EO and i wil eat sombodys for if dont i wil not get no indiana wedin cake i see you are all trying to get maried because i have gone war to eat reble and take bleu pills never mind my time is coming and i wil catch some of you a naping but all i ask of you is not to do no more for my time must be next if not i wil stay here a mong the rebles whilst i live and i would not had that to have gone of no way for i would have give five dolar bil to have seen gorge marry if i was to home i would come and have fun i wonder if old charles allen was there if he was i know him and mathias and Joseph Pease had plenty of fun and if had ben you would had fancy fun just got the word yesterday and i thought i perhaps if

i would write today i might get some of the cake for i know
fern has yet some and i want a piece of it has to be five years old
and i dare an other of my cusins to get maried with out i am
there or with out i die or the rebles feeds me to hevy then if
they will go on at such against my orders they will have go but
mathias must not marry until i come home for i intend to have all
of my connections to my wedding and tel me why in the devil if
you got something good to eat all of that good posom coon rabit
black squirls and i heard rooster crow yesterday morning and just
be low here they say there is a plenty good deer and turkey and
dem dar great big fat hogs and dont you know that i will have
good time 25 our boys was down in the woods other day and
50 rebles got after them and they got to an in trenchment and
fired on the rebles and they took wings of the morning in retreat
and they got out of in trenchment and the rebles seeing that
there was not many of them and they come a again the captain
seeing a gun boat which was making it ways to them the captain
run a little distance back give the gun boat sign and she opened
fire on them and [NEXT WORDS OBSCURED BY PAGE
CREASE] retreat for something give my love to all of the friends
dont give the seces an inch but come john howard on them no
more at present john posey to mathias embry write to me soon
a gain to foly island south carolina

    John Posey Co. D
    mass 55th Regiment in care of Captain Nunt which is a
    good father to us

febr uary the 20 1864 dear cusin it is with the greats of pleasur
that i do take my pen in hand to in form you that i am well at
presnt and do hope when these few lines comes to hand may find
you en joying the same blesing we have left Charles newton be
hind a gain we have left the sandy shores of South car lina and
to day finds us in the State of Floridai and we are once more on
the en tire land it is a new and big thing for the privalig of some
where to go has been a fool to us we left foly island on the 12 a
bout noon and landed in Jacksonville Florida on the thirteenth
a bout 5 o'clock in the after noon and i was one of the first thats
on guard and went on post immediately landing

the country here reminds to me more of home than any place els i have seen in the south it is as level as ever i saw the weather is in growing order peach and chery have put forth their bloom there is plenty of hogs and chickens here the boys are a faring wel and hav ing plenty of fun Charles newton was well but a bout the time e left vaginia some of the boys had the smal pocks and said ther was a great dager them having it and he was left and un til the fact was ascertained that thier is no danger we have been on an ex pedition last Saturday and Sunday we ventured a bout 30 miles west on the jacksonville & the gainy ville rail road we got a nest of hornets but did not stay long we went there like old sober men but when we came back we came back like gay and wel trained men when we started we did not get any orders to close up but we never mind we wil get be hind them some of these days the troops are a moving back to ward them a gain and this time we are a going to get them be fore us and then we wil show them how to shoot no more at present write a gain soon to the 55 massachusetts John Posey company D only i can not write any more for i am in a hurry mathias embry You need not write to any certain place only 55 massachusetts in care of Captain William Nut Company D

we have forty miles of the rail road in our possession

---

i want you to know that i have not got any leters you or your mother since the 10 of march more than that i have not had more than 5 leters from the hole family i think it is the hieth of con tempt i wil you one month mor to write and if you do not when i write and let you know things is you wil wel write tel al the friends to write and when you write to my Dear mother tel her i am wel and doing

---

may the 16 1864 Dear cusin

it is with the greats of pleasur that do take pen in hand to inform

240

you that i am wel at present and i hope when these lines comes to hand may find you enjoying the same blessing i lay down last night and laughed prety near al night and got up this morning with a duble stamp resolation and feel as hapy as knighton gale 16 degrees a bove the sky times are good here i expect we wil be paid of in a few days and of corse what litle i get wil be sent home as soon as i get it you must do the best you can i can not be with you al though you are dear to me and sight of you al wil be great to me you must be satisfied for i am al right if i had my choice to day stay here or go home under the present circumstances i give you the honor of a friend i would prefer staying i am beter satisfied now and have ben so evry since i left home than ever i was for three years previously i am in beter health now than i have ben for nearly five years i out of one thing in to an other and i am glad that i am a way from home and in the regiment

i am a soldier for uncle Sam and i will obey and stay with his men as long as it suits me if that is til i am gray i use to long to come home but i foand that was not making the thing gay i cal my self a reble roater and in the confederate country i stay as my girl tender if you please and be sure you do it as wel as i would treat or ought to treat my self remember we are a nation that have ben greatly opresed and our kind President is making slow but a sure efort to open up the way for us and my dear cusin it is a glorious blesing and great many others are engaged in this glorious under taking and al people of our color ought to be hapy and give our noble President al the praise that the tongue could ex press and every other individual that are now engaged in cause You are all supose to be up and a doing not idle and waist time and i am certain you will not waist your money your friends are watching for your apearance of improvement You al must move there is no ex cuse for you what ever the white people said the colored people could not dril now we have we have prove it that we can dril as good as any other nation on the globe now prove to them that you can prove and show the something els we are yet on the foley is land the boys are al wel and doing wel give my love to the friends as soon as you get this and see this report You must give three chers for the fortune that hapened in our regiment our Seargent John F. shorter of ohio is promoted second luitenant huraw hur-

241

aw huraw no more at present John Posey of the 55th masatusets regiment company great big

D

To ma thias em bry

June the 3 1864 dear sir

it is with greats of pleasur that i do take my pen in hand to in form you that i am wel at present and i hope when these lines comes to hand may find you enjoying the same blesing the boys are al wel and and doing wel time are pleasant here the mule stil remains contented i wish to tel you of the fight we had though perhaps you have heard three or five i wrote since but not having a corect report of afairs as we have heard diferent al con fidence to believ it is so that thier was 18 kiled and 30 wounded i hav not time to write to you as wish but wil say of the truth i hav had no leters from or your mother since the 10 of march and as evry body els are a geting leters i think it must be from yor neglict i think i wil have to continue in the field wher i am the most respected no more at present give my love to al the friends and write soon again

John Posey of the 55th massatasets regiment company D S.C. Foley island.

A Note On Sources

Anyone delving into the history of the 55th Massachusetts begins with the advantage that it is one of a relatively few African American Civil War regiments to have a published history. Compiled by a committee of white officers from the regiment and based to a large degree on the journal and letters written by one of their number (Colonel Charles B. Fox), the resulting *Record of the Service of the Fifty-fifth Regiment of Massachusetts Volunteer Infantry* (1868) is a book of great merit graced by prose that walks the fine line between the extremes of "just the facts" and the flowery excesses of the more florid examples of that genre.

A curious item often cited in bibliographies of the 55th Massachusetts is Burt G. Wilder's *Fifty-fifth Regiment of the Massachusetts Volunteer Infantry, Colored: June 1863-September 1865*, 1914. The "book" is a mere eight pages long and, in column inches at least, devotes more space to Wilder's idiosyncratic footnotes to the text, which reproduces a rambling discourse he presented about the regiment in which he served as surgeon. A later version (1919) is re-edited to conform to a passion developed by Wilder in the interim for a form of simplified spelling.

A modern pamphlet worthy of acquisition in regard to the 55th is Steven D. Smith's *Whom We Would Never More See: History and Archaeology Recover the Lives and Deaths of African American Civil War Soldiers on Folly Island, South Carolina*, published by the South Carolina Department of Archives & History in 1993. Also on the 55th's bookshelf is Wilber H. Luck's self-published *Journey to Honey Hill* (Washington, D.C., Wiluk Press, 1985).

Other published material with a direct connection to the 55th consists of letters or speeches by white officers of the regiment. Norwood P. Hallowell, first commander of the 55th, is well represented in the *Selected Letters and Papers of N.P. Hallowell*, 1963. Charles Bowditch, a young officer who served with the regiment on Folly Island in 1863-1864, saw no combat action, and eventually transferred to the 5th Massachusetts Cavalry, is the subject of "War Letters of Charles P. Bowditch," published in the 1923/24 volume of *Massachusetts Historical Society Proceedings*. Another young officer, Robertson James (brother of the novelist

Henry), has letters quoted in Jane Maher's *Biography of Broken Fortunes*, 1986.

Manuscript representation of the 55th is surprisingly strong thanks in good measure to the Burt G. Wilder papers at Cornell University. Wilder, one of the surgeons serving in the 55th, went on to a distinguished post-war career in medicine and, near the end of his life was determined to write a history of his regiment. Toward that goal he gathered clippings, wrote many letters to other survivors (black and white), and obtained photographs of men associated with the unit. It is a collection of unparalled content regarding the 55th and contains a good selection of material about the 54th Massachusetts as well.

The treasures of the Wilder collection aside, the next best repository of materials regarding the 55th is to be found in the Boston area. The valuable files of the Massachusetts Historical Society contain the "55th Regiment Massachusetts Volunteer Infantry, Association of Officers Record," with a good deal about the outfit. The Massachusetts National Guard Supply Depot in nearby Natick contains many Military Officer's Records, including correspondence from the regimental surgeon. At the Massachusetts State Library will be found the Alfred S. Hartwell papers, containing much valuable correspondence (official and private) from the best officer to lead the 55th.

The remaining principal source for manuscript materials regarding the 55th Massachusetts is the National Archives in Washington, wherein will be found the regimental Compiled Service Record, the Regimental Books and Papers (in Record Group 94), the official reports on the moral condition and history of the regiment sent in by regimental chaplain John R. Bowles (all of which are contained in this volume), and the Proceedings of General Courts Martial (Record Group 153). Also valuable was the multivolume microfilm collection titled "The Negro in the Military Service of the United States, 1639-1886."

Index

Mt. Pleasant, South Carolina 191
Murphy, Pvt. J. 126

Napoleon gun 128, 195, 196, 201
Neptune, U.S.S. 93
Nashville, Tennessee 95n
National Archives 223
National Tribune [Washington, D.C.] 168, 169, 186
Neptune, U.S.S. 19
New Bedford, Massachusetts 60
New York 73, 148, 149, 178, 235
New York, 26th 171
New York, 47th 83n
New York, 48th 83n
New York, 54th 28, 111, 131, 133, 134, 136
New York, 56th 25, 195, 203, 207, 214, 219, 220
New York, 103rd 19, 20, 22, 109n, 111, 121, 131, 133-136
New York, 127th 134, 195, 205-207, 210, 211, 214, 217-220
New York, 144th 205, 206, 208, 215, 219, 220
New York, 154th 195
New York, 157th 195, 205, 207, 214, 219, 220
New York Artillery, 3rd 195, 216, 218
New York City, New York 34, 35, 44, 82n, 113, 172
New York draft riot 73n, 148
New York Harbor 167
New York Herald 21, 36, 220n
New York Ledger 55
New York troops 15, 112, 115
New York World 36
New Berne, North Carolina 14, 35, 36, 37, 38

Newton, Pvt. Charles 42, 54, 67, 69, 236, 239
North Carolina 34, 35, 42, 194, 200, 236
North Carolina, 1st 56n, 73, 94, 97, 115, 133
North Carolina, 2nd 37, 42, 56, 236
North Carolina Colored Regiment, 1st 15, 18, 25n, 37, 38, 57, 63, 78, 91, 131
North Carolina Colored Regiment, 2nd 15
North Carolina Colored Regiment, 3rd 15
North Edisto River 21
Northhampton County, Virginia 134n
Nutt, Capt. William 53, 55, 69, 112, 115, 166, 169, 184, 230, 239, 240

Ogeechee River 193, 194
Oglesby, Cpl. D. 162
Ohio 13, 14, 85n, 105, 149
Ohio, 25th 169, 195, 205, 208, 211, 216, 217, 220
Ohio River 187
Olustee, Florida 18, 22, 69n, 77n, 78, 80, 87, 91, 94, 97, 99, 106, 115, 116
Orangeburg, South Carolina 29, 180-182
Overland Campaign 112n
Overton, Pvt. Thomas 162

Paducah, Kentucky 187
Palatka, Florida 18, 69, 71, 72, 81, 82-84, 89, 97, 98, 106, 173, 225
Palmyra, Missouri 228
Parker, George 47, 236
Parker, Cpl. Thornton 162

South Carolina Cavalry, 3rd 26, 194, 201
South Carolina Colored Regiment, 1st 44, 79n
South Carolina Colored Regiment, 2nd 25n, 79n
South Carolina Institute of Archaeology & Anthropology 16
South Carolina troops 218
South Mountain, Battle of 14
Southern Department 169
Spear, Cpl. James 131
Spears, Sgt. David 162, 172, 174
Spears, Henry 174
Spencer, Pvt. P. 162
Springboro, Ohio 129, 138, 169
Springfield rifle 109
Stafford, Pvt. C. 161
Standish, U.S.S. 20
Stedman, Sgt. William J. 122, 126
Stephens, Sgt. George E. 111
Sterns, Maj. George L. 10, 95
Stevenson, Pvt. J. W. 163
Stewart, Pvt. E. J. 162
Stoddard, Lt. George G. 217
Stono Inlet 20
Stono Landing 145
Stono River 20, 132, 137
Sturgis, Maj. James 58
Sumner, Sen. Charles 154
"Swamp Angel" 40

Tanner, Pvt. Bolden 118
Taylor, Cpl. George W. 118, 161
Taylor, Pvt. John 118
Taylor, Lt. Gen. Richard 200
Taylor, Pvt. Samuel 118
Tennessee 188
Tennessee River 188
Tenvey's Landing 199

Thomas, Pvt. E. 162
Thomas, Brig. Gen. George H. 193
Thomas, Maj. Gen. Lorenzo 226
Thomas, Sgt. Samuel P. 43n, 44n
Thomasville, Georgia 200
Thompson, George 140n
Thompson, Pvt. I. H. 126, 127
Thurber, Capt. James D. 126, 168
Tiger Island, South Carolina 20, 121, 131
Titus, Lt. Edgar H. 196, 217
Toombs, Brig. Gen. Robert A. 200, 201
Torrey, Capt. William H. 81, 233
Trenholm, George Alfred 182
Trotter, Richard S. 139
Trotter, Sgt. Maj. James Monroe 44, 62n, 72, 110n, 123, 127, 139, 143, 157, 161, 166, 180, 181, 184, 213, 231
Tuper, Lt. Col. Ansel 189
Turner, Sgt. O. 163
Tyler, Lt. Col. Rockwell 195

United States 17, 29, 62, 144, 146, 147
United States Army 33, 102, 187, 225
United States Cavalry, 5th 125
United States Christian Commission 225-227
United States Colored Troops 113
United States Colored Troops, 2nd 56
United States Colored Troops, 3rd 42n, 43n, 57, 79
United States Colored Troops, 4th 125

Endsheets: "Marching On!"—The Fifty-Fifth Massachusetts Colored Regiment Singing John Brown's March in the Streets of Charleston, February 21, 1865, *Harper's Weekly*, March 18, 1865, pp. 165-6.

"MARCHING ON!"—THE FIFTY-FIFTH MASSACHUSETTS COLORED REGIMENT SING